Edward Lee Stuart Horsburgh

**Waterloo**

A Narrative and a Criticism

Edward Lee Stuart Horsburgh

**Waterloo**

*A Narrative and a Criticism*

ISBN/EAN: 9783337141806

Printed in Europe, USA, Canada, Australia, Japan

Cover: Foto ©ninafisch / pixelio.de

More available books at **www.hansebooks.com**

BY

# E. L. S. HORSBURGH, B.A.
QUEEN'S COLLEGE, OXON.

ἀλλ' ἤ τοι μὲν ταῦτα θεῶν ἐν γούνασι κεῖται

METHUEN & CO.
36 ESSEX STREET, W.C.
LONDON
1895

# PREFACE.

I MADE an attempt a year or two ago to put before an audience at the Royal Institution a narrative of the Campaign of 1815, together with an abstract of the volume of evidence which eighty years has accumulated around the events of the four days over which it extended. It was then suggested to me that the expansion of my lectures with a view to publication might serve a useful purpose, notwithstanding the fact that the literature upon the subject which already exists would fill a good-sized library. The works of Charras, Clausewitz, Siborne, Chesney, Ropes, and many others, are well known to all students of military history, but owing either to their length or to their severe and technical style, they are but little read by the general public. The present volume, based upon a close study extending over many years of all the available authorities, claims, within a reasonable compass, to present the conclusions of experts upon controversial points, to suggest solutions to problems about which experts are in conflict, and to give a concise and faithful narrative of evenst.

I have to thank Captain H. de Gruchy of Oswestry, Salop, for the opportunity so kindly afforded me of examining several interesting papers and pamphlets from the pen of Marshal Grouchy, many of which were presented to Captain de Gruchy's father by the Marshal himself. Among these documents, however, there was none not already known to critics of the campaign.

Amid the mass of conflicting evidence and diversity of view which surrounds and obscures the subject I have endeavoured to pick an independent path, and have, it is hoped, supported every statement of an opinion by abundant evidence drawn from the official records and from the best English and foreign treatises.

Two years ago, when the substance of these pages was delivered in the form of lectures, none of the three brilliant soldiers — Lord Wolseley, Lord Roberts, and Sir Evelyn Wood—had yet begun to publish those remarks upon the campaign which have recently appeared in the *Pall Mall Magazine*. I should have hesitated before presuming to undertake a subject which had already engaged the attention of such authorities upon the art of war, but when once undertaken, there was no option but to proceed with it. Moreover, the appearance of the *Pall Mall Magazine* articles has not perhaps rendered such a little book as this entirely superfluous.

All students of Waterloo must find pleasure in acknowledging the value of Col. Maurice's work upon the campaign. His articles in the *United*

# PREFACE

*Service Magazine* are by far the most scholarly contributions to the subject made by an Englishman in recent times.

It was the dictum of one of Oxford's most brilliant scholars and critics — the late Thomas Clayton, dear to *The Spectator*, and still living in the affectionate memory of his friends—that " every gentleman should know at least one campaign by heart." This was his epigrammatic way of commending the study of military history to his friends. It is a study which presents to the student all the charm which an abstruse problem offers to the mathematician, a new force to the scientist, a disputed text to the scholar. There is undoubtedly a disposition among English people to-day to know all that is to be known about the final overthrow of England's greatest antagonist, and it is with the view of at once gratifying and stimulating the very legitimate curiosity which exists about Waterloo that the following pages have been written.

E. L. S. H.

*June*, 1895.

# CONTENTS.

## CHAPTER I.
INTRODUCTORY . . . . . . 1-10

## CHAPTER II.
I. Character and strength of the French, Prussian, and Anglo-Dutch armies.—II. Remarks on their commanders and their subordinates . . . . . 11-24

## CHAPTER III.
THE SCHEME OF OPERATIONS . . . 25-30

## CHAPTER IV.
I. Napoleon's order of movement and the passage of the Sambre.—II. The Prussian dispositions. Zieten's corps retrogrades on Fleurus.—III. Wellington's dispositions in view of the French advance.—IV. Further progress of the French left and centre.—V. Ney and the occupation of Quatre Bras.—VI. Concentration of the Anglo-Dutch Army.—VII. Summary . . 31-49

## CHAPTER V.
### THE MORNING OF JUNE 16TH.
I. Wellington and his army on the morning of the 16th; his statements to Blücher; their value.—II. Blücher's stand at Ligny.—III. Advance of the French right on Ligny. —IV. Attitude and conduct of Ney on the morning of the 16th.—V. Ney's dispositions before Quatre Bras.—

# CONTENTS

VI. Napoleon on the morning of the 16th ; his general plan of campaign as distinguished from his particular plan for the day; modification of his morning plan to suit the circumstances of the afternoon.—VII. Respective dispositions of Blücher and Napoleon for the battle of Ligny ; Napoleon's plan of battle ; positions and numbers of the forces engaged . . . . 50-84

## CHAPTER VI.

### THE BATTLES OF THE 16TH.

I. The Battle of Ligny.—II. The Battle of Quatre Bras.—III. Napoleon's delay in beginning battle.—IV. The D'Erlon Episode.—V. Summary . . . 85-114

## CHAPTER VII.

### THE 17TH OF JUNE—(WELLINGTON AND NAPOLEON).

I. The Line of Blücher's Retreat.—II. Wellington's determination to Retreat.—III. Position of the French Army on the morning of the 17th; delay at Quatre Bras and on the Right.—IV. The Retreat on Waterloo.—V. The position at Waterloo ; Wellington's dispositions.—VI. Views and expectations of Wellington in standing at Waterloo.—VII. Anticipations of Napoleon in taking position.—VIII. Summary . . . 115-143

## CHAPTER VIII.

### GROUCHY'S MARCH ON THE 17TH AND 18TH OF JUNE, UP TO THE OPENING OF THE BATTLE OF WATERLOO.

I. Grouchy despatched in pursuit of the Prussians.—II. Arrangements and instructions which governed his march.—III. Grouchy at Gembloux ; the two versions of the 10 P.M. despatch.—IV. Grouchy's determination to advance on Wavre.—V. The sound of the Cannonade at Waterloo.—VI. General criticisms and observations on Grouchy's movements . . . 144-175

# CONTENTS

### CHAPTER IX.

#### THE MORNING OF THE BATTLE.

I. Napoleon's Formation in Order of Battle on the 18th.—
II. Wellington's Formation.—III. Analysis of the Duke's Force and Position.—IV. Delay in beginning the Battle.—V. Napoleon's Despatch to Grouchy before the Battle.—VI. Prussian Movements on the Morning of the 18th . . . . . 176-196

### CHAPTER X.

#### THE BATTLE OF WATERLOO.

I. Napoleon's general plan and the attack on Hougomont.
—II. D'Erlon's infantry attack.—III. First appearance of the Prussians at St Lambert.—IV. Observations on Napoleon's conduct of the battle and on the difficulties of ascertaining the facts.—V. The attack on La Haie Sainte.—VI. Cavalry charges on the British right and centre.—VII. The battle with the Prussians around Planchenoit.—VIII. The charge of the Imperial Guard.
—IX. Wellington's advance and rout of the French.—
X. Lobau at Planchenoit protects the line of retreat for the main army.—XI. Pursuit of the French by the Prussians . . . . . 197-245

### CHAPTER XI.

#### CRITICAL EXAMINATION OF THE BATTLE OF WATERLOO.
#### (FRENCH SIDE.)

I. Napoleon's delay in beginning the battle.—II. His methods of attack at Hougomont and La Haie Sainte.
III. D'Erlon's formation in columns of attack.—IV. Ney's employment of the cavalry.—V. The expediency

# CONTENTS

of retreat at various periods of the battle.—VI. The attack by the Imperial Guard.—VII. Napoleon's physical condition at Waterloo.—VIII. Napoleon's generals at Waterloo . . . . . 246-272

## CHAPTER XII.

### CRITICAL EXAMINATION OF THE BATTLE OF WATERLOO.

(WELLINGTON AND BLÜCHER.)

I. Wellington's Defence.—II. Colville's Division at Hal.—III. Blücher's Co-operation; could it have been earlier or more effective? . . . . 273-289

## CHAPTER XIII.

### THE FOREIGN TROOPS WITH WELLINGTON AT WATERLOO.

I. The King's German Legion.—II. The Hanoverians.—III. Brunswick Contingent.—IV. The Dutch-Belgians 290-302

## CHAPTER XIV.

### GROUCHY AT WAVRE.

Grouchy follows the Prussians to Wavre—Receipt of Napoleon's 10 A.M. despatch—Grouchy confirmed in his design of attacking the Prussians—Prussian dispositions at Wavre—The battle at Wavre on the 18th—Receipt of Napoleon's 1 P.M. despatch—Its effect on Grouchy's dispositions—Early morning of the 19th—Thielemann's determination to attack—Success of the French on the 19th—Grouchy receives the news of Waterloo—Determination to retreat on Namur—Grouchy's conduct of the retreat—Conclusion . . . . 303-310

APPENDIX . . . . . 311-312

# CHAPTER I.

## INTRODUCTORY.

THE reappearance of Napoleon in the early spring of 1815 was to all Europe as if the Devil were unchained. It is indeed as the Arch-Fiend, in various aspects, that he is presented to us in numerous contemporary caricatures. Few things are more extraordinary than that concentration of European hatred which, in the early part of this century, was focussed upon a single individual. The passions he had roused, the fear and detestation with which he was regarded, had accomplished the apparently impossible. They had brought about, if only for a moment, a real European union. The eighteenth century is strewn with the remains of Definitive Treaties, Leagues, and Sanctions. The incurable jealousies among the great powers had played Napoleon's game in 1805, in 1806, and in 1809 no less effectually than his own victories, but the European union which a century had failed to effect was accomplished by five years of Napoleonic domination. The coalition of 1814 marched against one man, to the cry of "War to the Emperor, peace to the nation." The methods of the French Revolution had taught the crowned heads of Europe the value of specious cries, and "Peace to the cottage, war to the palace," was now parodied against its authors. But the coalition of 1814 was not merely an association of crowned heads and governments. It was a coalition of peoples. It had been the peculiar work of the French Revolution to rouse the spirit of nationality in Europe. "The Genius of Freedom," which Goldsmith had seen in 1755 "entering France in disguise," had seized upon the French people. From France it penetrated far and wide, and everywhere, in the early flush of revolutionary enthusiasm, the French were received as deliverers, carrying to down-trodden and oppressed peoples the unknown blessings of "Liberty, Fraternity, and Equality." Fired at first by genuine sympathy for the oppressed, the French were nearly as good as their watch-words; but human nature is stronger than watchwords, and aggrandisement, if it be easy, is irresistible. Napoleon was not the author of the infamous policy which enslaved nations while pretending to liberate them, but he was an apt pupil in that school. In his treatment of Venice in 1797 he bettered his teachers, though later he far outdid his own early efforts by his policy in Northern Italy, in the German States, and in Spain.

Such a policy brings with it its own retribution. "*Quisque suos patimur manes*," and the spirit of nationality, once invoked, can hardly be allayed.

# INTRODUCTORY

In Napoleon we see the victim of poetic justice, a conqueror conquered by the weapons he had himself thrust into his enemies' hands. The familiar name given to the battle of Leipsic—"The Battle of the Nations"—is not only a commentary upon some of the most important aspects of the French Revolution,—it also expresses the net result of Napoleon's career.

The European unity which Napoleon's own mistakes had produced was not, however, proof against success. To overthrow Napoleon was its only object, but that accomplished, forthwith the old international jealousies reappear. After Napoleon's first abdication the Congress of Vienna had to reconstruct Europe. Each power had its own separate interests to secure; each feared the aggrandisement of the other. The epigram of Talleyrand—"Le Congrès danse, mais ne s'avance pas"—points to the fate of coalitions when their main purpose has been effected. No sooner did the Congress get to business than it got to quarrelling, and it seemed as if open hostilities between the negotiating powers could scarcely be averted. It was at this moment that Napoleon landed from Elba, and the reappearance of the common danger drew the coalition together again in order to avert it.

It is beyond the purpose of this investigation to relate the personal or political details of this adventurous quest—how a majority of the French people acquiesced in Napoleon's reinstatement—

how the army rushed to his standard—how the generals who had been sent against him rallied to his cause—how the Bourbon King, Louis XVIII., so newly established, fled to Belgium—how, in three weeks from the time of landing, Napoleon was once more in possession of the Tuileries.

The fact was that the Bourbons "had learned nothing and had forgotten nothing." They thought that to put back the hands of the clock was to put back the march of time, that to ignore the Revolution and all the new forces and ideas which it had stirred up was to make it as though it had never been. Thus the Bourbon princes, Louis XVIII. and Charles of Artois, were utterly out of touch with the new lines of thought which twenty years of Revolution had established, utterly behind the times which they were called upon to control. Moreover, Louis XVIII., disguise it how he might, was a foreign-made Sovereign. He was imposed upon France, not freely chosen of the French people. In the nature of things there could be little sympathy between the France of 1814 and a Bourbon of 1789; while equally in the nature of things, Napoleon, so long as he lived, could scarcely fail to have a strong hold on France. In spite of the conscription, in spite of the heavy weight of his taxation, in spite of the blood and treasure which he squandered, France could not forget that in her hour of turmoil it was Napoleon

# INTRODUCTORY 5

who had given her what she chiefly needed—repose; that it was Napoleon who, in the great years of European war, had given her what she chiefly craved—glory.

He also brought to the situation a prestige with which no Bourbon could vie; with his personality was associated the splendour of continued victories and of territorial aggrandisement; to him attached the recollection that, while he ruled, France had gained a position of preponderance in Europe such as she had never known under any Bourbon —not even under Louis XIV.

Though it was perhaps natural that the Bourbons should fly and that Napoleon should be received, yet the real difficulty was to maintain permanently the position thus easily acquired. Looking at Napoleon's chances, it may perhaps be said that they were desperate from the outset. He found himself confronted once more by Europe in arms. Unity succeeded discord in the councils of the Congress of Vienna. An Anglo-Dutch army of over 100,000 men was already in Belgium, co-operating with a Prussian army even larger. Of the great powers, Russia, Austria, Spain, of the lesser powers, Portugal, Denmark, Sweden, and the minor German States required but a short period to enable them to put armies into the field proportionate to their European status. In course of time Napoleon would have to reckon with about three-quarters of a million of men, irrespective of those already arrayed against him.

His first step, therefore, after his re-establishment, was to negotiate for peace. "A noble arena," he declares in his letter to the allied Powers, "is now opened to sovereigns. I will be the first to descend into it. After having exhibited to the world the spectacle of great combating, it will be sweeter henceforth to exhibit no other rivalry but that of the advantages of peace, no other strife but that of the felicity of nations." Such negotiations, however, were hollow to the core. No one can have been more convinced of their futility than the Emperor himself. Europe had already sufficient experience of what Napoleon, firmly seated upon the Imperial throne, meant for her; she was already sufficiently versed in the value of Napoleonic assurances. Apart from this, Napoleon's hold over France had always been based upon military success. A continued series of great military achievements had alone maintained him even in his season of unlimited power; it was impossible to maintain a position intrinsically weaker without victories even greater than those of the past. Yet as a move in the game of politics his pacific negotiations were shrewd and strengthening. Their rejection seemed to throw the onus of the renewal of hostilities off his shoulders on to those of the allies, and he was able to pose as the defender of the Liberties of France against the foreign enemies who would dictate to her both a policy and a king. It is from 1814 and 1815 that the Napoleonic legend dates. The

# INTRODUCTORY 7

hopes which the French people so long continued to entertain of the Imperial house, the easy confidence with which they permitted themselves to be gulled in 1851, alike take their origin from the days when Napoleon the Great put off the *rôle* of conqueror for that of " Liberator."

The issue then could be decided only by war, and the question for Napoleon was whether the ensuing campaign should be conducted on offensive or defensive principles. Though his military career had been mainly an offensive one, yet the campaigns of 1814, which closed it, had displayed him as a master of defensive tactics. A definite invasion of French territory by hostile forces presented certain political advantages were he to permit such an invasion to take place. It might be possible thereby to rouse the national spirit of France in a way that would recall the days of '92 and '93. The cry of " La Patrie en danger " might work the same wonders as it had worked then, and delay would offer further facilities to his talents as a diplomatist. Napoleon did not forget that he was the son-in-law of the Emperor of Austria, and he perhaps imagined that Austria would show the same tardiness to combine against him as she had shown in 1813. With delay the European coalition might break up—in any case he might foment the jealousies, conflicting interests, and mutual fears of the Powers which had played his game in the past, and might play it now. Was it wise to precipitate hostilities when so much might be gained by evading them?

But, on the other hand, delay, whatever its advantages, was impossible. The odds against him were so enormous that his only hope of reducing them lay in promptly defeating his enemies *seriatim* and at once. It is doubtful if France would have submitted herself voluntarily to another invasion. To test her endurance again was to court a second fall, while prompt success in offensive operations would render her attachment to the Imperial cause doubly secure. If startling victories could be gained at the outset over enemies already in the field, the effect upon enemies not yet in the field might be incalculable. If only England and Prussia could be routed, it was at least doubtful whether Austria and Russia would continue the contest.

In estimating the military position of Napoleon and the allies respectively, just before the Waterloo Campaign began, it is evident that, however formidable in appearance were the forces already in the field to oppose him, there were on the other hand many chances in his favour against them. War waged by armies acting in combination can never present that unity of action and singleness of purpose which a sole commander can bring to bear upon the conduct of his operations. And yet never in warfare are unity of action and singleness of purpose more essential than in the

# INTRODUCTORY 9

direction of a combined movement, such as Wellington and Blücher had agreed upon. Napoleon was one, and uncontrolled. All the resources of France could be moved by the absolute power of his single will, and his army, however inferior in numbers, was infinitely more coherent than the armies opposed to him. Napoleon was a keen student of the campaigns of Frederick the Great, and doubtless had before his mind that crisis in the Seven Years' War, when his master in the military art was confronted by a situation not dissimilar to his own. Just as supreme military genius, acting alone, had gained the advantage then over a cumbrous and ill-assorted coalition, so genius now, equally unimpeded, might secure similar results.

Thus a determination to adopt offensive tactics might prove decisive of the issue. While Napoleon's main plan and its general details would be preconceived, prearranged, and certain, the operations of the allied commanders must depend on his movements. While it might be rash for them to concentrate in expectation of attack on any given point, it might on the other hand be fatal not to do so. There was no certainty that, take what step they might, it would not be fraught with disaster. Moreover, the allied lines of communication offered so many alternative points of attack, each holding out such solid advantages to an enemy, that the element of uncertainty must be regarded as an important factor in the situation, a factor undoubtedly operating in favour of Napoleon.

It was, therefore, with good hopes of success that Napoleon resolved upon an offensive campaign.

Having spent two months in reorganising the military forces of the country, and having posted all his available troops in convenient positions on the Belgian frontier, on June 12th he left Paris to conduct in person the campaign of Waterloo.

## CHAPTER II.

I. Character and strength of the French, Prussian, and Anglo-Dutch armies.—II. Remarks on their commanders and their subordinates.

OF the three armies in the field on the 15th June 1815, the French was unquestionably superior to that of either Wellington or Blücher. The superiority consisted not so much in numerical force as in the quality of the troops. The first step towards a proper comprehension of the campaign is to know the respective efficiency of the troops engaged in it, and for this purpose an examination of the composition of the three armies must necessarily preface an account of the work which they were called upon to perform.

### I.—*The French Army.*

Napoleon brought to the field* five corps of infantry, four cavalry corps, and the Imperial

| | | |
|---|---|---|
| * 1st Corps. | D'Erlon, | 19,939 |
| 2nd Corps. | Reille, | 24,361 |
| 3rd Corps. | Vandamme, | 19,160 |
| 4th Corps. | Gérard, | 16,000 |
| 6th Corps. | Lobau, | 10,465 |
| Imperial Guard, | | 20,884 |
| 1st, 2nd, 3rd, 4th Cavalry Corps. Grouchy, | | 13,784 |
| Miscellaneous, | | 3,500 |
| | | 128,093 |

These are Charras' figures. Gourgaud says, 115,500.

Guard, making a total of rather more than 128,000 men, with 344 guns.

Little complaint could be made as to the quality of these troops. It is true that, during Napoleon's absence in Elba, the army was undergoing a process of reorganisation, and that Napoleon himself had occupied the brief period since his return in moulding this work of reconstruction to his own advantage. The army, therefore, was to some extent in a transition state, and had other circumstances rendered such a course possible, Napoleon would doubtless have delayed the campaign until this work of reorganisation was completed. But while admitting that Napoleon had commanded better armies than this one, on the whole he must have regarded himself as fortunate in being able to collect so numerous a force, and of such excellent quality. The Peace had brought back into France a large body of veterans who had been confined in the various prisons of Europe, and it was of these that Napoleon's Waterloo army was largely composed. In all the ranks there was scarcely a man who had not served before. The troops were well-trained, well-tried, and efficient.

But the value of troops is in a large measure dependent on the officers who command them. Napoleon himself was commander-in-chief. The advantage which his presence in the field gave to his side has been variously calculated. A contemporary estimated his absence as worth

## THE FRENCH ARMY 13

40,000 men to his opponents, and with this estimate the Duke of Wellington agreed.

"Yes,"* said the Duke, "Bonaparte was certainly the best of them all, and with his prestige, worth 40,000 men."

Certainly his personal presence was of immense value, though perhaps not to be exactly calculated in round numbers. It is often said that Napoleon was not himself at Waterloo—that physical incapacity made it impossible for him to exhibit his true qualities as a leader, and it is undoubted that he had become increasingly subject to strange fits of lassitude and depression, which seized him even in the heat and excitement of an engagement. This is a matter deserving of attention, and further reference will in due course be made to it, but the rapidity, readiness, skill, and resource which he displayed throughout the campaign, give conclusive proof that when his strange malady was not actually upon him, his eye was not dim, nor his natural force abated.

Of his lieutenants, Ney, Duke of Elchingen and Prince of Moskowa, played by far the most active part throughout the campaign, but Ney only joined the army on the 15th June, when the advance on Belgium had already begun. He was therefore strange to his command and to his subordinates, and was, moreover, lamentably deficient in staff-officers. Considering the importance of the position allotted to Ney—he was given the command

* The Croker Papers, edited by Louis Jennings, M.P., iii. 276.

of the left wing—disadvantages more trifling than these were capable of exercising an important influence upon the conduct of the campaign.

Far more serious, however, was a certain want of harmony between the views of Ney and Napoleon as the campaign proceeded. Each commanded throughout the 16th and during part of the 17th June an independent force acting in combination with the other. Perfect unity of plan, perfect harmony of mind, should have existed between the commanders. This was not the case, and despite the personal bravery repeatedly displayed by Ney, even to the point of recklessness, a considerable share of Napoleon's failure must be laid at his door.

Napoleon's chief of the staff was Soult, Duke of Dalmatia. It is odd to find in this position a man who for years had held independent command. In the Peninsula Soult had been Napoleon's second self, and had frequently met the Duke of Wellington on equal terms of command. But whatever his skill as a responsible leader, in his new position as chief of the staff he failed to display that activity and capacity which might have been expected of him.

Davoust, who had been for so many years Napoleon's lieutenant in North Germany, was a man of great initiative, skill, vigour, and resolution. He was probably a better soldier than either Soult or Ney. Napoleon, however, refused to avail himself of Davoust's services on this

## THE FRENCH ARMY

campaign, for he considered it essential to leave as Governor of Paris, during his absence, a man of tried capacity in civil as well as military affairs. It may well be doubted if this decision was a wise one, for on many occasions during these momentous days, the dominating force and energy of Davoust might have been exhibited to the lasting advantage of the Imperial cause.

Not only was Davoust absent, but Napoleon was further weakened by the loss of Berthier, his former well-tried chief of the staff, who had now joined his fortunes to those of Louis XVIII., and of Marshal Mortier, the Commander of the Imperial Guard, who was seized with illness as the campaign opened. Lannes was dead. Masséna, gorged with wealth, thought only of preserving it, and his cautious trimming between the Bourbons and the Empire was rewarded by the undisguised mistrust of both. Murat was at Naples. It must be admitted that more perhaps depended on Napoleon's personal activity and control than was usual in his campaigns, for he was wont to rely upon his lieutenants not merely for obedience, but for co-operation—for an intelligent insight into the full meaning of his plans—and co-operation such as this was not forthcoming in the Waterloo Campaign.

In command of the cavalry, and very shortly to be raised to the more responsible position of commander of the right wing, was the Comte de Grouchy, Marshal of France, a man whom an evil destiny has doomed to be regarded as the scapegoat of the campaign, the author of all the disaster which brought it to a close.

Grouchy could boast of thirty-five years' service in the cause of France. Appointed second lieutenant in the regiment La Fère in 1780, when he was only fourteen years old, he was a captain four years later, and for the three years immediately preceding the Revolution he held a commission in the "Gardes du Corps" of the king.

On the outbreak of the Revolution he gave immediate evidence of his political sympathies by resigning his post in the King's Guards and taking service in the army as newly organised by the Constituent Assembly. When the monarchy was overthrown, Grouchy served the Republic, and when, by a decree of the Convention, nobles were excluded from holding commissions in the Republican armies, he at once enlisted in the ranks, declaring with much spirit that he could not be debarred from shedding his blood, as a private soldier, in the interests of his country. The reaction which followed the death of Robespierre proved favourable to Grouchy, and he was restored to his command, being gazetted General of division at the same time as Masséna, Soult, and Moreau. In the wars of La Vendée he rendered conspicuous services against Stofflet and Charette, and being here associated with General Hoche, Grouchy from the first conceived an unbounded admiration for the personal and military qualities of that best servant

## THE FRENCH ARMY 17

of the Republic. As second in command under Hoche he played an important part in the expedition to Ireland in 1796, and it was certainly through no fault of his that that enterprise had so grotesque and disastrous an issue for France.

He watched the rise of Napoleon with suspicion, and was not included in the list of officers who accompanied the Egyptian expedition of 1798. He was thus available for service against the Austrians in Italy, where, as second in command to Joubert, he exhibited considerable talent both in the field of diplomacy and of war. At Novi he fought desperately, was badly wounded and made prisoner, nor did he return to France until after Marengo had been won by Napoleon, now first Consul of France. Profoundly suspicious of the Napoleonic dispensation, he had even from his place of captivity protested against the *coup a'état* of Brumaire, which he regarded as the enslavement of the Republic. Upon his return to France he attached himself as firmly to Moreau as he had previously attached himself to Hoche. But notwithstanding his distrust of the Consular system, his undoubted military capacity secured him the position of Inspector-General of Cavalry, and from this time Napoleon, though regarding Grouchy's political principles with suspicion and dislike, never failed to find him high employment in his successive campaigns. He was at Ulm in 1805. He commanded the cavalry at Jéna in 1806, he received the Grand Cross of Bavaria

B

for his gallantry at Eylau, and the Grand Cordon of the Legion of Honour upon the battlefield of Friedland. In 1808 he was Governor of Madrid, and covered the retreat of the French army when King Joseph evacuated the capital, but like Talleyrand, Caulaincourt, and all far-sighted politicians, he dissented strongly from Napoleon's Spanish policy, nor did he hesitate to express the dissatisfaction which he felt. He obtained his recall from Spain in order to serve in Italy under Prince Eugene, and his skilful manœuvres, which brought him with his army over the Italian frontier on to the field of Wagram, secured a due recognition when he was appointed Commander of the Iron Crown, Colonel-General of the Chasseurs, and a Grand Officer of the Empire. In the Russian Campaign of 1812 he contributed to the victory of the Moskowa. He covered the retreat of the army from Moscow, holding a position of peculiar trust and dignity as commander of the "*escadron sacré*," that squadron in which all the private soldiers were officers of the grand army, and whose special mission it was to guard the person of the Emperor. In 1813 he declined the commands which Napoleon offered him, for he judged the cause of the Emperor to be now dissociated from the cause of his country, but after the disasters of that year, when he saw France threatened by invasion, he proffered his sword for the defence of the frontiers, and was once more appointed to the command of the cavalry. In the campaign which

## THE PRUSSIAN ARMY 19

followed he conspicuously proved his worth, and it was in return for a series of brilliant services rendered " in other circumstances, and notably at Friedland, at Wagram, and on the plains of Champagne," that he was named Marshal of France in April 1815.

This summary of the chief events in Grouchy's military career, brief though it is, is nevertheless somewhat out of proportion to the notices contained in these pages of the other commanders in Napoleon's Waterloo army. But Grouchy looms so large in the history of the campaign, that a peculiar—even if misplaced—interest attaches to him. To the public, not only in England but in France, he is known by a single episode in his career, by his association with Napoleon's overthrow at Waterloo. A somewhat wider knowledge of the man explains the conduct of Napoleon in committing to Grouchy so great a weight of responsibility in the campaign, and also enables us to form a sounder judgment as to Grouchy's own fitness for the task imposed upon him.

II.—*The Prussian Army.*

The Prussian army consisted of four * grand corps, numbering in all over 124,000 men. Of

|  |  |  | Ropes' Estimate. | Chesney's Estimate. |
|---|---|---|---|---|
| * 1st Corps. | Ziethen, | . . | 32,692 | About 31,000 |
| 2nd Corps. | Pirch, | . . | 32,704 | ,, 32,000 |
| 3rd Corps. | Thielemann, | . | 24,456 | ,, 24,000 |
| 4th Corps. | Bülow, | . . | 31,102 | ,, 30,000 |
| Non-combatants, | . | . . | 3,120 |  |
|  | Total, | . . | 124,074 | 117,000 |

these nearly 12,000 were cavalry. There were 312 guns. Most of these troops had served before, and may be regarded as efficient soldiers. Some of them were animated by something of Blücher's enthusiasm against Napoleon, but some, on the other hand, had served under the Emperor in his campaigns of 1811 and 1812. These men had come under his spell, and their fidelity when acting against him was doubtful. As a fact, however, the Prussian army maintained its cohesion well throughout the campaign, and no dangers arose from the disaffection of any considerable number of the troops. The commander-in-chief, Marshal Prince Blücher, was a dashing officer, who dated his military experience from the Seven Years' War. He had commanded against Napoleon in person with success at the Katzbach in 1813, but had sustained a succession of defeats on the French frontier in the campaign of 1814. As a strategist he was defective and old-fashioned as compared with Napoleon or Wellington, but he was heartily beloved by his men, who appreciated his pluck and daring, and he was ably served by his chief of staff, Gneisenau, on whom fell much of the responsibility for the conduct of affairs.

Gneisenau worked out upon the field the plans which he had developed in the study. He was the Moltke of 1815. A master of detail, he never allowed detail to master him at the expense of general principles. To him has been assigned

# THE ANGLO-DUTCH ARMY 21

the credit, perhaps on insufficient grounds, of the decision,* after Ligny, to conduct the retreat on a line parallel with that of the British Army —thus maintaining communications with Wellington, though sacrificing the Prussian base at Namur,—a decision which practically decided the fate of the Campaign.

The Corps Commanders were steady, sterling soldiers, who knew their duties and discharged them well—Bülow, indeed, had exercised independent command successfully at Dennewitz in 1813—and there existed between them a spirit of co-operation and good-feeling which was to exercise important effects upon the issue of Waterloo.

### III.—*The Anglo-Dutch Army.*

The Anglo-Dutch Army † was a heterogeneous collection of British, Germans, Dutch-Belgian, Brunswick, and Hanoverian troops, all under the command-in-chief of the Duke of Wellington.

* See page 117.

† 
| Ropes' Estimate. | | Chesney's Estimate. | |
|---|---|---|---|
| British Force, | 31,253 | 1st Corps. Prince of Orange, | 25,000 |
| King's German Legion, | 6,387 | | |
| Hanoverians, | 15,935 | 2nd Corps. Lord Hill, | 24,000 |
| Dutch-Belgians, | 29,214 | Reserve. Duke of Wellington, | 21,000 |
| Brunswickers, | 6,808 | | |
| Nassauers, | 2,880 | Cavalry. Lord Uxbridge, | 14,000 |
| Engineers and non-combatants, | 1,240 | Artillery and Engineers, | 10,000 |
| | 3,717 | | 94,000 |

## WATERLOO

The Duke called it "the worst army that had ever been got together," and indeed it was unreliable as regards each component part. The British contingent did not include, except to a very small extent, those troops who had served with such credit in the Peninsula, for they had not yet returned from the seat of war in America. The Dutch-Belgians and Brunswickers were of doubtful loyalty, and of as doubtful value in the field. The men of the King's German Legion were fit to rank with the British contingent, but there were very few of them, and of the British contingent only a small number had served before. The army in the field numbered in all about 94,000 men, of whom 14,500 were cavalry. There were 196 guns.

The burden of controlling this motley force fell solely upon the shoulders of the Duke of Wellington. He assumed all the responsibility, but his powers were absolute. His confidence in himself was great though quiet, and he neither asked for advice nor allowed it to be offered. He was of the school which holds that genius consists in the capacity for taking pains, and from the first beginning of his military career he had studied the art of war in its minutest details. "One must understand," he said, "the mechanism and power of the individual soldier—then that of a company, a battalion, or brigade, and so on—before one can venture to group divisions and move an army. I believe I owe

## THE ANGLO-DUTCH ARMY 23

most of my success to the attention I always paid to the inferior part of tactics as a regimental officer. There were few men in the army who knew those details better than I did. It is the foundation of all military knowledge." He had practised his principles of warfare in India and in the Peninsula with eminent success, and though he had never met Napoleon, he had beaten with ease all the French marshals who had been sent against him. If Napoleon's absence was equivalent to the loss of 40,000 men, the Duke of Wellington's presence was certainly worth much. Sir William Fraser relates a story, which is not, it is hoped, beneath the dignity of history, to illustrate the Duke's value in terms of men. A sentry in the Peninsula was keeping guard for a detachment of troops exposed in a position of great danger. The Duke unexpectedly appearing, the sentry cried out, "God bliss your crooked nose! I'd rather see it than 10,000 min." Possessed of the absolute confidence of the allied sovereigns, of his officers and men, and with a corresponding confidence in himself, it was certain that even with his unpromising materials the Duke would make a bold stand for victory. He was a master of defensive as Napoleon was of offensive tactics, and a contest between them under conditions favourable to the development of the highest powers of both was certain to afford a military spectacle of more than ordinary interest.

The force commanded by the Duke was, however, entirely inadequate to the task of destroying Bonaparte. Nor was such a task ever assigned to it by the Allied Powers or undertaken by Wellington. The duty of defeating him lay with the two allied armies acting in combination. Just as the hopes of Napoleon lay in frustrating this combination, so the hopes of the allies were dependent upon maintaining it.

Of the other commanders in the Anglo-Dutch army it is unnecessary to speak. None held any independent position of command such as that occupied by Ney or Grouchy in the French army. Their duties were to obey orders, and this, with the Duke in command, they were willing and prompt to do. No particular military capacities have ever been claimed for the Prince of Orange or for the Duke of Brunswick. Lord Hill was a sound divisional officer, Lord Uxbridge a dashing cavalry leader ; Sir Thomas Picton, though unfortunately out of favour with the Duke in 1815, was worshipped by his men and very capable in the handling of them.

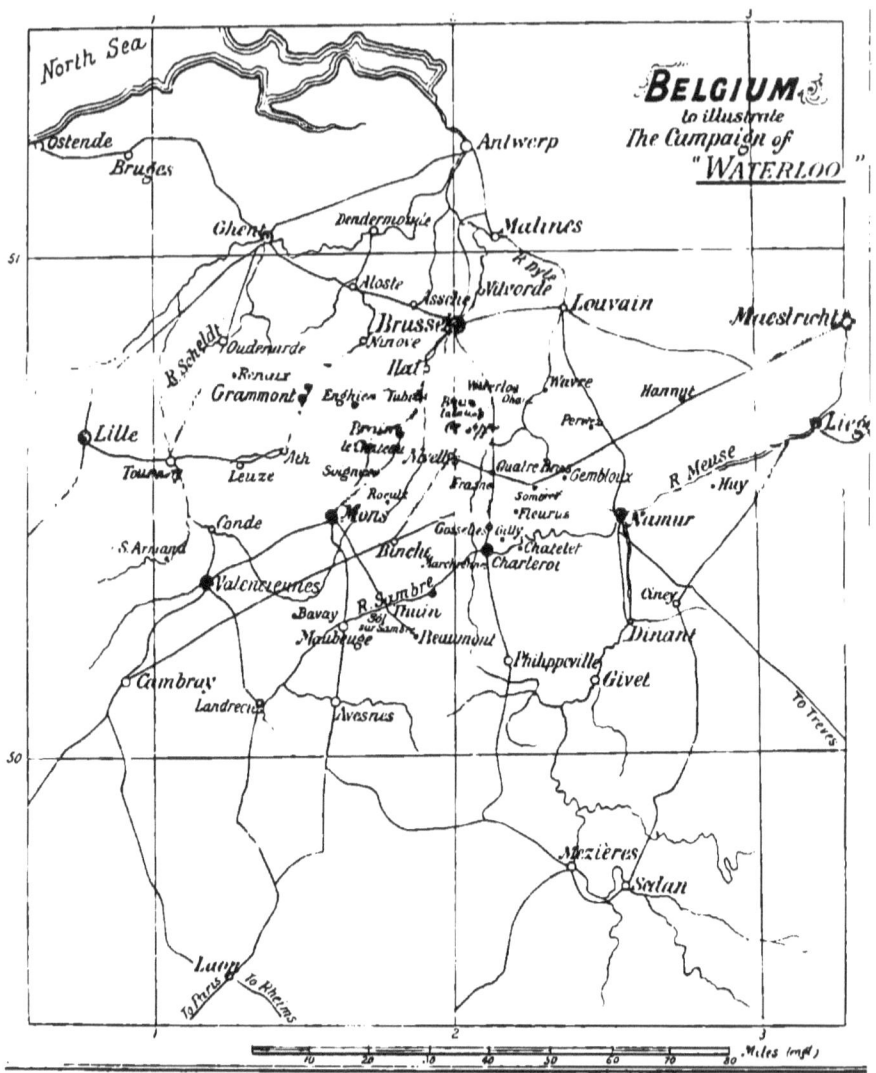

PAGE 24.

# CHAPTER III.

### THE SCHEME OF OPERATIONS.

NAPOLEON'S plan of campaign was necessarily dependent upon the positions occupied by the allied armies.

The Anglo-Dutch forces lay in cantonments around Brussels, extending westward to Ghent, Oudenarde, and Tournay; southward to Nivelles and Mons. Wellington's base of supplies was Ostend, a port which offered him favourable means of communication with the fleet and with England. The Prussian base was Namur, but the cantonments of the Prussian army extended far beyond that point—to the westward as far as Charleroi, southward to Dinant and Rochefort, and eastward to Liége.

The distance from Namur to Ghent is 70 miles, from Namur to Brussels about 40 miles, from Tournay to Liége more than 100 miles ; and thus at the outset we are struck by the wide extent of country covered by the allied troops, and the extreme length of their lines of communication. As a consequence of this, rapid concentration in the event of a surprise or any other emergency would be difficult. A skilful and energetic opponent might force a general engagement upon either or both of the allied armies before half their troops could be rallied to the field, thus affording a chance of cutting the communications on which they were dependent for any combined operations, or of defeating each in detail before any concentration in force could be effected. Moreover, in the event of such a contingency, it was probable that the defeated army would retire upon its base. Now the bases of the Anglo-Dutch and Prussian armies were divergent. Every step towards Ghent and Ostend would take Wellington further away from Namur: every step towards Namur would take Blücher further away from Ghent and Ostend. Thus, in the event of defeat, there would be small chance of combining again, and the loss of combination involved the loss of the campaign.

But, on the other hand, so many alternative routes, as lines of attack, were open to Napoleon, that any premature concentration on the part of the allied generals might be fatal. He might attempt to intervene between the two armies by marching direct upon Brussels, and this was very much the course which he actually adopted, or he might attempt to sever the communications between Blücher and his base by marching towards his right or those between Wellington and his base by marching towards his left. This latter course was the one which the Duke consistently maintained to the end of his life would have been, strategically speaking, the

## THE SCHEME OF OPERATIONS

most advantageous for Napoleon to adopt. This may or may not be so, but in any event three things are clear.

1. That the allied line was dangerously extended.
2. That to concentrate within a more limited circuit of ground, until the line of attack was definitely declared, was perhaps more dangerous.
3. That the situation offered to Napoleon several alternative courses, the uncertainty as to which of them he would take being a distinct source of disadvantage to the allied generals.

It has often been stated that Napoleon's plan was to separate the allied armies: it should rather be said that his object was to annihilate them in detail.

The situation of Blücher's forces, nearer by some miles to the French frontier than the army of the Duke of Wellington, rendered it probable that the Prussians would be the first to concentrate upon news of Napoleon's advance. The character of Prince Blücher rendered it probable—though by no means certain—that, once concentrated or even partially concentrated, he would fight. The scattered dispositions of the Anglo-Dutch army in their cantonments rendered it improbable that they could be concentrated in any efficient force in less than two days. A strong detachment from the main French army could at any rate hold them in check, while Napoleon was disposing of the Prussians—and the Prussians once out of the way, he could then turn his uninterrupted attention upon Wellington. Thus there were very good chances that, with secrecy and rapidity combined, Napoleon might be able to fall upon the Prussian army, with a force little inferior to it (perhaps an even greater force if the Prussian concentration was only partially effected), and cripple it severely, if not annihilate it altogether, before any support could be rendered by its Anglo-Dutch allies. If these possibilities were realised, the Prussian army would be either incapacitated for further service in the campaign or *separated* from its allies, for it was fairly presumable that, if defeated, it would retreat in the direction of its base, leaving Wellington's army entirely unsupported.

Thus a movement direct upon Brussels by the main *chaussée* from Charleroi offered to the French many advantages over the alternative lines of attack. An advance by the right or by the left, with a view of cutting off either Wellington or Blücher from their respective bases, might undoubtedly have secured great results, but one result must inevitably have been to bring the allied armies together. Together they would have numbered nearly 230,000 men, to whom Napoleon could oppose little more than half that number. Whatever advantages he might gain would quickly be recovered from him, and he would find himself compelled to accept battle, in a position probably not of his own choosing and against enormous odds, whereas his actual plan offered him a distinct prospect of engaging the allies separately with forces in each case superior or very little inferior to their own.

# THE SCHEME OF OPERATIONS 29

Napoleon's design, as just stated, is not quite the one with which he is commonly credited. The general supposition is that his scheme was first to separate and then to fight. We have the authority of Wellington and Bonaparte himself for stating that his scheme really was to fight first, believing that separation would naturally follow. It is true that Napoleon's line of march, straight up the Charleroi-Brussels road, seems to indicate an intention of getting between the armies. Hence it has been assumed that he intended to operate in the space between them, and to seize crucial points in their line of communications, but "the space intervening between two armies cannot be an object of operation. It would be very unfortunate if a commander like Bonaparte, having to do with an enemy of twice his strength, instead of falling upon the one half with his united force, were to light on the empty interval and thus deal a blow in the air. . . . Bonaparte chooses therefore the direction between the two armies, not in order to separate them by wedging himself between them, but because he might reasonably expect to find Blücher's force in this direction and to fall upon it, either united or in separate corps."*

One further fact may be stated in support of this view of Napoleon's general idea. Had he desired to seize the crucial points in the allied line of communication with a view merely to separate them, he would, as a glance at the map will show, have seized Sombref and Quatre Bras.

* Clausewitz. Der Feldzug von 1815. Kap. 22.

Not only did he not occupy Sombref, but he took good care "above all not to occupy Sombref."* Neither was Quatre Bras occupied on the first day of the campaign (15th June), though it would have been easy, and for other reasons very advisable, to occupy it. The essential thing was that Blücher should fight with his communications with Wellington open. It was probable that he could be induced to fight, for he would have hopes of being supported; but with his communications closed, it was probable that he would withdraw, to concentrate again in a position more favourable to combined operations.† The occupation of Sombref "would have caused the failure of all (Napoleon's) movements, for then Marshal Blücher would have been obliged to make Wavre the place for the concentration of his army, the battle of Ligny would not have taken place, and the Prussian army would not have been obliged to give battle."

The truth of Napoleon's own statements, particularly after the event, is of course open to doubt, but where his subsequent statements tally with his action at the time, there is no reason for treating them with suspicion.

Having now considered the numerical force, calibre, and *moral* of the three armies, the strategy which Napoleon determined to adopt, the position of the allies in their cantonments, and the general plan of operations which the Emperor hoped to carry out, we are able to proceed to the campaign itself.

* Napoleon. Correspondence.   † *Ibid.*

# CHAPTER IV.

## THE 15TH OF JUNE.

I. Napoleon's order of movement and the passage of the Sambre.—II. The Prussian dispositions. Zieten's corps retrogrades on Fleurus.—III. Wellington's dispositions in view of the French advance.—IV. Further progress of the French left and centre.—V. Ney and the occupation of Quatre Bras.—VI. Concentration of the Anglo-Dutch Army.—VII. Summary.

### I.

NAPOLEON had ordered the concentration of his troops around Charleroi, and in the early days of the month of June the various corps of which his army was composed broke camp and marched to the rendezvous. By the 14th the concentration was effected skilfully, silently, and with great rapidity. Military critics are agreed as to the magnitude of this operation and the ability with which it was directed. Chesney calls the arrangements "simple in theory, but a mighty problem to work out in practice." It is certain that at the beginning of the campaign, at any rate, Napoleon exhibited no falling-off from his own high standard of military science.

The army thus concentrated, Napoleon left Paris on the 12th, and was at Beaumont on the 14th. He now issued to the troops his famous manifesto, in which he calls upon them to remember the glories of the past, the unequal odds under which at Jéna and Montmirail he beat "these same Prussians, to-day so arrogant," and the horrors of the English prisons. He reminds them that the coalition is insatiable, but that like madmen, they are blinded by a moment's prosperity. If they enter France it will be but to find a tomb. Perils and hardships have to be encountered, but with constancy all will be well. "*Pour tout Français qui a du cœur, le moment est arrivé de vaincre ou de périr.*"

From Beaumont on the same day Napoleon issued his "order of movement," in which, with great detail, he explained the order of march for the morrow. The precise hour at which each corps was to move, the disposition of its baggage, and its situation relative to the rest, is here carefully pointed out. The 1st and 2nd corps, under D'Erlon and Reille respectively, forming the left wing of the army, were to advance, the one at 2.30 A.M., the other at 3 A.M., upon Marchienne-au-Pont and Thuin. The 3rd and 6th corps, forming the centre, were to march at 2.30 A.M. upon Charleroi. The 6th corps was to support the 3rd, while the Young Guard was to follow the movements of the 6th.

The 4th corps, which constituted the right, was also ordered to advance upon Charleroi at three o'clock, though, by a later order, it was to cross the

## THE 15TH OF JUNE

river at Châtelet some way to the right. It was to take care to direct its movement in line with that of the 3rd corps, so as to arrive in front of Charleroi as nearly as possible at the same time as that corps, and the Commanders of the three leading columns, Reille, Vandamme, and Gérard, with Pajol, commanding the 1st Cavalry Corps, were to be in constant communication one with the other, so as to arrive before Charleroi *en masse*.

Accordingly, in the early morning of the 15th, the movement thus prescribed was begun. The left advanced at the appointed hour, and at Thuin fell in with the Prussian outposts. These fell back beyond Charleroi, and the bridge across the Sambre at Marchiennes was by ten o'clock in the hands of the French.

The advance of the centre column was delayed and thrown into some confusion by the fact that Vandamme did not get his orders. He was to have started at 2.30 A.M., but, as a fact, he did not set out till 7 A.M. Pajol's cavalry, therefore, which was at the head of the column, found itself unsupported, and it was not until the afternoon that the error was fully rectified. This *contretemps*, however, did not prevent the capture of the bridge at Charleroi before noon.

The right, under Gérard, moved more slowly. Its start was delayed by the fact that some of the divisions composing it had not yet been fully concentrated. When at length its march began, fresh confusion arose by the defection to the enemy of Bourmont, who commanded the leading division. Gérard did not, therefore, reach the river till late in the afternoon, and certainly did not cross it till evening—perhaps one half of his corps did not cross until the early morning of the 16th.

But, on the whole, due allowance being made for errors in execution and for accidents, Napoleon's order was effectively carried out upon the 15th. Before proceeding to trace the movements of the columns further we must pause to examine the positions of the allies and their movements consequent upon Napoleon's advance.

## II.

At 2.30 A.M. on June 15th, the hour of the French advance, the allied armies were still in their cantonments. The first Prussian corps (Ziethen) was at Charleroi and beyond it at Fontaine-l'Evêque, Marchiennes, and Thuin, and therefore was the first to come into collision with the enemy. Blücher was at Namur, and upon receipt of information that the French were in motion, he immediately gave orders for the concentration of his army in the neighbourhood of Sombref. A glance at the map, however, will show that this concentration could not be effected completely in less than forty-eight hours, for Bülow, with the 4th corps, was at Liége, and the distance between Liége and Sombref is about

## THE 15TH OF JUNE

fifty miles. Thus Napoleon's hopes of confronting the Prussian army before it was fully collected seemed in a fair way to be realised. The 3rd corps (Thielemann), cantoned on the Meuse around Dinant, and the 2nd corps (Pirch) at Namur were equally in positions of isolation as regards Ziethen. Consequently, while concentration was in process, it rested upon Ziethen and upon Ziethen alone to resist the advance of the French army in force. Ziethen's corps consisted of less than 33,000 men, and was thus wholly inadequate for purposes of effective resistance. Its only course was to fall back, which it did, upon Sombref, thus taking up its part in the general movement for concentration. This retrograde movement by a corps in the face of an army was an operation of extreme delicacy and attended by great risks. Ziethen was equal to his responsibilities, and though, perhaps, he may be accused of some degree of negligence in not destroying the bridges at Marchiennes and Châtelet, yet in the conduct of the retreat itself he was never at fault, and his operations on this occasion are cited as a model for future commanders to follow under similar circumstances.* Fortune certainly favoured him materially in the failure of Gérard, with the French 4th corps, to fulfil his part in the general movement. Had Gérard come up upon Ziethen's left flank while the centre column was pressing him in front, his orderly withdrawal would certainly have been impossible,

* Sir E. Hamley. "Art of War."

and his whole corps might have been put *hors de combat* for the rest of the campaign.

It is impossible to over-estimate, in the study of campaigns, the importance of apparently trifling details. Speculation on what might have been is, in a sense, an empty amusement, but, on the other hand, it may be legitimately indulged in for the purposes of illustration.

Gérard's delay was partly due to Bourmont's defection, but it was due much more to the fact that his corps was not properly concentrated at the moment prescribed for its advance. Some of the divisions were half-a-day's march behind time. Had Gérard been properly concentrated, he might have reached the river in line with the centre column "*à la hauteur du 3$^{me}$ corps*," as Napoleon put it. Thus situated, he would have been in a position to fall on the flank of Ziethen's retreating force. This movement might have destroyed an entire Prussian corps, discomposed Blücher's whole scheme of concentration, and perhaps rendered the battle of Ligny impossible. Such speculations are useful if they serve to emphasise the fact that, on the loss of half-a-day's march somewhere between the 7th and 14th of June, depended the chance of destroying one-fourth of the Prussian army. Illustrations of the same essential principle in war, the importance of minute detail in the conduct of a campaign, will be multiplied in the course of this study.

As it was, the concentration of the Prussian

## THE 15TH OF JUNE

army—always excepting Bülow's corps—was duly effected in the neighbourhood of Sombref in the course of the 15th and early morning hours of the 16th of June.

### III.

Wellington's army was also in its cantonments at the moment of the French advance. No concentration whatever of the Anglo-Dutch troops had taken place up to the 15th. Napoleon was thus allowed to cross the river, to advance his columns, and to interpose between the allies practically without any opposition from the Anglo-Dutch army. Hence arises the story that the allied generals were taken by surprise. It has, however, already been explained that the Duke of Wellington acted upon a deliberate principle. He determined to maintain his position round Brussels, because upon Brussels the Netherlands depended. He covered a wide extent of ground by his dispositions, because he was uncertain what Napoleon's line of attack would be, and because he was desirous of being prepared for any event. Whether he was wise in his policy of delay is one matter, whether he was taken by surprise by Napoleon's rapidity is another. There is sufficient to account for delay without the theory of surprise. The Duke consistently maintained that his action was right. Critics are now almost unanimous in holding that he was wrong : "in place of waiting to see where the blow actually fell, the armies should have been instantly put in motion to assemble

Nor was this the only error. The line of cantonments occupied was greatly too extended."*

The plan of combination between the two sections of the allied armies was also very loosely defined. We have seen that from his knowledge of the man, Napoleon expected that Blücher would accept battle, even with no definite assurance of support from Wellington, and this, at Ligny, Blücher actually did.† On the other hand, it was most improbable that Wellington would stand against the French without definite assurances of support from Blücher. It is obvious that neither should have risked a decisive engagement—unless positively compelled to do so—without the support of the other. And yet no agreement to this effect had been come to beforehand, and at the outset of the campaign the armies were so placed that they could not help each other even if they would. The ultimate results should not blind us to the defects of those who won the victory, and great as the Duke of Wellington's genius undoubtedly was, there is an unpleasant spice of truth—as far as this campaign, at any rate, is concerned—in Napoleon's dictum, that "*La Fortune a fait plus pour lui qu'il n'a fait pour elle.*"

It was about three o'clock in the afternoon of the

---

\* Sir J. Shaw Kennedy. But, on the other hand, premature concentration on Wellington's part towards his left would exactly play Napoleon's game if he were advancing by way of Mons to cut the Duke's communications with his base of supplies.

† Further detail on this point will be found in c. v. § 2, p. 57.

# THE 15TH OF JUNE 39

15th that the Duke received information that the French were in movement, and had attacked Ziethen before Charleroi. This was all the news which he received up to ten o'clock in the evening of that day. These reports, however, led the Duke to issue a Memorandum for the movements of the army. Orders were given to concentrate the troops in certain situations, such as Ninhove, Grammont, Braine-le-Comte, Nivelles, and Enghien —all of them well to the westward of Napoleon's line of advance, while later orders, supplementary to these, definitely ordered the 3rd division of British Infantry to Nivelles, where the Prince of Orange was to have already collected his 2nd and 3rd divisions. These orders show us the Duke still doubtful whether Napoleon's attack on Charleroi was not a feint, and still maintaining his troops in such a position as to admit of ready concentration south-west of Brussels in the event of the main attack being directed towards his right.

## IV.

In the meantime the leading French columns had pressed steadily forward beyond the river. The centre, which was under the immediate control of the Emperor in person, passed through Charleroi in the afternoon, drove the Prussians from the position they had taken up at Gilly, and by night-time was bivouacked to the south of Fleurus — "*maîtres de toute la position de Fleurus*," as the bulletin of the day states.

The progress of Gérard upon the right has already been traced, and the effects of his partial failure demonstrated. The operations of the left have been traced up to the fulfilment of Napoleon's first orders. The bridge at Marchiennes had been seized, and the Prussian outposts at that point and at Thuin driven in. Further orders were now given to Reille to cross the river, to take position on the Brussels road, and to advance on Gosselies. D'Erlon, with the 1st corps, was to support him and second his operations. Later orders to D'Erlon were more emphatic,—he was to join himself to the 2nd corps at Gosselies. These instructions Reille proceeded to obey, and it was while he was moving on Gosselies that Marshal Ney, who had arrived at Charleroi a few hours before, took command of the whole left wing, composed of the corps of Reille and D'Erlon. He promptly carried the advance still further to Frasne, driving Prince Bernard of Saxe-Weimar's brigade back to Quatre Bras, and a body of Prussians which had been stationed at Gosselies, to Fleurus.

D'Erlon, however, with the 1st corps, was by no means so active in executing his instructions. At the moment when the 2nd corps was bivouacked at Frasne, D'Erlon, far from supporting it, was not yet entirely across the river. In fact, there now began that system of delay, for it can be characterised by no milder term, on the part of the 1st corps, which was to have

**POSITIONS OF THE ARMIES ON**
**JUNE 15th 1815**

The advance of the various corps and their halting places at night are marked at the broad lines.

# THE 15TH OF JUNE

such a serious effect upon the operations of the next day.

## V.

Marshal Ney, who, at the eleventh hour, was entrusted with a capital command, possessed a reputation second to none as a brilliant and daring leader. Few people recognise him under his Imperial title of Marshal "Prince of Moskowa." Everyone knows who is meant by "the bravest of the brave." It would be untrue, in view of the services which he rendered in this campaign, to say that he was half-hearted in Napoleon's cause, but certainly his adherence to it was tardy, and it is obvious from his conduct in the campaign that his reliance upon the judgment of his chief was no longer implicit. He was, moreover, under a disadvantage, from the fact that he joined the army late, and that he was deficient in staff officers, as already stated. But most of all, perhaps his reputation has suffered from the fact that the first orders he received from Napoleon at Charleroi were verbal orders, and so no authoritative documentary evidence is before us whereby we may test exactly how far he obeyed his instructions and how far he disregarded them. At the very outset of the campaign a controversy meets us upon the subject of Ney's action on the 15th. It has been seen that, immediately on assuming his command, he pushed on the pursuit of the Prussians from Gosselies to Frasne, but it is contended that this was not enough, that Quatre Bras was his true objective point that evening, that he had been ordered to seize it, that no difficulties interposed to prevent him, and that yet he refrained from carrying out his instructions. The stern fight for the possession of Quatre Bras which occupied the following day is pointed to as a commentary upon his negligence the evening before— an effect of wilful disobedience, a cause, or part of the cause, of subsequent disasters at Waterloo.

This question takes us back to Napoleon's general plan of campaign. Quatre Bras and Sombref are the two points on the Nivelles-Namur road by which communications were maintained between the allied armies. It has been seen that to seize both these points of communication was no part of Napoleon's general plan. He indeed "took good care not to occupy Sombref," for reasons already stated. Why, then, should he desire to occupy Quatre Bras? If the occupation of Sombref was likely to prevent Blücher from fighting because his communication with Wellington would be cut, logically the occupation of Quatre Bras would have had a like effect. If, in view of an engagement with the Prussians, Napoleon's only demand upon his left wing was that it should prevent Wellington from bringing assistance to Blücher, Ney, at Frasne, on the night of the 15th, was sufficiently near to Quatre Bras to ensure his occupying Wellington on the following day. If, however, Napoleon expected that Ney should not only occupy Wellington, but should be able to detach a reinforcement to the assistance of the main army in the coming battle with the Prussians, the question of the occupation of Quatre Bras on the 15th assumes another aspect. Ney in possession would be in a much stronger position than Ney trying to gain possession. Comparatively few troops would be sufficient to hold the place already won, and the surplus might then readily be detached along the Namur road in order to take the Prussians on the flank at the crisis of the morrow's battle. The advantage of such a manœuvre might more than compensate for any possible disadvantage which the occupation of Quatre Bras might imply. If Blücher, as a direct consequence of that occupation, should determine not to fight — his logical and wisest course—then the Emperor's whole plan was dislocated; but if he were true to his character,* he was sure to fight, if only his communications at Sombref were undisturbed, and in this event a French detachment marching from Quatre Bras along the Namur road would take Blücher in flank and rear at the moment when he was heavily engaged with Napoleon on his front, and thus the defeat of the Prussians would be rendered certain and decisive. The occupation of

* I am unable to accept Herr Delbrück's view, expressed in his "Life of Gneisenau," and emphasised in the "*Preussische Jahrbuch*," Nov. 1894, that Blücher yielded unhesitating and absolute obedience to Gneisenau throughout this campaign. This view, if accepted, would oblige us to leave Blücher's own personality entirely out of account. But Delbrück's whole article is audacious rather than conclusive.

Quatre Bras was therefore worth risking, and Ney was certainly expected to occupy it. The argument thus far does little more than prove that, if there were strong reasons for not occupying the place, there were reasons equally strong for doing so. It does not help us to a decision respecting the instructions which Napoleon gave to Ney. And, indeed, to argue this point of instructions is like beating the air, for there is only one single piece of contemporary documentary evidence which is of service in guiding our views. This is the bulletin of the army for the 15th June, published in the *Moniteur* upon the 18th June. In this bulletin it is stated amid a large mass of information as to the positions of the army, that Ney's headquarters that evening were at Quatre Bras. Here is a statement strictly official, drawn up long before any controversy was raised, and therefore entirely impartial—a paper, moreover, which is undoubtedly authentic—and which seems to be conclusive. It is inconceivable that such a statement could have been made if orders to occupy Quatre Bras that evening had not been given. All the hearsay evidence of after years, which with so much toil has been raked together for the purpose of exonerating Ney and supporting the facts as put forward by his family, is as nothing when compared with this one written piece. We are therefore forced to the conclusion that Napoleon's verbal orders to Ney on the 15th were to occupy Quatre Bras, and that Ney

# THE 15TH OF JUNE

neglected to fulfil these instructions, being content that his vanguard should lie at Frasne.*

Apart from the fact that it shows Ney in a hesitating and cautious mood—not entirely confident in the soundness of the Emperor's judgment—the matter in truth has not that importance which has been attributed to it. So long as the position was in the hands of the French before Wellington had time to move to the support of Blücher, it mattered little whether it were seized on the 15th or early on the 16th. Therefore we need feel no surprise that, as far as the manœuvres of the first day went, the Emperor was entirely satisfied. The dilatoriness of D'Erlon with the 1st corps, and of Gérard with the 4th, was, of course, to be regretted, but, with this exception,† "all the Emperor's manœuvres had succeeded in accordance with his wishes."

## VI.

While the French troops were in bivouac, confidently awaiting the morrow, and resting

* The argument in the text has been directed as far as possible to the question of Ney's *instructions*, and whether he fulfilled them or not. The argument of Clausewitz, which is very forcible, is directed to the *strategy* of the movement on Quatre Bras, and on strategical grounds he shows that Napoleon expected far more from Ney than the Marshal could possibly accomplish. We have not, however, to deal at present with the abstract question as to which of the two, Napoleon or Ney, was in the right according to the theory and practice of war, but are concerned only with Ney's orders, and how far he fulfilled them. The more general bearings of the case will be discussed in the next chapter.

† N. Correspondence.

after a hard day's march, in the Anglo-Dutch army all was astir, and the troops were rapidly concentrating upon the points specified in the Duke's orders.

But these points—Ninhove, Grammont, Braine-le-Comte, Nivelles, Enghien, etc., were far away from Quatre Bras, which was to be assaulted next day by the French, and it was necessary, therefore, for the Duke to issue still further orders to direct his various divisions to concentrate there. Everyone knows that this concentration was effected, as far as it was effected at all, in a very straggling sort of way—that the troops were not at Quatre Bras massed to withstand the enemy at the moment when the attack began, but that some were there, and that others kept arriving all through the afternoon, until at last a very respectable force was collected upon the field, though not amounting to much more than three-eighths of the Duke's whole available strength. These facts certainly confirm the opinion, already quoted, that the English line of cantonments was "much too extended," and they also tend to create an impression that the Duke must have delayed considerably in issuing those supplementary orders which resulted in a partial concentration on Quatre Bras. It is indeed difficult to fix upon the exact time when his determination so to concentrate was arrived at. There is evidence to show that all was settled, and the orders despatched, before the Duke went to the Duchess

## THE 15TH OF JUNE

of Richmond's ball that night, but if this was so, why did the troops arrive so tardily? The Duke's own words to Lord Bathurst are: "*In the meantime* I had directed the whole army to march on Les Quatre Bras," but this expression is very indefinite. Judging only by the way in which the troops arrived upon the field on the afternoon of the 16th, it may be strongly inferred that the Duke's orders for concentration at Quatre Bras were not issued till after he returned from the ball, shortly before leaving Brussels, between seven and eight o'clock in the morning. There are indeed two orders to Lord Hill, dated "Brussels, June 16th," which seem to contradict the assertion that the Duke had "directed the whole army to march on Les Quatre Chemins." Being dated "Brussels," they must have been written before the Duke left the city—that is, early in the morning — and they direct Lord Hill "to move the 2nd division of infantry upon Braine-le-Comte immediately," whither the cavalry had already been ordered, and "the first division of the army of the Low Countries, and the Indian brigade . . . to Enghien." Now these orders do not indicate an intention of concentrating at Quatre Bras, but are rather in harmony with the orders of the evening before, which seem to mark Nivelles as the point fixed upon in the Duke's mind. The whole matter is complicated by the fact that no definite orders to concentrate at Quatre Bras are anywhere to be found ; we have to rest upon the Duke's assertions and reports, and upon that evidence which is better even than written orders, the fact that in course of time troops to a considerable number did put in an appearance there. It is difficult, however, to escape the conviction (1) that the Duke was badly served by his intelligence department on the 15th, for he did not receive news from the front till the evening ; (2) That, misconceiving Napoleon's plan, the concentration at Quatre Bras was perilously delayed, and was indeed in the nature of an after-thought, orders for concentration elsewhere having already been issued. It is certain that on the night of the 15th-16th June, the only troops actually at Quatre Bras in position to oppose Ney were the brigade of Prince Bernard of Saxe-Weimar, 4000 strong, and that they were there, not as a consequence of the Duke's orders, but in direct opposition to them, the Prince of Orange having been instructed on the 15th, "to collect his 2nd and 3rd divisions (of which Prince Bernard's brigade formed a part) at Nivelles"—a point six miles to the westward of Quatre Bras.

## VII.

Summarising the operations of the 15th, we find—

1. That Napoleon, with the French centre, had driven the 1st Prussian corps before him, and

taken position to the south of Fleurus, ready for an engagement with Blücher next day: that owing to accidents the centre was not supported by the right in such a manner as Napoleon had directed and hoped, but that by night-time the right was collected and in position,—that the left, under Ney, had, as far as the 2nd corps was concerned, acted with energy, driving Prince Bernard from Frasne, and occupying that position, though it is questionable whether Ney should not have pushed still further, and occupied Quatre Bras,—that the first corps was unaccountably slow in its progress, and entirely failed to fulfil its instructions to support and join itself to the second.

2. That three out of the four Prussian corps were in course of concentration in the neighbourhood of Sombref, Bülow being at such a distance that he would require, reckoning from midnight of the 15th, at least twenty-four hours to join the main army.

3. That the Duke of Wellington, only hearing the news from the front in the evening, issued orders for the concentration of his army in the neighbourhood of Nivelles — only 4000 troops being at Quatre Bras, and those by accident— but that subsequent orders were issued, though copies are not forthcoming, some time in the night or early morning of the 16th, directing a concentration on Quatre Bras.

## CHAPTER V.

### THE MORNING OF JUNE 16TH.

I. Wellington and his army on the morning of the 16th; his statements to Blücher; their value.—II. Blücher's stand at Ligny. —III. Advance of the French right on Ligny.—IV. Attitude and conduct of Ney on the morning of the 16th.—V. Ney's dispositions before Quatre Bras.—VI. Napoleon on the morning of the 16th; his general plan of campaign as distinguished from his particular plan for the day; modification of his morning plan to suit the circumstances of the afternoon.—VII. Respective dispositions of Blücher and Napoleon for the battle of Ligny; Napoleon's plan of battle; positions and numbers of the forces engaged.

### I.

THE Duke of Wellington rode out of Brussels between seven and eight o'clock in the morning, but before leaving he had received from his Deputy Quarter-Master-General, Sir W. De Lancey, a Memorandum purporting to state the actual situation of the army at seven o'clock A.M. Fortified with this information, the Duke rode to Waterloo, passed Picton's brigade, which was halted there, and had not yet received orders to advance, and arrived at Quatre Bras about ten o'clock. Having surveyed the position, he despatched a letter to

## THE MORNING OF JUNE 16TH

Blücher, giving him information as to the situation of the army.

"*On the heights beyond Frasne,
June* 16, 1815.   10.30 *a.m.*

"MY DEAR PRINCE,—My army is situated as follows :—

"The *Corps d'Armée* of the Prince of Orange has a division here and at Quatre Bras, and the rest at Nivelles.

"The Reserve is in march from Waterloo to Genappe, and will arrive at noon.

"The English cavalry will be at the same hour at Nivelles.

"The corps of Lord Hill is at Braine-le-Comte.

"I do not see much of the enemy in front of us, and I await news of Your Highness and the arrival of troops in order to decide my operations for the day.

"Nothing has appeared on the side of Binche, nor upon our right.—Your very obedient servant,

"WELLINGTON."

A comparison between this document and the Memorandum of Sir W. De Lancey shows that Wellington, in giving information to Blücher, depended almost implicitly upon the Memorandum. It becomes a matter of the first importance therefore to see if the situation of the army really was what Sir William's "Disposition" and Wellington's letter to Blücher stated it to be.

The text of the Memorandum is therefore sub-

"Standard" - 3/7/96

Several objects of much interest were disposed of yesterday by Messrs. Debenham and Storr, at their auction-rooms, King-street, Covent-garden. One, which produced a very lively competition, was a general officer's gold cross for the Peninsular Campaign, with clasps for Talavera, Nive, Salamanca, Vittoria, and St. Sebastian. It was presented to Colonel William Howe De Lancy, and was especially interesting from the fact that the recipient was Quartermaster General on the Staff of the Duke of Wellington at Waterloo, where he received his death wound, and the Duke, in his Despatch, after stating that the Quartermaster General was killed by a cannon shot in the middle of the action, went on to say, "this officer is a serious loss to his Majesty's service, and to me at this moment." The biddings started at 50*l*., and ran up to 550*l*., at which the cross was sold. Another gold Peninsular medal, for the battle of Talavera, 1809, awarded to Lieut. Colonel Henry Seymour, 23d Light Dragoons, fetched 60*l*.

# 52 WATERLOO

joined, and notes attached to each paragraph, with a view of estimating its accuracy. (**Black print** denotes *the document;* small print, *notes.*)

**DISPOSITION OF THE BRITISH ARMY AT SEVEN O'CLOCK a.m., 16th JUNE.**

**1st Division.** Had arrived at or moving on **Braine-le-Comte, marching to Nivelles and Quatre Bras.**

By the supplementary orders of the previous evening, 10 P.M., June 15th, the first division (Cooke's) was to move from Enghien upon Braine-le-Comte. It arrived there at 9 A.M., halted till noon, awaiting orders. Cooke, on his own responsibility, ordered the advance to Nivelles; arrived there at 3 P.M. Thence ordered to Quatre Bras, a seven miles' march; came up about 7 P.M.

**2nd Division. Braine-le-Comte, marching to Nivelles.**

The 2nd division (Clinton) by 10 P.M. orders was to move from Ath to Enghien. These orders only arrived at 10 A.M., 16th; division reached Enghien at 2 P.M; Braine-le-Comte at 12 (midnight). Thus the 2nd division was nowhere near Quatre Bras on the day of the battle.

**3rd Division. Nivelles, marching to Quatre Bras.**

By the 10 P.M. orders the 3rd division (Alten) was "to continue its movement from Braine-le-Comte upon Nivelles." It arrived at Nivelles at noon.

**4th Division. Oudenarde, marching to Braine-le-Comte.**

The 4th division (Colville) ordered (10 P.M. orders) upon Enghien.

From Brussels to Oudenarde was at least 40 miles, the orders therefore would arrive about 5 A.M.

# THE MORNING OF JUNE 16TH 53

Oudenarde to Enghien 40 miles, and on to Braine 55. This division was quite unavailable for service at Quatre Bras, and probably was not reckoned upon by the Duke for that action.

### 5th Division.  Beyond Waterloo, marching to Genappe.

The 5th division (Picton) left Brussels about 5 A.M. Waterloo is 11 miles distant. It certainly was not "marching to Genappe" at 7 A.M., for it did not leave Waterloo till 1 P.M.

### 6th Division.  Assche, marching to Genappe and Quatre Bras.

The 6th division (Cole's) was at Assche, 7 A.M. No orders for it on 15th.

### 5th Hanoverian Brigade.  Hal, marching to Genappe and Quatre Bras.

This brigade (Vincke) was situated as stated. It may have been marching as stated.

### 4th Hanoverian Brigade.  Beyond Waterloo, to Genappe and Quatre Bras.

This brigade (Best) came up together with Picton's division about 3 P.M. It was at or close to Waterloo at the hour stated.

### 2nd Division, 3rd Division,  } Army of the Low Countries {  At Nivelles and Quatre Bras.

These divisions (Prince of Orange) were ordered, at 10 P.M. on the 15th, to collect at Nivelles. The 2nd division (Perponcher) was at Quatre Bras, but the 3rd (Chassé) only reached Nivelles about noon.

# 54 WATERLOO

1st Division, Indian Brigade, } Army of Low Countries { At Sotteghem, marching to Enghien.

1st Dutch-Belgians (Bylandt) and 7th Dutch-Belgians (Anthing, or the Indian Brigade), were situated as stated, and perhaps were so marching.

## Major-General Dörnberg's Brigade and Cumberland Hussars, beyond Waterloo, marching to Genappe and Quatre Bras.

These troops had been ordered on 15th " to march upon Vilvorde, and to bivouac on the high-road near to that town." They had to come from Mons, 45 miles. They could not have reached Vilvorde, much less be "beyond Waterloo," at 7 A.M.

## Remainder of the Cavalry, Braine-le-Comte, marching to Nivelles and Quatre Bras.

The 10 P.M. orders of the 15th had directed the Cavalry on Enghien. These orders received at 6 A.M. on the 16th. At 7 A.M., therefore, these troops were still close to their cantonments at Ninhove, and did not reach Quatre Bras till the fight was over.

## Duke of Brunswick's Corps. Beyond Waterloo, marching to Genappe.

The Duke of Brunswick's contingent arrived shortly after Picton's division to the support of Prince Bernard's Brigade at Quatre Bras. It left Brussels at 5 A.M.

## Nassau. Beyond Waterloo, marching to Genappe.

Kruse's Nassau contingent did not arrive to take part in the action. The Nassauers engaged were a part of Prince Bernard's Brigade. Kruse's division could not have been "beyond Waterloo," therefore, at the hour mentioned.

It should now be clear, and reference to the maps will make it clearer still, that the Duke of Wellington's army was by no means situated as the Duke stated that it was in his letter to Blücher. Doubtless he had a right to expect that his chief-of-staff would supply him with correct information, and to this extent he was justified in his announcements to the Prussian leader; but, at the same time, very little reflection was required to demonstrate to him convincingly that in some particulars it was erroneous even in the case of those troops which were nearest at hand, and whose movements and position were therefore capable of the most accurate definition. To take one example only, the Duke had himself passed Picton's division at Waterloo as he rode to Quatre Bras. It was halted there to await orders to march either on Quatre Bras or Nivelles as the Duke, from his observations at the front, might decide. It was not moved forward from Waterloo till one o'clock. Nevertheless, the Duke informs Blücher that at 10.30 "the Reserve (of which Picton's division was a part) *"is in march from Waterloo to Genappe, where it will arrive at noon."* The same kind of criticism may be extended to most of the other statements in the Duke's letter. We can, therefore, scarcely be surprised if Gneisenau, who never cordially trusted the Duke of Wellington, believed that it was his intention deliberately to deceive the Prussians as to his ability to support them in the coming battle in order to induce them to fight, and so hold the French in check while the Anglo-Dutch concentration was being effected.* Such a course of conduct is entirely foreign to the Duke's character, nor has any evidence, other than the Memorandum, been brought forward to support it, but it was not unnatural or improbable that such a suspicion should be entertained, especially in the mind of one not cordially disposed to the Duke.

There cannot be a doubt that Wellington was himself deceived by Sir W. De Lancey's Memorandum. Serious consequences might have followed from the mistake. The Duke himself determined to stand at Quatre Bras under the impression that a sufficiency of troops would be upon the ground in time. Had he known the real state of the case, he probably would have come to a different decision, for at no time during that engagement were there forces enough on the field to withstand Ney's united command, and of course Wellington could not reckon upon the accident, which, as will be seen, kept that force disunited, one-half of it being altogether unavailable for the battle. Thus, from too confident reliance upon mistaken information, the Duke ran the risk of a serious defeat at Quatre Bras; while Blücher, at Ligny, was induced to hope for assistance from his ally, which, in fact, it was impossible to render.

In view of the charges still made by Prussian authorities against the Duke of Wellington, a

* Delbrück's " Life of Gneisenau," published 1880.

# THE MORNING OF JUNE 16TH 57

separate section must be reserved for a more particular consideration of the matter from a Prussian point of view.

Having surveyed the front at Quatre Bras, Wellington rode over to Bry for the purpose of holding personal communication with Blücher. Baron Müffling, the Prussian *attaché* on the Duke's staff, and Gneisenau were present at the interview. Müffling has given an account of what took place, and it appears that the Duke reiterated the statements of his letter. The question arose as to the support to be rendered by the Anglo-Dutch army to the Prussians in the coming engagement, and the Duke, it is said, undertook to come if he were not himself attacked. It is evident that he expected nothing serious from the French upon his own front, for as he left Blücher he said, "I will overthrow what is before me at Frasne, and will direct myself on Gosselies," thus clearly indicating that he either entirely misconceived the strength of the French under Marshal Ney, or else that he was confident of finding practically his whole army at Quatre Bras upon his return from the interview. The Duke then rode back to Quatre Bras, where, upon his arrival at three o'clock, he found the battle already in progress.

## II.

We must now trace the movements of the Prussians upon the 16th up to the time when the battle of Ligny began, reserving the consideration of the engagements for a separate section.

Shortly after dawn Ziethen was under orders to march, and he withdrew from Fleurus to take up position at St Amand. The 2nd corps moved up to support the 1st, and occupied a position behind it. Thus these two corps formed the Prussian right and centre. The 3rd corps took position later in the day, extending from Sombref to Balâtre, and formed the left of the Prussian army. These movements were on the point of completion when the Duke of Wellington came over to Bry, and they lead to the conclusion that Blücher had already determined to stand his ground, before any personal consultation with the Duke had taken place. This fact has an important bearing upon another vexed question of the campaign. Did Wellington promise to support Blücher in the battle of Ligny, and did Blücher fight relying upon that promise? *

There can be no doubt that help was expected, and that Wellington expected to be able to render it. The conversation which took place between him and Blücher at Bry ran chiefly upon the direction from which that help should come, and we have heard Wellington declaring his intention of overthrowing whatever was before him, and promising to come " if I am not attacked myself." But all this does not constitute evid-

* See Appendix.

## THE MORNING OF JUNE 16TH

ence to prove that Blücher would not have taken position for battle at all but for Wellington's assurance. If so, why did he not gain the assurance before taking position? There is no document of either the 15th or 16th conveying any such assurance. The Duke's letter of 10.30, already quoted, may have given rise to an expectation of assistance, but it could have done no more. It is reasonable to suppose that after his defeat Blücher would have alluded to Wellington's failure to redeem his promise, had such a promise been actually made, and that he would have felt some personal resentment against Wellington as the man who had played him false and exposed him to disaster, but it is notorious that no such feelings existed in Blücher's mind, and no such allusions appear in his report,

The whole arrangements, in fact, were of a piece with that loose system of combination under which the allies had acted all along. They were to act together, but the terms of their co-operation and the methods of effecting it had never been defined.

At the same time, it would appear to be extreme rashness on Blücher's part to engage the enemy with one whole corps of 30,000 men absent from the field, and with no assistance to count upon from his ally,—to oppose his 80,000 men to what he supposed to be Napoleon's whole force. Blücher was, however, of an impulsive character, apt to mistake hopes for realities, and there is no doubt that he both expected the arrival of his missing corps in time to take part in the battle, and also some degree of assistance from the Duke of Wellington. This being so, he was perhaps justified in determining to fight rather than to retreat still further in the face of the enemy, and thus disspirit his troops at the very opening of the campaign.

III.

We now come to the operations of the two wings of the French army on the morning of the 16th.

Dealing first with the right and centre, whose movements involve little subject for controversy, and which were under Napoleon's more immediate control, we find that upon the morning of the 16th, the Emperor wrote a letter from Charleroi to Marshal Grouchy, entrusting him with the command of the 3rd and 4th corps, "as commander of the right wing" of the army. This letter could not have been written later than eight o'clock A.M. To these troops were added the cavalry of Pajol, Milhaud, and Excelmans, and with them Grouchy is directed to advance forthwith to Sombref—the cavalry and the 3rd corps (Vandamme) leading—the 4th corps (Gérard) to follow immediately, though by a different road, in order to avoid any crowding (*encombrements*) at Fleurus, whither the Emperor was about to direct the Reserve. Napoleon expresses his intention of attacking the enemy if at Sombref, or even if it

## THE MORNING OF JUNE 16TH

was to be found as far back as Gembloux, in order that it might be cleared out of the way. He would then be able with no loss of time to combine his operations with those of the left wing, and be free to march on Brussels next morning, or possibly the same evening. He concludes by telling Grouchy that he has no reason to expect, from reports to hand, that the Prussians will be able to oppose to him more than 40,000 men.

These movements Grouchy proceeded to effect, the Emperor himself with the Guard coming up to Fleurus before one o'clock, and the left wing was promptly formed in order of battle, in accordance with Napoleon's plan of attacking the enemy wherever he should find him.

The 6th corps (Lobau), numbering rather more than 10,000 men, seems to have been strangely neglected in Napoleon's orders. It had bivouacked the evening before close to Charleroi, and, indeed, was not across the river. It was allowed to remain there throughout the morning of the 16th, no orders for its advance being despatched till the battle of Ligny had actually begun. Eventually it was directed to move to the support of Napoleon, but only arrived on the field as the battle was ending, and it took no active part in the engagement. Thus Napoleon, apparently with deliberation, refused to avail himself of the services of 10,000 men, whose prompt interposition at a critical moment might have been of inestimable value. It is even stated by Charras that Lobau was left a discretion as to which wing of the army he should follow, though eventually instructed to attach himself to the right and centre.

Several inferences may be drawn from Napoleon's conduct in respect to this corps. Taken together with the statement to Grouchy, that the Prussians could not oppose to the French more than 40,000 men, it may be regarded as an indication that Napoleon, being deceived as to the strength of the enemy which he was about to meet, neglected to bring up Lobau because he supposed he would have no use for him, or that, as is more probable, at a moment when his whole army was engaged against the allies, the Emperor may have thought it prudent to retain a reserve of 10,000 fresh troops which he might employ as occasion should direct, in case of disaster on either wing. Further allusion will be made to this matter in discussing the battle of Ligny itself; for the moment it is sufficient to note that throughout the morning of the 16th the 6th corps was in bivouac near Charleroi.

### IV.

The movements of the left wing, under Ney, now demand attention, and with them considerable controversy is associated.

After conducting the operations of his wing until the close of the 15th, the Marshal returned to the Emperor's headquarters, where, over supper, a lengthy interview took place. Whatever may have been the exact tenor of Napoleon's earlier

# THE MORNING OF JUNE 16TH 63

verbal instructions as to the occupation of Quatre Bras, there can be no doubt that Ney reported at this interview what he had actually done—that Quatre Bras had not been occupied—that only his advance columns had got as far as Frasne, and that D'Erlon was scarcely yet across the river. If Grouchy was present at this interview, this must be the occasion to which he refers when he says that he had himself heard Napoleon * " blame Ney for having suspended the movement of his troops upon the 15th, instead of keeping himself to the execution, pure and simple, of his instructions, which ordered him to march on Quatre Bras." None the less the blame, if blame there was, cannot have been very severe, nor can it have interrupted the friendly relations existing between Ney and his master. It may be assumed that Napoleon gave the Marshal an outline of the operations he proposed for the day which was about to dawn, for upon his departure we find Ney conferring with Reille at Gosselies, and ordering him to set out as soon as he could, and get his troops together at Frasne. This may or may not have been in consequence of Napoleon's instructions. No written instructions reached Ney till after 10 A.M., and it was not till an hour later that Reille actually moved forward from Gosselies. We have therefore to consider whether, in the absence of definite written instructions, Ney was fulfilling his duty in

* Observations by Grouchy on Gourgand's Narrative (Philadelphia, 1818).

remaining quiescent during the early morning hours of the 16th.

If, throughout this campaign, nothing more was expected from such commanders as Ney and Grouchy than a blind adherence to the letter of their instructions, then it will not be difficult to justify in the main their entire course of action; but, as has been said, Napoleon looked to his immediate subordinates for co-operation as much as for obedience. He took them very completely into his confidence, explained to them his hopes and projects in terms very different from those of peremptory command, and expected, and had much right to expect, as full an appreciation of the spirit as of the letter of his instructions. Assuming that a certain latitude was allowed to Ney over and beyond his formal orders, it cannot be maintained that, even on abstract grounds, the Marshal was justified in adopting a course of inaction from sunrise until eleven o'clock A.M. For there was definite work to be done, left over from the day before, to which the instructions of the day before, in the absence of others, clearly applied, and this work was to collect the tardy corps of D'Erlon, and bring it up to the support of Reille. Here there can be no question as to orders. Every order given to D'Erlon on the day before was to the effect that he was to keep close to Reille, "*vous prendrez des positions qui vous* rapprocheront *de Reille—pour* appuyer *Reille et le* seconder *dans ses opérations—l'intention est que*

## THE MORNING OF JUNE 16TH 65

*vous ralliez votre corps . . . pour* joindre *le 2^{me} corps, d'après les ordres que vous donnera M. le Maréchal, prince de la Moskowa* " (Ney).

Nor can there be any question that these precise orders had not been carried out. We left the 1st corps at Marchiennes, upon the Sambre. There it remained throughout the remainder of the 15th, three of its divisions bivouacking on the north bank of the river, but one division, at evening time, had not yet come up, and so was not across the Sambre that day.

The work of Ney, therefore, was clear. If there were no fresh instructions from the Emperor, there were the incompleted instructions of the day before to fulfil.

The first communication which passed between Napoleon and Ney shows the anxiety of the former upon this very matter. He wishes to know " if the first corps has operated its movement, and what is this morning the exact position of the 1st and 2nd *Corps d'Armée.*" The Emperor had to learn that, far from seconding, supporting, or joining Reille, at 6 A.M. in the morning the whole of the 1st corps was not yet across the river, and no part of it was more than a short march in advance of Marchiennes. There is no intention here of fixing upon Ney the original backwardness of this corps. His responsibilities did not begin till five o'clock in the evening of the 15th, but from that moment he was bound to use every effort to consolidate his force, for as long as it was disunited it

E

was ineffective for the full execution of the task assigned to it.

At the same time it is impossible to attribute Ney's inaction to any natural dilatoriness or want of energy. We may presume that he was acting on general principles, and must look at each part of his conduct in relation to the whole. Upon the 16th, while the battle of Quatre Bras was in progress, in spite of precise instructions to the contrary, Ney proposed to keep half his available force in reserve at Frasnes. It may therefore be inferred, with very considerable probability, that throughout there was a deliberate intention on Ney's part to keep the 1st corps well in the rear, in order that it might act as a reserve to his wing, ready to support him in the event of disaster to the 2nd corps. In his judgment such a course was safe and prudent. It was such a course as Napoleon himself adopted in regard to the 6th corps. We must not quarrel with Ney for having a judgment of his own. It has been specially claimed for Napoleon's generals that they were expected to co-operate with their master, not merely to obey blindly. But when Ney, on his own judgment, ventured deliberately to follow a course opposed to his instructions from head-quarters, it is certainly not unfair that he should be called upon to bear the responsibility for any ill effects which followed from such a determination.

The first instructions of the 16th sent to Ney from head-quarters have already been alluded to. They evince Napoleon's anxiety to know exactly how it stood with the 1st corps. In this first letter, which arrived about 6 A.M., there is, it is true, no word about Quatre Bras, no suggestion that it is to be occupied immediately, much less any precise orders to that effect. But then in this letter there are no orders at all. It is a letter conveying and demanding information. Ney is told that Kellermann's cavalry has been directed on his wing, and is asked for information as to the position of his own force; and the answer to the question, why no definite instructions were given to seize Quatre Bras, is that Napoleon wanted definite information before he could issue definite instructions.

Early in the morning Napoleon wrote a letter to Ney, similar in character to the letter to Grouchy already referred to. In this letter the Emperor is extremely confidential; he details his own plans and the instructions given to Grouchy, declares his intention of attacking the enemy and clearing the road as far as Gembloux. There, according to events, he will decide upon his future course. Ney is to be ready to march on Brussels the moment Napoleon's decision has been arrived at. He may even arrive at Brussels at seven o'clock the next morning. To effect this purpose Ney is to dispose his troops in front of and around Quatre Bras, extending a division to Marbais to be in touch with the battle on the right, and these dispositions are to be so made "that at the first order, your eight divisions can march rapidly and without obstacle to Brussels."

Following immediately upon this letter came the formal orders from Soult, in which he is instructed to take position at Quatre Bras. It is clear from the tone of these orders that little resistance was looked for from the side of Brussels, and that the movements of the 16th, as far as the left wing at any rate was concerned, were expected to be as leisurely and unopposed as those of the day before. But it was not long before news reached head-quarters of the real state of the case. Soult had heard of masses of troops on the side of Quatre Bras. He therefore writes again to Ney with supplementary instructions "Reunite the corps of Counts Reille and D'Erlon, and that of the Count of Valmy (Kellermann), who is this instant starting to join you; with these you should beat and destroy any hostile forces which may present themselves." How far Ney was from carrying out these instructions is seen in the orders of the following day. In them Soult was instructed to say, "The Emperor has seen with pain that you did not yesterday reunite the divisions. They acted in isolation, and consequently you suffered losses. If the corps of D'Erlon and Reille had acted together, not an Englishman of the force which attacked you would have escaped."

Ney's first duty, therefore, on the morning of the 16th, was to hasten the progress of D'Erlon's

# THE MORNING OF JUNE 16TH

dilatory corps, and to join it to the corps of Reille, but throughout the day the two corps remained disunited, with consequences disastrous to both wings of the French army.

Not only did Ney fail to consolidate his force, but he also neglected to occupy Quatre Bras early on the morning of the 16th. Admittedly, it would have been easy to occupy it at any time up to noon or one o'clock, for Ney's force, if combined, amounted to more than 40,000 men, while the ground was held only by a part of the Prince of Orange's divisions, no English reinforcements beginning to arrive till after two o'clock.

Various considerations may be put forward to account for this. First of all, the Marshal was assuredly unaware how small was the force in occupation of Quatre Bras, for, owing to the nature of the ground, it was difficult to gain precise intelligence, or to form accurate estimates. Moreover, he had not merely to reckon with the enemy actually upon the ground, but with those hostile forces which were hurrying to the scene of action. Wellington, he knew, was rapidly concentrating his army, and the French left wing was in danger of being confronted at any time by 80,000 men. Caution, therefore, was the first essential in face of such a possibility, for it was only by extreme caution that 40,000 men could manœuvre to any advantage in face of double their numbers.

In the second place, Ney's own force actually in hand was by no means so strong as it was made to appear on paper. Not only was the 1st corps far behind, but one division of the 2nd—that of Girard—had been detached from the left wing, and was operating in support of Grouchy near Fleurus. Reille's corps was thus weakened for Ney's purposes by about 5000 men, and so, instead of 40,000, he had not, in the absence of D'Erlon and Girard, 25,000 men available for an immediate advance.

Again, an immediate movement on Quatre Bras would, as the map plainly shows, throw Ney considerably to the front of the main army; but it was an essential principle of the general scheme of operations, that the two wings should advance simultaneously, and should keep as far as possible *la même hauteur.* Hence it is urged by Clausewitz and others, that Ney was right in timing his forward movement to keep pace with that of Napoleon, and that it would have been an act of inexcusable rashness to outstrip the movement of the main army. "Ordered as he was to advance *tête baissée* along one road, could he tell whether, when at last he raised his head and eyes, he would not find himself outflanked by hostile columns on the right, and above all on the left, and pinned to the ground he stood on? . . . What general has ever been asked to advance with 40,000 men along a single road into the very midst of the enemy's forces?"\*

Forcible as these considerations are, they do

\* *Feldzug von* 1815. Kap. 36.

not excuse Ney. The quotation from Clausewitz ends with a question which is almost in the form of a challenge. Both question and challenge are met by a reference to Ney's instructions. He was ordered to advance on and beyond Quatre Bras with the force entrusted to him, and events were soon to prove that, had he concentrated his corps, and obeyed his orders, he would not have had to face these problematical dangers. When, as has been said, he assumed the right to an independent judgment, he assumed the responsibility for its consequences, and if those consequences were disastrous, the blame must in justice fall upon him.

## V.

The formal instructions to Marshal Ney, to which allusions have been made, were as follows :—

"CHARLEROI, 16*th June* 1815.

" M. LE MARÉCHAL,—The Emperor orders you to put in movement the 2nd and 1st *Corps d'Armée*, as well as the 3rd Cavalry Corps, which has been put at your disposal, in order to direct them upon the intersection of the roads called Les Trois Bras (Quatre Bras), where you will cause them to take position. . . . His Majesty desires, if there is no obstacle, that you should establish one division with cavalry at Genappe, and he orders you to carry another division towards (*du côté de*) Marbais. . . .
"DUC DE DALMATIE."

Ney's dispositions, however, were by no means such as were prescribed. Reille was still at Gosselies at 10.15 A.M., for he wrote to Ney from that place, announcing that information had arrived to the effect that the Prussians were forming at St Amand, and that as a consequence he should postpone his own movement until the receipt of further orders. It was not till nearly noon that the 2nd corps left Gosselies, and in due course it was formed up for action at Quatre Bras.

The 1st corps was still in the neighbourhood of Marchiennes and the river at 11 A.M. According to D'Erlon's own statement, it was not till between 11 and 12 A.M. that he received his marching orders—namely to take position at Frasnes, with three of his four divisions, and to direct the fourth on Marbais. D'Erlon was engaged in executing this movement when the battle began at Quatre Bras, and he reached Frasnes about 5 P.M.

Kellermann's dragoons were posted at Frasnes and Liberchies, where also were the divisions of the Guard commanded by Lefèbvre-Desnouettes and Colbert.

Thus, at 2 P.M., at which hour the engagement at Quatre Bras began, Ney had only Reille's three divisions in position. The bulk of his force was in reserve at Frasnes, or engaged in marching on that point, and this notwithstanding his precise instructions to "reunite the corps of D'Erlon, Reille, and that of the Count de Valmy (Kellermann)."

## VI.

"I have adopted as a general principle of this campaign the division of my army into two wings and a reserve." In conformity with this announcement, made to Ney in his morning letter of the 16th, Napoleon wrote to Marshal Grouchy investing him with the command of the right wing, which was to consist of the 3rd and 4th corps, and of the cavalry corps of Pajol, Milhaud, and Excelmans.

The 6th corps and the Guard made up the reserve, which was under the immediate direction of the Emperor in person. The reserve formed the centre of the army, and was so disposed as to be able to support the operations of either wing, according to circumstances. It could also be strengthened by reinforcements detached from either wing, as occasion might require.

The left wing numbered about 40,000 men, the right wing nearly 50,000, the reserve rather more than 29,000 men.

Such being the general principle underlying Napoleon's dispositions, it is necessary to examine the particular plan of operations which the Emperor sketched out for the day of the 16th, for it is of the first importance to recognise clearly the distinction between the general plan governing the campaign as a whole, and the particular plan governing the operations of a single day.*

* The failure to recognise this distinction invalidates the argument which Clausewitz applies to this part of the subject.

Nor is this the only distinction which it is essential to have in mind. The march of events upon the morning of the 16th was destined to produce important modifications in the scheme of operations as originally laid down for the day, so that in the morning we see a set of instructions issued to meet the situation as Napoleon conceived it in theory; in the afternoon the dispositions and instructions were based on the actual facts of the case as learned from practical experience and observation.

It is from the morning letters to Ney and Grouchy that we are able to grasp Napoleon's first ideas of the situation which confronted him.

In the letters to Ney, Napoleon informs the Marshal of his intention to attack the Prussians if he meets with them, and to explore the road as far as Gembloux. This done, he will decide upon his future movement, and the instant his decision is made, Ney is to be ready to march on Brussels. "I will support you with the Guard, which will be at Fleurus or Sombref, and should wish to reach Brussels to-morrow morning." Therefore (*donc*) Ney was to dispose his troops partly in front of Quatre Bras at Genappe, partly around that point, and partly at Marbais, a point midway between Quatre Bras and Sombref. The object of placing a division at Marbais, as Soult makes clear to the Marshal, was that it might be ready to support either Grouchy at Sombref or Ney himself at Quatre Bras according to circumstances, and to

## THE MORNING OF JUNE 16TH 75

explore the roads in all directions, but particularly in the directions of Gembloux and Wavre.

The letter to Grouchy instructs him to march with the right wing to Sombref. "If the enemy is at Sombref, I wish to attack him. I even wish to attack him at Gembloux, and to seize that position, my intention being, after making myself acquainted with these two positions, to march this night and operate with my left wing against the English. Lose not a moment therefore. . . . Communicate constantly with Gérard, so that he may be able to assist you in attacking Sombref, if it be necessary. . . . All the information which I have is to the effect that the Prussians cannot oppose to us more than 40,000 men.

"As soon as you have made yourself master of Sombref, it will be necessary to send forward an advance guard to Gembloux to reconnoitre all the roads which converge on Sombref, at the same time that you will establish your communications with Marshal Ney."

The first point to which these letters draw our attention is Napoleon's uncertainty in regard to the Prussian army. He proposes to attack the Prussians "if he meets with them." He anticipates no difficulty in occupying Sombref—indeed, his objective point is rather Gembloux than Sombref. Evidently, in his opinion, the Prussians were far from being fully concentrated. If Ziethen from Charleroi were supported by Pirch from Namur, that was about the extent of the force which Blücher would have to oppose to him, and so he persuaded himself that he had to deal only with some 40,000 men, against whom, using Grouchy's force alone, he could place 50,000 in the field.

He is also quite at ease on the subject of the the Anglo-Dutch army. No resistance to Ney at Quatre Bras is expected. The march on Brussels would be unimpeded, for the Emperor proposes to arrive there "to-morrow morning." The results of the 16th, according to Napoleon's ideas in the morning, would be the occupation of Genappe, Quatre Bras, Gembloux, and Sombref, the overthrow of such Prussian corps as had effected a concentration, and the disappearance of all obstacles to an uninterrupted march on Brussels.

At the moment when the Emperor was transcribing these confident anticipations to his lieutenants, Blücher was rapidly concentrating three-fourths of his army at and about Sombref, and Anglo-Dutch troops to the number of 25,000 men were pressing hastily on Quatre Bras to support Prince Bernhard in the defence of that position.

Conclusions very unfavourable to Napoleon have often been drawn from a comparison of his intentions with the true facts of the situation. He is accused of exhibiting arrogant self-confidence in combination with an almost wilful self-deception. But the case is capable of quite another interpretation, for the contention is, to say the least, tenable, that on general principles of strategy his judgment of the situation was a correct one. That judgment was based upon knowledge which in the main was accurate. He knew that the concentration of the Prussian army was by no means complete, and on general principles he was justified in assuming that Gembloux, or even Wavre, was the point on which that concentration would be made. Gembloux was nearer to Namur than Sombref, and was nearer for Bülow in his march from Liége. In fact, while concentration at Sombref was sure to be partial, at Gembloux it might have been complete. He also knew that Wellington was not in any proper sense of the word concentrated at all. His own arrangements excluded the possibility of any effective support being at present given by Wellington to Blücher or by Blücher to Wellington, and therefore, in Napoleon's opinion, it would be the height of imprudence in either of the allied commanders to risk a general engagement upon that day. To do so would be to play into his hands—for he could oppose to the Prussians on the one hand a force which, even if inferior in numbers, was yet, by superiority in military qualities, capable of inflicting upon them a severe defeat, while on his left wing Ney could certainly hold in check, if not entirely overthrow, any force which Wellington, in the backward state of his concentration, might be able to put into the field. Could he suppose, in default of actual observation, that his enemies would thus play his game for him? But even if they did, his general plan for the day was not thereby invalidated. On the contrary, much of it would still hold good in spite of the altered state of affairs, and the result would be more decisive than he had at first ventured to anticipate. Instead of merely inflicting a check upon his adversaries, the chance would be offered him of disposing of them both in the course of a single day.

It was about 10 A.M. when Napoleon began to entertain suspicions that his movements for the day would not be so uninterrupted as he had at first supposed. At that hour he learned " that the enemy was displaying masses of troops on the side of Quatre Bras," and it was then that he imperatively ordered Ney to unite his corps, and with his forces thus consolidated, to beat and destroy all the hostile forces which might display themselves. He then proceeded in person to Fleurus, and upon his arrival he learned that the Prussians, according to all appearances, were taking position in force with a view to a general engagement. He was not inclined to credit these reports, and it was not until he had himself inspected the Prussian position that he was convinced of Blücher's intention to stand and fight. From the vantage ground of a windmill a little in front of the town he was able to observe the whole disposition of the Prussian army, and it taught him in a moment all that he needed to know. Instead of 40,000 men, he saw before him three-fourths of Blücher's force. From its extended line he could read the Prussian

# THE MORNING OF JUNE 16TH 79

general's intention of reaching forward one hand to Wellington upon his right, and the other to Bülow coming up upon his left. Convinced that neither Wellington nor Bülow could render any assistance, Napoleon at once formulated his plans, so as to gain the utmost possible advantage from the imprudence of his adversary, and the plan of attack which he now developed was of a character to result in the complete overthrow of the Prussian army.

We now turn to the examination of this plan, which was to govern the operations of the French army throughout the remainder of the day. Napoleon's earlier schemes, communicated in the morning to Grouchy and to Ney, may be dismissed from our minds, except in so far as they were still partially applicable to the new situation. His movements, far from being entirely dislocated by Blücher's unexpected demonstration in force, were only rendered the more vigorous and the more decisive, and with marvellous skill he adapted all the essential features of his original design to serve the purposes of the unlooked-for opportunity which was now before him. Blücher, as Napoleon expressed it, was "taken *en flagrant délit*," and it only remained to mete out to him the punishment due to his rashness and temerity.

With the Prussians in force before him, and with masses of troops displaying themselves at Quatre Bras, there was no longer a question of occupying, practically without resistance, Quatre Bras and

Genappe on the one hand, and Sombref and Gembloux on the other. Manœuvres were to give place to action, and the problem before Napoleon was how to make action most decisive against one, if not both, of the enemies he was about to meet.

The first essential was to prevent the allied armies from rendering each other any support. For this purpose his original plan was still efficient. The left wing would hold Wellington in check at Quatre Bras, while the right and the reserve would contain Blücher. The division which Ney had been ordered to post at Marbais would not only intervene directly between the allies, but could be utilised with crushing effect against one or other of them, as circumstances might direct.

All anxiety on the score of a junction between the allies being removed, it remained to determine, should it prove impossible to secure a decisive triumph on both wings, against which of the opposing armies the main effort was to be directed. Every consideration pointed to the Prussian army as the true point of attack. Any conspicuous success gained against the 90,000 men then on the ground would involve the demoralisation of the whole Prussian contingent; it would retire in confusion upon its base, thus separating itself, with every step in retreat, further and further from its ally; nor, even when reinforced by Bülow's additional 30,000 men, would it be in a position for several days to assume an offensive attitude, and

# THE MORNING OF JUNE 16TH

in the meantime Napoleon could dispose of Wellington at his leisure.

Moreover, the very dispositions of the Prussians, in order of battle, exposed them to such a defeat as that upon which Napoleon calculated; while in the case of Wellington only a small portion of his troops could possibly be on the ground at Quatre Bras, and any success gained over him then could only be of a partial and indecisive character.

The main idea, therefore, in Napoleon's mind in drawing up his plans for the afternoon of the 16th was this, that the main business of the day rested with him and with the right wing at Ligny, Sombref, and St Amand, while the duty of Ney was first to contain Wellington, and then to second Napoleon's operations against Blücher.

It was this main idea that Ney, as we shall see, entirely failed to grasp.

## VII.

The Emperor's plan of battle against Blücher was governed altogether by the dispositions of the old Marshal himself. These were by no means such as to secure the approval of the Duke of Wellington. He was at Bry while the Prussians were being placed in position, and expressed to Sir Henry Hardinge his opinion that "if they fight here, they will be damnably mauled." Exposed along the hill slopes to the full fire of the enemy's artillery, their superiority in numbers was likely to be more than counter-balanced by Napoleon's superiority both in skill and position. The Prussian army had been drawn up in order of battle, with its right extending as far as Wagnelée, its centre at Ligny, and its left reaching in a south-easterly direction from Sombref to Tongrines and Balâtre. The inferences from this formation clearly were that the Prussian right were endeavouring to keep open the communications with Wellington, and that the Prussian left was similarly employed in relation to Bülow and the town of Namur. If this were so, the left could take no very vigorous part in the coming engagement, for its operations must necessarily be confined to the immediate neighbourhood of the main *chaussée* to Namur. It would therefore be sufficient to occupy the Prussian left by false demonstrations, while the main effort was directed against the right or the centre, or both simultaneously.

Having inferred that the Prussian left might be comparatively neglected, Napoleon had yet to decide whether he should direct his full force upon the right, or confine himself to an endeavour to break the Prussian centre. Either alternative offered some special advantages. By attacking the right, he would be drawing nearer to his own left wing, and, moreover, would, if successful, be forcing the Prussians away from their allies. By breaking their centre he would be in a position to roll up the Prussian army upon its wings, and to effect its total ruin. The fertile genius of the

# THE MORNING OF JUNE 16TH

Emperor was equal to devising a combination which, if properly carried out, would secure the advantages of both these courses. His plan was to demonstrate in strength against both points, but more especially against the right. As a result, Blücher would detach his reserve in increasing numbers to the support of his menaced wing. At the favourable moment the French reserves would be launched against the centre, thus denuded of its full complement of defenders, and the Prussian line would be utterly broken. Simultaneously with this movement, a detachment of 10,000, or even possibly 20,000 men, would arrive from Ney, and would take the Prussian left in flank and rear; penetrated in the centre and outflanked upon the right, general confusion would overtake the whole army, and it would be, if not annihilated, at least crippled by a blow from which it would take long to recover.

Such was Napoleon's scheme for the conduct of the battle of Ligny. It remains to see how far he was able to execute it.

The first step towards its execution was to secure the co-operation of Ney. To this end a despatch was sent to the Marshal, dated Fleurus, 2 P.M.

"The intention of his Majesty is that you should attack what troops are before you, and that, after having vigorously driven them in, you should fall back on us, in order to assist in surrounding the (Prussian) corps, of which I have just spoken."

At 3.15 P.M. another despatch followed, more

specific in its terms, and much more vigorous in its language.

"At this moment the engagement is very pronounced. His Majesty desires me to tell you that you should manœuvre at once, so as to envelope the enemy's right, and fall *à bras raccourcis*, upon his rear. This army is lost if you act with vigour. The fate of France is in your hands.

"So hesitate not a moment to execute the movement which the Emperor orders, and direct yourself upon the heights of Bry, and St Amand to assist in a victory perhaps decisive. The enemy is taken *en flagrant délit* at the moment when he is seeking to form a junction with the English."

In the meantime the French army was formed up for the attack. In front of St Amand were posted the three divisions of Vandamme's 3rd corps. Girard's division was in reserve, with the cavalry of the 3rd corps (Domon) upon the left.

The three divisions of Gérard's 4th corps, with its cavalry (Maurin), were in front of Ligny.

Grouchy, with Pajol's and Excelman's cavalry —soon to be supported by one of Gérard's divisions—observed the Prussian left.

The Imperial Guard, with Milhaud's cuirassiers, were in rear of Gérard and Vandamme, in reserve, while Lobau's 6th corps was at Charleroi, from whence it was ordered to move on Fleurus.

The total French force, exclusive of Lobau, was about 68,000. The Prussians numbered about 20,000 more.

# CHAPTER VI.

## THE BATTLES OF THE 16TH.

I. The Battle of Ligny—II. The Battle of Quatre Bras—III. Napoleon's delay in beginning battle — IV. The D'Erlon Episode—V. Summary.

## I.

THE battle of Ligny began about half-past two in the afternoon and lasted until after nightfall.

The first attack was by Vandamme upon the village of St Amand. It was followed within half an hour by Gérard's attack upon the village of Ligny. Throughout the afternoon the contest for these positions was carried on with desperate fury on both sides. The houses both in Ligny and St Amand were for the most part built of stone, and stood each in its own little plot of ground, which contained a garden, perhaps an orchard, and some out-buildings. The Prussians had taken full advantage of every means of defence. From crenellated walls, from every window, from the shelter of each bush and tree, a furious fire was poured in upon the advancing French, and bloody hand-to-hand contests went on in the streets. As often as the French secured possession of one or other of the villages, so often did Blücher send in reinforcements to drive them out again, and in this way, as Napoleon had foreseen, his reserves were being rapidly exhausted.

The Emperor on his side as resolutely refrained from putting in fresh troops. Gérard, Vandamme, and Girard fully understood that they were to expect no support until Napoleon judged the decisive moment to have arrived, and thus it is estimated that, after three hours' fighting, 10,000 fewer troops had been employed on the French than on the Prussian side. In this fact lay the real secret of Napoleon's ultimate success, and the knowledge that Lobau was advancing with 10,000 additional troops gave Napoleon ample confidence that the issue would be favourable to himself.

In the meantime Grouchy, upon the French right, was engaging Thielemann's corps. Here the struggle was less intense, for it was Grouchy's business to demonstrate rather than to attack in earnest. It was sufficient if he continually menaced Blücher's communications with Namur, for as long as they were threatened it would be impossible to draw upon the Prussian left wing for support to the right and centre.

By five o'clock all Blücher's troops were engaged. Amand-la-Haye was in the hands of Girard, but the division of Pirch and the cavalry of Jürgas were now joined to Ziethen's division in an endeavour to recover it. Vandamme held St Amand,

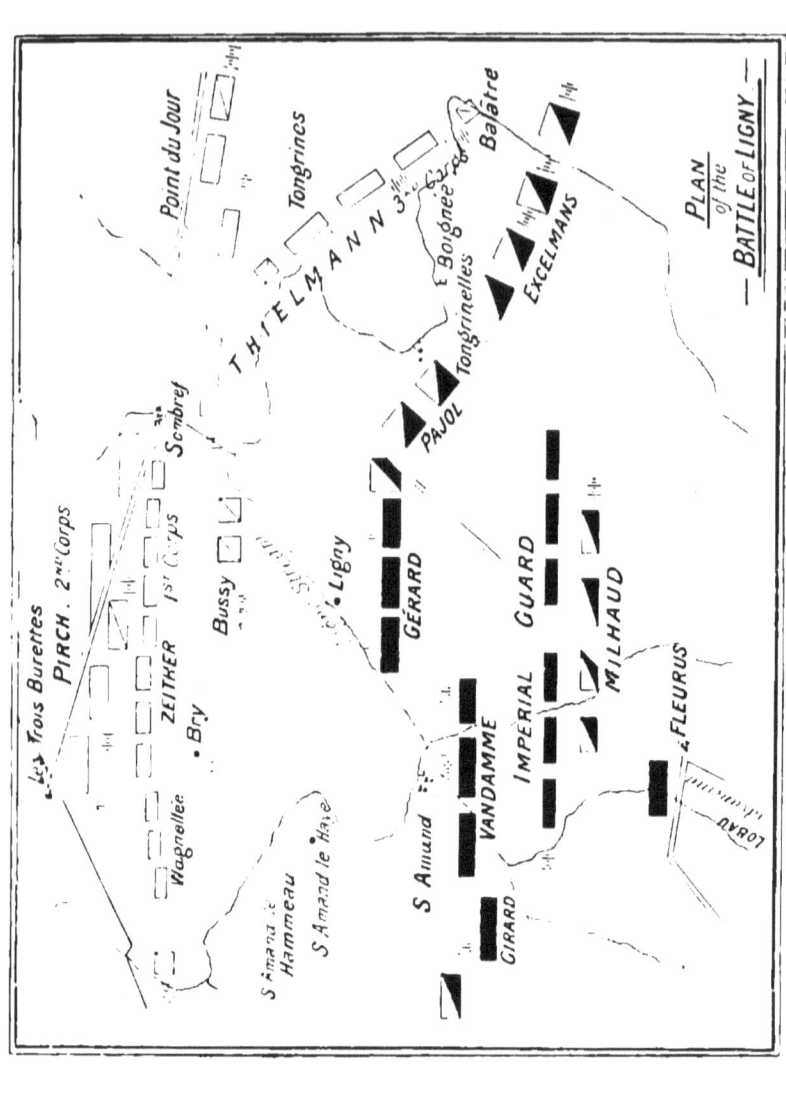

## THE BATTLES OF THE 16TH 87

though hotly pressed by superior forces: Gérard was in possession of Ligny, though his corps had suffered fearfully in the struggle, and he was desperately in need of succour.

Napoleon judged the crisis to have arrived. It was now 5.30 P.M. Moving forward the guard from their station in front of Fleurus, he put himself at their head and directed them against the Prussian centre. Scarcely had this movement of his reserve begun than it was arrested. A report from Vandamme informed the Emperor that a strange corps had appeared upon his left, and seemed as if about to take him *en revers*. In view of this demonstration it was essential to take instant measures to ascertain its meaning, and in the meantime the advance of the guard in force was suspended.

In due course it was discovered that the strange troops upon the left were the 1st corps of the French army under Count D'Erlon advancing to the support of Napoleon.

Apparently, therefore, Ney had fulfilled his instructions. The plan of battle which the Emperor had devised was answering his anticipations point by point. The violence of Girard's and Vandammne's attack had deceived Blücher into the supposition that his right was the vital point: his centre had been weakened to strengthen his forces at Wagneiée and St Amand—all his reserves were now employed in action, and this was the moment when his centre was to be attacked by the full force of the Imperial Guard, and when 20,000 fresh troops under D'Erlon were about to take him simultaneously in the flank.

But this was precisely the moment when Napoleon's star began to wane.

For it was not until 7.30 P.M. that he learned definitely that the strange corps was D'Erlon's, and not a reinforcement coming to the assistance of Blücher. Consequently the suspended movement of the Imperial Guard was not resumed until after a lapse of two hours. It was during this interval that the 3rd and 4th corps suffered most severely at Ligny and St Amand, and the delay cost Napoleon several thousand men.

At 7.30 the day would soon be over, and instead of four hours in which to complete the defeat of the Prussians, scarcely two remained before darkness set in: the delay therefore rendered the victory less complete, and the pursuit of the defeated enemy less vigorous. But more important still, it was not in accordance with Ney's instructions that D'Erlon's corps was advancing to the field. On the contrary, his movement was in direct opposition to them. Before the 1st corps had time to render any assistance in the battle in progress before its eyes, a peremptory order from Ney at Quatre Bras recalled it to his side, and as a result neither at Ligny nor at Quatre Bras did it fire a shot. The fourth section of this chapter will be devoted to an investigation of this deplorable blunder and its consequences. Here it can only be noted in re-

# THE BATTLES OF THE 16TH

gard to its immediate effects upon Napoleon's dispositions and the issue of the battle of Ligny. At the moment when Vandamme perceived the unknown corps upon his flank, he was at the end of his resources. Blücher in person was rallying the scattered division of Pirch, which had been sent to the support of Ziethen, but had retired before the furious onslaught of the French infantry. One of Vandamme's divisions was forced to give way, and St Amand-le-Hameau and St Amand-la-Haye once more fell into the hands of the Prussians. Napoleon therefore, while suspending the general advance of the Imperial Guard, none the less moved forward Duhesme with the Young Guard to the support of his shattered left. This timely reinforcement re-established the battle on that wing. Gérard in the centre in the meanwhile was performing prodigies of valour. Alone with his two divisions, for one had been withdrawn from him to the support of Grouchy, he held his own against twice his numbers, and still clung to Ligny with indomitable tenacity. At last the time arrived when Napoleon could with safety advance his reserves, and Friant's and Morand's battalions of the Imperial Guard marched straight on the Prussian centre. Weakened as it was by the withdrawal of so many brigades to the right, the centre first wavered and then gave way. An attempt to turn the French column upon its flanks was frustrated by Milhaud's cuirassiers. Blücher, at last recognising his deception, strained every nerve to re-establish his line, but without effect. He was himself thrown from his horse, and a charge of cavalry passed over him, only, however, with the effect of inflicting severe bruises upon the tough old veteran. The French Grenadiers and Chasseurs soon crowned the heights of Bry and Bussy upon which the Prussians had stood: Vandamme debouched from St Amand, driving the Prussian right before him: Grouchy met with equal success against Thielemann. To maintain the contest further was impossible, for the Prussians were in retreat throughout the length of their line. All that remained was to withdraw in as good order as the circumstances permitted, and favoured by the darkness which had now set in, and by the blunder which had robbed Napoleon of his reinforcements from Ney, Blücher was enabled to retire from the field with an army defeated indeed and exhausted, but none the less capable, when joined by the absent corps of Bülow, of rendering a good account of itself in the subsequent operations of the campaign.

## II.—*The Battle of Quatre Bras.*

The action at Quatre Bras began about half-an-hour before the battle of Ligny—that is to say, about two o'clock P.M.

It will be remembered that Ney had failed to carry out his repeated instructions to reunite the force under his command. D'Erlon was not yet at

## THE BATTLES OF THE 16TH

Frasnes, and it was Ney's intention, when he arrived there, to keep him in reserve at that point. Kellermann's dragoons were at Frasnes and Liberchies, while of Reille's four divisions of infantry, one, that of Girard, had been withdrawn for service at Ligny.

Thus, when the engagement began, Reille's three divisions—Bachelu, Foy, and Jerome, with Piré's cavalry, alone were in position facing the enemy, and even of these Jerome was not actually in readiness until three o'clock.

The part which had been assigned to Ney was to keep Wellington in check, so as to prevent any assistance from the Anglo-Dutch army moving to the support of Blücher.

But in view of the backward state of Wellington's organisation, a force of over 40,000 men was more than sufficient to effect this purpose. Ney, therefore, with a part of his force, was to manœuvre towards his right, in order to come up upon the Prussian right at Ligny, and crown the victory which Napoleon there hoped to gain. To accomplish this he was to sacrifice all ideas of a brilliant success on his own wing. This would come later, when Napoleon, having overthrown the Prussians, had joined his forces to those of Ney, as he purposed doing at the first opportunity. To contain Wellington with one part of his force, and to assist the Emperor with the other, would be productive of results which might prove decisive of the campaign—results more far-reaching than an absolute victory over the Anglo-Dutch army could entail. "It may be," said Napoleon to Gérard, as the battle of Ligny was beginning, "that the fate of the war will be decided to-day. If Ney efficiently executes my instructions, not a cannon of the Prussian army will escape. It is taken *en flagrant délit.*"

With such views on the part of Napoleon, the action at Quatre Bras began, but Ney regarded his task in a somewhat different light.

Ignorant of the number of troops the Duke of Wellington would be able to bring against him, and fully aware that every moment the number was increasing, Ney determined to proceed with the utmost caution. He kept a strong reserve behind him in case of need, and throughout the engagement he was more intent upon his own position than upon the position of the Emperor at Ligny. For this there is much excuse, but still the results of the 16th were far less decisive than they might otherwise have been.

Quatre Bras is situated at the junction of the main road from Brussels to Charleroi with the main road from Namur to Nivelles. A little to the south of the latter, and to the west of the former, was the Bois de Bossu, a wood which, as well as the village of Quatre Bras, was held by Perponcher's division of Dutch-Belgians, under Prince Bernhard of Saxe Weimar. No other troops—of the whole of Wellington's army—were present at two o'clock, when the engagement began. Ney drew up two of Reille's divisions—

## THE BATTLES OF THE 16TH 93

those of Bachelu and Foy—on each side of the Brussels-Charleroi road in such a manner that that road bisected his centre. They were supported by Piré's cavalry, while the division of Jerome, upon its arrival, took position on the right. No orders were sent to Kellermann to bring up his cavalry from Frasnes and Liberchies till the afternoon was well advanced.

The battle of Quatre Bras was a series of charges, on the right and left, for the possession of the Bois de Bossu and the village at the cross roads. Great credit is due to the Dutch-Belgians, who, though only 9000 strong, had yet held these positions undismayed by the proximity of such vastly superior forces. The first French attack was directed against the Dutch-Belgians alone, but at about 2.30, Sir Thomas Picton's division began to come up, and throughout the afternoon reinforcements of English and Hanoverian troops were arriving. This arrival in isolated detachments was, however, especially at first, a source of great danger to Wellington, and the cause to a large extent of the very severe losses which his troops suffered, for it was possible for the French to charge the English regiments while they were forming, and before they were prepared for the attack—notably this was so in the case of the 42nd Highlanders, two companies of which were pierced by the French lancers and overwhelmed while in the act of falling-in. Picton's division was largely made up of Highland regiments, the

3rd battalion of the Royal Scots, the 28th Highland regiment, and the 1st battalion of the 95th regiment, composing Kempt's brigade, forming the English left, while Pack's brigade, composed of the 44th, 79th, and 92nd Highland regiments, constituted the right. The Duke of Wellington was present in person almost from the beginning of the action, and exposed himself fearlessly. He was for a considerable period with his staff just in front of the 92nd regiment, which lined the ditch immediately in front of the Namur road and from that spot he directed the movements of his force and watched the fierce charges of the French Cuirassiers. One such charge swept the ground on which he had been standing only five minutes before. Picton's division was in turn supported by the Brunswickers, who arrived about three o'clock and were posted on the left. The Duke of Brunswick, their commander, displayed conspicuous personal gallantry, but fell, pierced by a musket ball, about seven o'clock in the evening. In the meantime repeated charges and counter-charges were being made upon the Bois de Bossu, and whenever the English were successful in expelling the French and debouching on to the open ground beyond, they were met by the fierce onset of the French cavalry before they could form, and were in turn driven back. Detachments of the French cavalry also manœuvred round the wood to their left, and thus were in position to charge the English the moment they emerged from the wood upon the

## THE BATTLES OF THE 16TH 95

open ground. Affairs were in a critical situation as the evening wore on, for the French had gained the Bois de Bossu, and had passed beyond it to the main road. It was now that the English Guards arrived, having marched from Enghien since 3 A.M. that morning. They immediately formed and forced the French to retire. It was a tremendous struggle—the French attempting to again outflank the English, but being met in their attempt by the 3rd battalion of the Guards, which had skirted the wood and was drawn up in hollow square upon its extreme western edge. When evening closed the cross roads and the wood were still in the occupation of our troops. Upon the French right and English left the fight was no less deadly. Ney soon discovered that his dispositions were insufficient to effect his purpose—so by five o'clock he had ordered up one brigade of Kellermann's dragoons from Frasnes. These plunged desperately and at once into the thick of the fight for Quatre Bras: but fresh reinforcements were now arriving to the Duke in quick succession. Halkett's brigade and Kielmansegge's first Hanoverians came up about six o'clock, followed by Cooke's division about seven, and it was clear that the French were outnumbered, and could only gain the contested positions by the arrival of fresh troops. Such support was momentarily expected, for Ney had already despatched orders to D'Erlon to bring up the 1st corps to take part in the battle. To his dismay he learned that the 1st corps had been turned off the road at Frasnes to attach itself to Napoleon's main army by a march on Bry. No chance, therefore, remained of re-establishing Kellermann's dragoons, which, notwithstanding the impetuosity of their onset, were repulsed between six and seven P.M. But even in this repulse we can trace the determined obstinacy of Ney only to employ a part, not the whole, of the troops entrusted to him. For but one brigade of Kellermann's heavy cavalry had been ordered up to the front. The other brigades were still maintained at Frasnes and Liberchies. Had Kellermann been in force, with his four brigades together, it is more than probable that the French operations on their right would have been crowned with success, even without the support of D'Erlon's divisions. As it was, not only did the Bois de Bossu and the cross roads remain in the hands of the Anglo-Dutch army, but it was able to occupy an advanced position beyond Quatre Bras —the French, when darkness set in, retiring to Frasnes.

Such was the action at Quatre Bras, when rather more than 53,000 men on both sides were engaged. Nearly 9000 in all fell in the battle, or about one in six. Wellington had collected altogether upon the field about 31,000 men—not one-third of his total available force; and the bulk of these had arrived in detachments as the engagement proceeded, peculiarly exposed to disaster while in process of formation. These facts and figures are

## THE BATTLES OF THE 16TH 97

an eloquent commentary upon the Duke's note to
Blücher, written in the morning, and to which full
reference has already been made. How completely
misinformed he was of the real whereabouts of his
troops, the progress of the battle was to make
abundantly clear. However much the Duke is
to be praised—and very justly praised—for his
cool and spirited conduct of the fight, for the
most part against superior numbers and troops of
very superior calibre to his own—nothing but
censure can be extended to arrangements which
left him exposed to such chances at so critical a
moment. For it is sufficiently evident that the
Duke's success depended upon chances which
he had no right to count upon, and which, in
fact, he did not count upon. Every account of
the battle of Quatre Bras, contemporary or critical,
goes to emphasise the desperate character of the
struggle, the doubt of victory, the half-expectation
of defeat. If this was so when Ney had only
22,000 men engaged, can it be denied that the
Duke would have experienced a severe defeat if
43,000 men had been brought against him? And
this was the force at Ney's disposal had he cared
to avail himself of it.

The fatal procrastination which allowed D'Erlon's corps to remain so far behind Reille, the
vagaries of D'Erlon, who, when called upon, was
not to be found, the over-caution which maintained
three out of Kellermann's four brigades in reserve
throughout the action, all these were chances on

which the Duke could not by any possibility calculate, and yet it was to these chances that he owed his success.

III.—*Napoleon's Delay on the morning of the 16th.*

It has been seen that the engagement at Ligny did not begin until 2.30 P.M., and that at Quatre Bras until about two o'clock. Thus, for purposes of active fighting, the morning hours were entirely thrown away. It was broad daylight at 3.30 A.M. The troops were not in position before Quatre Bras or Ligny until—putting it at the very earliest —1.30 P.M.

Napoleon therefore allowed at least ten hours to elapse before undertaking any directly offensive operations.

This delay has excited much criticism and controversy, and every writer on the campaign has made it the subject of his attention. Some see in it a large part of the cause of Napoleon's subsequent failure, and censure him severely for his inactivity; others regard it as inevitable,—the result of his situation and the nature of things; others, again, throw the responsibility for it upon Ney, or upon Gérard, or upon some other of Napoleon's lieutenants. Amid so many conflicting opinions it is difficult to feel assured that any conclusion is thoroughly sound and final: any explanation must necessarily be based to a large extent upon conjecture.

None the less a brief review of the circumstances

## THE BATTLES OF THE 16TH 99

upon the 16th may help to the formation of a correct judgment.

Napoleon began the day under an entire misapprehension as to the intentions of his opponents. His plan of action was communicated to the commanders of his wings about 9 A.M., and we have seen that it was based upon the supposition that no serious resistance would be offered that day by the allies to his operations on either side. Neither Wellington nor Blücher could be concentrated in force, and until their concentration was completed, or in a fair way to completion, Napoleon judged that they would not be rash enough to risk an engagement which might prove decisive of the campaign. Therefore, as far as the 16th was concerned, he would have to deal, on the right wing, with perhaps 40,000 Prussians at the most, while Ney, on the left, would have before him only such troops as Wellington could hastily muster from Brussels.

With these views, which on all general principles of strategy he was justified in entertaining, he limited his own operations for the day to the occupation of Genappe and Quatre Bras by Ney, and of Gembloux and Sombref by Grouchy.

To accomplish these objects, in view of the fact that little resistance was expected, there was no need of haste. The afternoon would amply suffice for their complete fulfilment. The morning would give to his soldiers the opportunity for that repose which they imperatively needed, and thus refreshed, they would be the more efficient for the work of the afternoon.

It was not until Napoleon actually saw the Prussians forming at St Amand, Bry, and Sombref that he could believe in the extent of his own good fortune; but having realised it, he lost no time in getting his army into position for immediate action.

It is claimed for the explanation here suggested that it possesses at least the merit of simplicity. It answers both to the facts of the situation and to the documentary evidence of the Emperor's ideas and intentions. It is not, however, the explanation usually put forward, and hence it may be well to glance for a moment at the opinions on the subject expressed by such experts as Clausewitz, Ropes, and Chesney.

Clausewitz considers that, in the nature of things, it was impossible to begin the attack upon the Prussians at Ligny until the afternoon. "The troops," he says, "had attacked the Prussian outposts as early as 4 A.M. on the 15th, had probably been marching, therefore, the greater part of the night, and had spent the whole of the 15th right into the night in fighting, or, at any rate, under arms or on the march, consequently it was impossible that an attack on Blücher at Sombref . . . should ensue in the early hours of the 16th.

"*Could* the real tactical encounter of the two main forces have taken place on the forenoon of the 16th, it would have been a monstrous mistake to delay it, for Blücher was still concentrating, as

## THE BATTLES OF THE 16TH

Bonaparte knew; and seeing that the total Prussian force was so very superior to the 75,000 men whom he could employ against it, it was of the utmost importance to give battle before they were all united. . . . But the French troops needed time to rest, to get their provisions, to cook, and, finally, to concentrate. All this could not be accomplished in a short summer's night."*

Clausewitz thus attributes the delay to the fact that a soldier's powers of endurance are limited, and the Duke of Wellington endorses this opinion.

Ropes thinks that Napoleon's delay was the result of Ney's failure to seize Quatre Bras, and to consolidate the corps under his command.

"The backwardness of D'Erlon's corps not only deferred the forward movement of the left wing, it seems to have delayed the advance of the main body. Until Napoleon could be sure that Ney, with the large force that had been assigned to him, was in march on his left . . . he seems to have been unwilling to move upon Blücher. . . . He postponed his own forward movement upon Fleurus and Sombref until Ney could move simultaneously upon Quatre Bras." †

Chesney considers that Napoleon was alone to blame for Ney's want of concentration and failure to occupy Quatre Bras, and he judges that the cause of delay on the morning of the 16th is to be found in the fact that "Napoleon had no idea that

* *Feldzug von*, 1815, Kap. 25.
† "The Campaign of Waterloo," ch. ix.

three-fourths of the Prussian army was collected in his front. As he was aware beforehand how their army was cantoned, and judged Blücher still to be near Namur, it follows that he believed himself in contact with their extreme right, which, unsupported, must needs give way and open his path to Brussels.

Chesney therefore agrees with the view expressed in the text as far as Napoleon and the Prussians are concerned, but he differs in regard to the responsibilities of Ney upon the left.

### IV.—*The D'Erlon Episode.*

It is much easier to estimate the effects of D'Erlon's wanderings upon the issue of the two battles of Ligny and Quatre Bras, and upon the campaign as a whole, than to penetrate the mystery which attaches to his movements.

The facts, however, up to a certain point are clear. D'Erlon, in obedience to Ney's instructions, was marching his corps from Marchiennes and Gosselies to Frasnes. Before reaching Frasnes, Durutte, who commanded the leading division, received further orders to direct his march on Quatre Bras. On arrival at Frasnes, however, an *aide-de-camp* met Durutte at the head of the column, and gave him instructions to march immediately to the support of Napoleon at Ligny. The 1st corps accordingly turned off the main *chaussée* to its right, and in due course appeared upon the flank of the armies engaged around St Amand between 5 and 5.30 P.M. Scarcely had it arrived when peremptory orders from Ney recalled it to Quatre Bras. The 1st corps, therefore, spent the day in marches and counter-marches, but rendered no assistance in either battle, for it did not reach Quatre Bras until the battle was over.

The mystery attaching to these proceedings begins when we endeavour to discover by whose order the 1st corps was turned aside to march on St Amand. If by Napoleon's order, why were his movements disconcerted by its approach, why did he not keep D'Erlon with him to operate upon the Prussian flank, instead of allowing him to march back again to join Ney?

The fact being established that D'Erlon's movement was directed in obedience to the order of somebody, the question as to who gave the order is narrowed down within three alternatives. It was either Ney, or Napoleon, or some one else.

It certainly was not Ney, for that Marshal was firmly convinced from the first that the order was given by Napoleon. In his letter to the Duke of Otranto, dated Paris, June 26th, 1815, Ney writes—
" The battle (of Quatre Bras) became general, and victory was no longer doubtful, when, at the moment that I intended to order up the first corps of infantry, left by me in reserve at Frasnes, I learned *that the Emperor had disposed of it* without advising me of the circumstance. The shock

which this intelligence gave me confounded me."

There is a tone of genuine astonishment about this letter which is an evidence that it expresses Ney's honest convictions, and his attitude of personal indignation against Napoleon, which was strongly marked on the morning following the battle of Quatre Bras, is another indication that his letter to the Duke of Otranto was not the outcome of an afterthought.

But Ney's convictions, however sincere, are not conclusive upon matters of fact. There is further evidence, in support of his opinions, which is entitled to be carefully weighed.

In his "Etudes sur Napoléon" (Paris, 1841), Lieut.-Colonel Baudus, attached to Soult's staff during the Waterloo campaign, says, that when the battle of Ligny was at its height, "Napoleon called me and said, 'I have sent an order to Count D'Erlon to direct his whole corps on the rear of the right of the Prussian army. Go and carry the duplicate of this order to Marshal Ney.'"

Baudus then goes on to say that both the Emperor and Soult urged upon him to insist with Ney that nothing was to prevent the execution of this order. "Tell him," said Napoleon, "that the important affair is here."

If, therefore, we believe Baudus, there is no longer a doubt about the matter. It was Napoleon who sent the order to D'Erlon.

But are we justified in implicitly relying on the

statement of Baudus? 1841 is twenty-six years after the battle of Waterloo, and in twenty-six years a man's memory may well become untrustworthy about great events, much more about matters of minute detail.

Moreover, the narrative bears a sufficient resemblance to the facts as we know them from official documents to justify the suspicion that Baudus was confused between the truth and his recollections of the truth. No form of error is more common or more misleading.

The order which Baudus carried was, he tells us, a duplicate. The original order, then, had been previously despatched. Now, at 3.15 P.M., when the engagement at Ligny was *en ce moment très prononcé*, an order was sent to Ney which has already been quoted. In it the Marshal was told that the fate of France was in his hands—that he was to lose not a moment in executing the movement which the Emperor ordered. There is a suspicious similarity between the terms of the order and the terms in which Baudus was entrusted with his mission. It is, at any rate, by no means improbable that Baudus was not the bearer of a further order in duplicate, but was carrying the duplicate of the 3.15 P.M. order.

In the 3.15 order there is not a word about D'Erlon's corps. Ney was instructed to direct a detachment on the heights of Bry and St Amand, but what particular troops he was to detach is not specified. The order was general in its tenor.

The Baudus order, if it ever existed, was particular.

If, therefore, we accept the supposition that Baudus, twenty-six years after the campaign, was confused in his recollections, his testimony to the effect that Napoleon was directly responsible for D'Erlon's movement falls to the ground.

In addition to this it is significant that no such order as that which Baudus asserts that he carried is in existence. Even if the duplicate has been lost, we might expect to find some traces of the original. Copies, moreover, would have been made before the order was despatched, but not a vestige of the order, its duplicate, or the copies of it has ever been discovered, nor was any allusion to these alleged orders made in the official despatches of the following day. Ney strenuously denied that any order of the kind ever reached him, and his denial carries as much weight as Baudus' assertion. In fact, the evidence in favour of the latter's narrative is not such as to carry conviction with it. It is certainly more credible that Baudus mixed up in his own mind an acknowledged order to Ney with an alleged order to D'Erlon, particularly as this supposition does not for a moment impugn his good faith, than that orders in duplicate, of which, probably, there were copies, should entirely disappear without having been received, and that both commanders—he who wrote them and he to whom they were written—should be confounded at an incident which, on the

## THE BATTLES OF THE 16TH

supposition that the orders were sent and received, must have occurred in conformity with the calculations of both.

According to D'Erlon's own statement, written in 1829, it was General Labédoyère, Napoleon's *aide-de-camp*, who showed him a pencil note which he was carrying to Marshal Ney, enjoining the 1st corps to march on Ligny. Labédoyère also informed D'Erlon that he had taken upon himself to communicate this intelligence to Durutte at Frasnes, and that the change of direction had already been made.

Colonel Heymés, however, chief of Ney's staff, says that it was not General Labédoyère but Lieutenant-Colonel Laurent who instructed the 1st corps to bend their march on St Amand, and once more we are met by a conflict of personal testimony. If the chief *aide-de-camp* of the Emperor was carrying a pencil note to Ney, it is legitimate to infer that the Emperor had sent him with the note. No such inference can be drawn from the presence of Laurent, for he was, comparatively speaking, an obscure member of the staff.

There are two facts, however, which, apart from all other considerations, seem to prove conclusively that Napoleon did not order D'Erlon's change of movement. The first is the surprise which the Emperor exhibited when the 1st corps appeared. At the most critical moment of the battle of Ligny he suspended an operation which was designed to be decisive, lest he might be taken on his flank by a hostile force. If he was expecting D'Erlon, could he have mistaken him for a moment for a hostile force?

The second fact is Napoleon's neglect to employ D'Erlon when on the field. When, in obedience to Ney's imperative order, the 1st corps marched back again to whence it had come, Napoleon made no effort to retain it. From this we may infer that he considered it as a part of Ney's wing, not of his; as subject to Ney's orders, not to his, and, therefore, as altogether outside his own sphere of operations.

Would he have so regarded the matter if he had himself summoned D'Erlon to his side?

Whether, when the corps had arrived, Napoleon would not have done better to use it himself, is another question not bearing on Napoleon's responsibility for the incident. The point, however, for the sake of convenience, may be referred to here.

La Tour d'Auvergne, whose treatise on the campaign is for the most part luminous and careful, states that the Emperor "reiterated his orders to D'Erlon" (to take the Prussian army *à revers*) indicating to him again the direction, so as to "avoid all indecision." He does not, however, produce any evidence for this statement, which is directly contrary to the account of the matter given by D'Erlon and Durutte, who, of all people, were likely to know the truth as to this particular.

## THE BATTLES OF THE 16TH

The Emperor then did not employ D'Erlon at Ligny, either because of the lateness of the hour, or through uncertainty as to the state of Ney's operations on the left, or because he supposed that D'Erlon already had his definite instructions from Ney. At the moment also his attention was wholly directed to the movement of his guard. This question is almost as difficult a one as the mystery of D'Erlon's appearance, but, as it is impossible to do more than guess at the motives which actuated Napoleon, the problem is not capable of a thoroughly satisfactory solution.

It was, however, undoubtedly an error, considering that the corps was on the field, and could scarcely be back with Ney in time to render any assistance upon the left, not to employ it at Ligny, where it might have proved very useful.

The arguments which have been applied to the incident as a whole point to a definite conclusion— the conclusion that neither Napoleon nor Ney ordered the oblique movement of D'Erlon's corps. It must then have been somebody else who did it. It was probably an officer from the headquarters' staff, either Labédoyère or more probably Laurent, who, knowing the tenor of the orders he bore, took it upon himself to change the direction of the march of the columns. From D'Erlon's subsequent statement in 1829, we may judge that he shared this opinion.

"Had General Labédoyère," he says, "a mission to change the direction of my column before having seen the marshal? I do not think so; but, in any event, this circumstance alone was the cause of all the marches and counter-marches which paralysed my *Corps d'Armée* during the day of the 16th."

With one more quotation from the official despatches, the matter may be dismissed. In a letter addressed to Ney from Fleurus next morning, Napoleon says—

"The Emperor has seen with pain that you did not yesterday unite your divisions. They acted in isolation, thus you experienced losses."

If the corps of Counts D'Erlon and Reille had been together, "not an Englishman of the corps which attacked you would have escaped. If Comte D'Erlon had executed the movement on St Amand,* which the Emperor ordered, the Prussian army would have been totally destroyed, and we should have made perhaps 30,000 prisoners."

In this passage Napoleon hits the true mark. Though Ney was assuredly not responsible directly for the D'Erlon blunder, yet had he in the morning consolidated his command in accordance with repeated instructions the blunder could not have occurred.

Whoever was responsible for the mistake, its effects were in every way disastrous.

At Ligny Napoleon's victory was delayed, and by delay it was rendered far less decisive than it

* *I.e.*, the movement ordered in the despatches sent to Ney at 2 P.M., and more especially 3.15 P.M., on the 16th.

would otherwise have been. The Imperial Guard broke the Prussian centre at Ligny about eight o'clock P.M. But for the uncertainty caused by D'Erlon's appearance this would have been done about 6.30. The daylight would have sufficed to push the Prussian retreat severely, and to ascertain its direction beyond possibility of error. As it was, the retreat was conducted in good order, and its direction was not thoroughly known to Napoleon thoughout the remainder of the campaign. That steady, solid movement to the northward which reconnected Blücher's communications with Wellington would have been frustrated, and it was this movement which won the battle of Waterloo. Much more disastrous would the Prussian defeat have been had D'Erlon been called upon to participate in the final struggle at Ligny.

At Quatre Bras the co-operation of the 1st corps would have ensured a victory over Wellington. It is impossible to doubt this in view of what Ney actually accomplished with only 20,000 men engaged. It is a simple problem in proportion. If Ney, with 20,000 men, could hold Wellington in check for seven hours, what could he have done with 40,000?

And had Wellington suffered at Quatre Bras a severe reverse, he could scarcely have adopted, on the following day, that policy of *reculer pour mieux sauter* which, at Waterloo, was crowned with such decisive success. Time would have been necessary for the reorganisation of his army, and an engagement such as Waterloo would have been postponed, perhaps indefinitely. For the Prussian retreat northward was conducted on the supposition that Wellington would stand and fight the French at Mont St Jean. The Prussians would assuredly have retired on their base but for the prospect of an *immediate* engagement, in which they might co-operate.

Thus, with D'Erlon either at Quatre Bras or at Ligny, the whole future of the campaign would have been other than it was. This is not to say that Napoleon would have succeeded ultimately, but undoubtedly a heavy reverse on either point would have rendered the prospects of the allies far more gloomy than on the evening of the 16th they actually were.

In attempting, as we have done, to estimate the effects of the absence or presence of 20,000 men, who might have been employed on either wing, we run some risk of falling victims to an unconscious confusion. We may end by imagining them employed on both wings at once, and drawing conclusions from premisses which are obviously absurd. This danger, it is hoped, has been avoided. And yet, perhaps, some such employment of D'Erlon's corps was not so impossible as at first sight appears. Let us split the corps in halves, allowing 10,000 men to Ney to support his battle at Quatre Bras. This brings Ney's effective force to over 30,000 men. It is by no means impossible that with this number Ney might have gained a real success.

The remaining 10,000 might, according to Napoleon's 3.15 order, have been despatched upon St Amand and Bry.

Coming up with a full knowledge of their mission, and at the crisis of the battle, this manœuvre might have effected all that Napoleon anticipated from it. This, of course, is speculation, but it was not impossible to materialise this speculation into a fact. It was this that Napoleon ordered and expected, and such a disposition of D'Erlon's corps was most in conformity with the actual situation which confronted each wing of the French army.

### V.—*Summary*.

The 16th of June was perhaps the most eventful day in the history of the campaign, and also the most important in the effects which it exercised upon the ultimate issue. The hour of five o'clock in the afternoon marks the turning-point when the fortunes of Napoleon began to decline, and the prospects of the allies to grow bright; and yet the honours of the day rested, on the whole, with the Emperor.

Instead of a day of mere manœuvres, he had been enabled to strike a heavy blow against three-fourths of the Prussian army. He had, in his own opinion, rendered it incapable, at any rate for some days, of taking any further part in the campaign; he had kept the allies asunder while maintaining his own position in strength between them.

Wellington, out of his whole army, had only succeeded in bringing to the field about one-third of its effective force, and, far from overthrowing whatever was in front of him, and directing himself on Gosselies, his utmost endeavours had only succeeded in gaining him a few yards more ground than his troops had occupied the evening before.

But, on the other hand, no decisive success had been gained by the French at Quatre Bras, and the Anglo-Dutch still interposed between them and Brussels. At Ligny the Prussians had been suffered to retreat in good order, and by withdrawing northward on Wavre, towards Wellington and their own reinforcements, they were more formidable after defeat than they had been before, for they had succeeded in veiling from Napoleon both their direction and their intentions.

Thus, by the very fact of his success, the Emperor was filled with a confidence that was at once misplaced and delusive, and from it all his subsequent false moves in the campaign took their origin.

# CHAPTER VII.

## THE 17TH OF JUNE.
### (WELLINGTON AND NAPOLEON.)

I. The Line of Blücher's Retreat—II. Wellington's determination to Retreat—III. Position of the French Army on the morning of the 17th; delay at Quatre Bras and on the Right—IV. The Retreat on Waterloo—V. The position at Waterloo; Wellington's dispositions—VI. Views and expectations of Wellington in standing at Waterloo—VII. Anticipations of Napoleon in taking position—VIII. Summary.

## I.

AFTER the battle of Ligny the Emperor rested upon his victory. "The Prussian army has been put to rout," he writes to Ney on the 17th. "General Pajol is pursuing it on the roads to Namur and Liége." This letter was written about 8 A.M., twelve hours after the fight was over. Yet during these hours Napoleon had made no attempt to pursue the Prussians, except, early in the morning, to send out Pajol with a division of his cavalry. Pajol's reports, no doubt, suggested the tone of confidence in which the Emperor wrote. The facts, however, were widely different from these confident suppositions. The Prussian army had not been put to the rout. After the battle,

Ziethen's corps retired in good order on Tilly, a village about two miles due north of Bry. Pirch's corps continued to occupy Bry until after midnight, when it followed Ziethen. Thielemann's corps remained in occupation of Sombref until ordered to retire on Gembloux, while Bülow, after marching all day, arrived at Sauvenières in the early hours of the morning. Within six hours after the battle the Prussians were better concentrated than before. Nor was it the Prussian army which Pajol was pursuing on the roads to Namur and Liége. More than 10,000 men who had taken part in the battle deserted when the battle was over, and made their way along the Namur road. In addition to these there were plenty of stragglers and wounded men, as is always the case after a hot engagement, who had drifted away from the main body, and would naturally be making their way towards the Prussian base. The prisoners captured by Pajol's cavalry were from these straggling detachments. As for the main body, it entirely escaped observation, and was every moment interposing a greater space between itself and the French army. The very measures, therefore, which Napoleon took added to his deception, and he whose success had so often depended upon neglect of the strict rules of war, could hardly be brought to believe that his enemies had imitated his example, and for the purposes of greater ultimate advantage, had determined to risk the loss of their base. The

# THE 17TH OF JUNE

risk, indeed, was very great. The Prussian soldiers carried with them but very scanty rations, and by a retreat northwards it became doubtful how soon fresh supplies could be brought up. The ammunition, too, was a source of anxiety, for all that Blücher had with him had been exhausted at Ligny, and he was in ignorance as to whence or when fresh supplies would be forthcoming. Nothing can exceed the pluck and daring of a determination arrived at in the moment of disaster, to court privations, hunger, and fatigue, if only the communications with the Anglo-Dutch army might be maintained.

The chief credit for this determination must be given to Gneisenau, Blücher's chief-of-staff. The Marshal himself had been severely bruised and shaken in the course of the battle of Ligny. His horse fell dead upon him, and two successive cavalry charges passed over his prostrate body. No sooner was he rescued than he was on horseback again, though now over seventy years of age, but he was in no condition to conduct the further operations of his force, and this duty therefore fell to Gneisenau.

It may be doubted what that General really meant by directing the line of Ziethen and Pirch's corps on Tilly. It is a fundamental rule in war that a defeated army retreats upon its reinforcements, and Bülow's columns, as yet wholly unemployed, were heading fast towards Gembloux. It may therefore have been that Gneisenau considered a northerly line of retreat was, in any event, a good direction to take, as tending to concentrate the army, and that this decision by no means committed him to following this line further when once his immediate purpose was accomplished. Be this as it may, in the course of the night each corps of the Prussian army was under orders to march on Wavre,—Ziethen and Pirch by way of Gentinnes and Mont St Guibert, Bülow and Thielemann by way of Walhain.

## II.

The Duke of Wellington received no news of his allies until about nine o'clock on the morning of the 17th. The Prussian commanders have been blamed for neglect in this respect, but it appears that, immediately after Ligny, information had been sent to Wellington informing him of the result of the battle, but that the officer who carried the despatch had been wounded, and so was unable to deliver it. Certainly the receipt of communications of such importance should not have been made contingent upon the chance disasters which might occur to an individual *aide-de-camp*. It is unnecessary, however, to discuss here the serious consequences which this want of information might have involved; for the present it is sufficient to note the fact that, at 10 A.M., the Duke's army, now powerfully reinforced, though not even yet completely concentrated at Quatre Bras, was still

## THE 17TH OF JUNE

in position at and beyond that point, completely isolated, and exposed, without prospect of support, to the conjoint attack of both wings of the French army. There was no alternative but retreat. It was an unpleasant necessity, and liable to expose the Duke to much ill-natured criticism. He was mindful of the persistent misrepresentation which had followed him throughout the Peninsula campaigns, and he evidently expected the same kind of thing now. His composure, however, was quite undisturbed, and his decision was arrived at with singular promptitude. "Old Blücher," he said to Captain Bowles, "has had a damned good licking, and gone back to Wavre, eighteen miles. As he has gone back, we must go too. I suppose in England they will say we have been licked. I can't help it; as they are gone back, we must go too." "He made all the arrangements for retiring," says Captain Bowles, "without moving from the spot on which he was standing, and it certainly did not occupy him five minutes."

The retreat was immediately begun, and by evening the Duke's army was in position at Waterloo.

### III.

We may now return to Napoleon and consider his movements in relation to these operations. His general plan of action had been sketched in his letter to Grouchy of the previous day. "My intention is, after having defeated the Prussians, to set off this night, and to operate with my left wing, which Marshal Ney commands, upon the English." This was written when he expected but little resistance from the Prussians, but the fact that resistance had been in force, and had been protracted, did not necessarily affect his general design. It was not now possible "to set off *this night*" but there was nothing to prevent his setting off quite early in the morning. Eventually he did proceed on exactly the lines he had himself laid down the day before. We have therefore—as no new plans had to be devised, nor any important changes introduced into those already existing—merely to consider the reasons which induced Napoleon to delay his movement on the morning of the 17th. The question must be examined from two sides—his delay in ascertaining the facts about the Prussian retreat, his delay in attaching himself to Ney for offensive operations against the English.

In regard to the first point, two hours of the battle of Ligny having been lost by the unexpected appearance of D'Erlon, darkness intervened to prevent any efficient and vigorous pursuit of the Prussians.\* Nor at a later time was a pursuit in force practicable. Napoleon had not to deal with the Prussians alone. He must, in fulfilment of his plan, operate promptly against the English. For this purpose he required to keep his troops well in hand, and also, not to exhaust those who were comparatively

\* The Prussians, however, did not allow darkness to prevent their vigorous pursuit of the French after Waterloo.

## THE 17TH OF JUNE

fresh, and on whom he relied to defeat Wellington. Hence any pursuit of the Prussians must be entrusted to those who had borne the brunt of the fight at Ligny—that is, to the troops of Vandamme and Gérard, composing the 3rd and 4th corps. These men were thoroughly exhausted. Not only had their ranks been thinned by severe losses—it is estimated that 12,000 French fell at Ligny—not only had they fought with great persistency and fury for eight hours, but they had sustained the fatigues of a long march begun in the early morning of the 15th, and only ended by the order to form in line of battle on the 16th. There are limits to the soldier's powers of endurance, and those limits may well have been reached by the time Ligny was over. We do not, therefore, blame Napoleon for failure to pursue energetically and in force. We blame him for not observing the line of the enemy's retreat. A small cavalry detachment was despatched in the wrong direction, —why was no reconnaissance made on the roads to Tilly and Gembloux? The fatigues of the soldiers can be no excuse here, for Napoleon had plenty of cavalry upon his right wing which had only been slightly engaged. Instead of detaching Pajol and Excelmans on the Namur road, why should not Excelmans have explored towards Wavre? It is perfectly clear that both Napoleon and Soult were so certain, on abstract grounds of reasoning, that the Prussians had gone in the direction which ought in theory to have been taken, that they did not think it worth while to explore the roads in any other direction. Two hours more daylight on the 16th would have rendered such a misapprehension impossible.

In regard to the second point, why did Napoleon delay to attach himself to Ney, and immediately begin operations against the English?

Here again the fatigues of the soldiers cannot be alleged as an excuse. The Emperor at no time proposed to utilise for his attack upon Wellington the troops of Vandamme and Gérard. Apart from these he had the Guard. The Guard had certainly been employed at Ligny. They had fought with conspicuous valour from seven o'clock until perhaps 9.30, but throughout the afternoon they had been spectators of the scene, and a few hours' rest were sufficient to recruit their energies. He also now had the 6th corps of Lobau, which had not been employed at all, and on his left wing there was D'Erlon, none of whose 20,000 men had fired a shot. He had, therefore, 50,000 troops, exclusive of those who had fought at Quatre Bras, to which may be added three divisions of Kellermann's dragoons, and Lefèbvre-Desnouette's division of the cavalry of the Guard, which Ney had not employed, with which to attack the Anglo-Dutch army on the 17th. Wellington, at Waterloo on the 18th, could only oppose about 68,000 men to the French army. Before Quatre Bras, on the 17th, the rivals would have been fairly equally matched in point of numbers, and Wellington

## THE 17TH OF JUNE

would have been quite overmatched in point of quality.

Napoleon's delay, therefore, must be accounted for on other suppositions than that his troops were fatigued and his forces inadequate. Napoleon's personal fatigue, however, was one factor in the situation, his want of information was another. It is to these causes that his delay may be attributed. The amount of work which the Emperor had got through since the opening of the campaign was enormous. He had personally superintended everything. He had to lay down the movements for Ney upon the left, for Grouchy on the right, and himself to lead the reserves. We see him supping with Ney at midnight on the 15th, and again astir a few hours later. On the 16th he must have been twenty hours in the saddle. His capacity for dispensing with sleep is proverbial, but none the less, when Ligny was over, he was terribly exhausted. Critics are sometimes apt to regard military affairs as if they were conducted by pieces on a chessboard. Armies are composed of men, and it is a man, subject to human weakness, who leads them. It may be true that to issue a few orders would not have taken much time, nor have added materially to Napoleon's fatigue, but this leaves out of consideration not only the physical but the mental lassitude which ensues upon the completion of some great piece of work—the disinclination to face even the smallest tasks which refer to the execution of another. It was but human nature that Napoleon should be content to leave matters as they were till next morning, when he could undertake the new work before him with energies renewed and mind and body refreshed by some hours of undisturbed repose.

But it cannot be denied that had he been more than man—had he been able to dispense with that much-needed rest—a great opportunity was before him, never to present itself again. But he was unaware of the fact,—his intelligence was at fault.*

Ney had sent no information upon the conclusion of the action of Quatre Bras of how things had gone with him that day. Early in the morning we find Soult writing to Ney under the supposition that his force was only now concentrated, and demanding exact information as to the position of his divisions, "and of all which is passing in front of you." As late as twelve o'clock this information had apparently not arrived. "His Majesty awaits your reports with impatience," Soult writes at that hour. The fact was that Ney was bitterly exasperated by the Emperor's supposed withdrawal of D'Erlon's corps from the operations at Quatre Bras, and it would seem that he expressed it by reserving information of what had passed and was passing upon his front. But all this time the opportunity was slipping away— the enemy were retreating. Had Napoleon known that the allied army was still before Quatre Bras,

* For the whole subject of Napoleon's physical condition in the campaign, see Chapter XI., § vii. and note. Also see page 145.

## THE 17TH OF JUNE

isolated from Prussian support, exposed to an immediate attack, it is impossible to imagine that he would have hesitated to march at early morning for the purpose of overwhelming it. Had this been done, say at 6 or even 7 A.M., it does not appear that anything could have saved Wellington from destruction. But in the absence of information from Ney, Napoleon was justified in assuming that the English had withdrawn in the night, for he could not know that the news of Blücher's defeat would not reach Wellington till nine o'clock in the morning. The blame for his inaction does not rest wholly upon the Emperor's shoulders. Ney must share the burden, in that he failed to display either initiative or activity at a time when, from a leader of his reputation, both might well have been expected.

Napoleon then contented himself on the morning of the 17th with recruiting the energies of himself and his troops, and by writing a letter to Ney, the contents of which have already been alluded to. He blames the Marshal's want of concentration on the day before. To avoid the possibility of any such misfortune in the future, very precise instructions are given. " The Emperor hopes and desires that your seven divisions of infantry and the cavalry shall be well together, and that together they should not occupy one league of ground, so as to have them well in hand and employ them at need." In the same letter the Emperor declares his intention of moving to his left by the Namur-Nivelles route. This would avert the possibility of an attack upon Ney by Wellington's troops, for they would immediately be exposed to destruction from such a flank movement by Napoleon; whether Ney should himself attack was left to his own judgment. "The intention of his majesty is that you should take position at Quatre Bras, as you have been ordered to do" (the day before), "but if that is impossible, report at once and in detail, and the Emperor will move, as has been described; if, on the contrary, there is only a rear-guard, attack it and take position."

Considering the temper and disposition of Ney on the morning in question, no very vigorous action was to be looked for from him, but it may be doubted if any was required beyond the prompt despatch of news to the Emperor's headquarters. As he read over his instructions, he may well have felt that they conveyed to him orders to remain as he was until Napoleon could join him.

It is true he was to take Quatre Bras, but it was recognised that he might be outnumbered there. He was to act according to circumstances, and he was to be the judge of the circumstances. Some hostile criticism has been levelled against Ney for not having attacked the Anglo-Dutch army himself on the morning of the 17th. Such a proceeding would certainly have been rash, though it might well have been successful. It scarcely follows, as some of Ney's defenders have asserted, that the order—

## THE 17TH OF JUNE

"If there is only a rear-guard, attack it"—constitutes proof positive that if there was more than a rear-guard he was not to attack it. In the one case there could be no doubt about the matter; in the other, Ney was to do what he thought best. If Napoleon had marched promptly by his left to the support of Ney, there could have been no time for hesitation or delay, but as it was, to attack with weakened forces troops which had just been strongly reinforced, might seem a mad and senseless proceeding. At the same time, it must be remembered that Ney had been reinforced too. He had now D'Erlon's corps of 20,000 men, in addition to the 15,000 who remained of Reille's corps after the engagement of the day before. He had at his disposition three untouched brigades of Kellermann's dragoons, and Lefèbvre-Desnouette's cavalry. He could put into the field in the early hours of the 17th at least 15,000 more men than were mustered when the action of the 16th was ended. Should he not have risked his now consolidated force against Wellington, even though the latter was now consolidated also, and outnumbered him by perhaps 10,000 men? Moreover, he had upon his right the main French army. A true comprehension of the situation must have made clear to him that he had only to apply for assistance to get it. Had he informed Napoleon at night or even early in the morning of the facts, a strong detachment could have arrived upon his right in three hours, and by eight o'clock Wellington might have been fully engaged, with every prospect of prompt success for the French.

We have evidence that Napoleon's co-operation in such an attack would have been immediate. When at length he heard what the actual situation on Ney's front was, he immediately despatched a corps of infantry and the Imperial Guard to Marbais, at the same time writing to the Marshal instructions " to attack the enemy at Quatre Bras in order to drive them from their position, while the corps at Marbais would second his operations." Can there be a doubt that the same action would have been adopted many hours earlier if the facts had been known earlier? We may admit that Ney was right in not risking an engagement against a superior force, but this admission does not excuse him for not taking vigorous and immediate steps to secure adequate reinforcements in order to effect so vital an object as the overthrow of the only enemy now remaining in the field.

But whatever might have been, the fact remains that the morning of the 17th was wasted, and the grand opportunity lost. Hearing nothing from his left, and being satisfied with the completeness of his own success upon the right, Napoleon determined to devote the day to the recuperation of his army. " *La journée d'aujourd'hui,*" he says, "*est nécessaire pour terminer cette opération*"—which operation is not distinctly specified, whether his own movements or Ney's, though, from the context

# THE 17TH OF JUNE 129

it may be judged that he refers to Ney's seizure of the position at Quatre Bras—"*pour compléter les munitions, rallier les militaires isolés et faire rentrer les détachements.*"

Thus it is that we see the Emperor, on the morning of the 17th, chatting with his generals on indifferent subjects, recalling incidents of the early days of the Revolution, and, with the exception of the one letter to Ney, taking no step to hasten or direct the movements of his wings.

At noon, however, he was active once more. He then set about preparing to move upon Marbais, with a view to forming a junction with Ney and prosecuting a vigorous attack upon the English by his left, and about the same hour he entrusted to Marshal Grouchy the task of following up the retreat of the Prussians with 33,000 men, a commission which has been the subject of eighty years of controversy and recrimination, and which marks a crisis in the history of the campaign.

## IV.

It was about one o'clock when Napoleon put himself at the head of his columns to march by the main *chaussée* to the support of Marshal Ney.

He took with him the Imperial Guard and the 6th corps of Lobau, all of them comparatively fresh troops, for they had taken no very prolonged part in the engagement at Ligny—indeed, Lobau had not been employed at all.

At Marbais he picked up the infantry and cavalry which had been despatched to that point earlier in the day, and appeared upon the flank of his left wing with over 30,000 men. Upon his approach Ney put his men in movement, the forces thus united pursuing the enemy who had been in process of withdrawal from Quatre Bras for now at least four hours. Napoleon must have perceived at last, with feelings of bitter chagrin, the opportunity which had presented itself to him in the early morning, and which he had omitted to grasp. If his general movement had begun earlier, the united French army, over 71,000 strong, would have appeared against the English army in a position of isolation, and only 45,000 strong.

There is small wonder that he should have felt indignant with Marshal Ney, not because he had not himself attacked the English, but because he had refrained from sending information which would have enabled Napoleon to seize the chance offered him. " They have ruined France," he said to D'Erlon, whom he found in advance of Quatre Bras. Perhaps he was thinking of his order to Ney the previous afternoon—" The fate of France is in your hands." Perhaps already he had a premonition of coming disaster. At two o'clock he was a different man to the Napoleon who at eleven o'clock was talking politics to his generals, pleased with the operations of the past and confident about the future. Instead of a holiday march he now had serious work before him, and

## THE 17TH OF JUNE

the due execution of it depended chiefly upon his own exertions.

The pursuit, however, was now urged with as much vigour as the fact that Wellington had already been four hours in movement would permit. It was impossible to approach the English main army; its march was entirely unimpeded, except "by fatigue, dust, heat, and thirst"—but the rear guard, which was made up of the cavalry led by Lord Uxbridge, supported by one division of infantry, had some smart skirmishes with the French vanguard. In one of these, at Genappe, the 7th Hussars were ordered to charge the head of the French column. Opposed to them were Lancers, strongly backed by Cuirassiers, and strengthened on each flank by strong bodies of cavalry. The ground was heavy, and the horses of the Hussars were leg-weary and jaded. Under such conditions the order was injudicious. Several English officers and over forty men were killed, and reflections were subsequently cast upon the regiment which were thoroughly undeserved. It was at the moment of this reverse that the 1st Life Guards were brought up and ordered to charge. Their weight and impetuosity carried everything before them, and the temporary check was speedily repaired. No second effort on the part of the English Guards was necessary, for "though we were to have given them another charge of the same sort," writes an officer of the 2nd Life Guards, "they thought it prudent not to expose themselves to our weight a second time." On the other side, the French Guards, marching at the head of the pursuing column, with six pieces of horse artillery, kept up a murderous cannonade against the English cavalry whenever the opportunity permitted. Throughout the afternoon the rain fell in torrents from a murky and thunderous sky—the air was heavy, hot and sultry—the fatigues and exhaustion of the soldiers were excessive, but on each side there was the same strict obedience to orders, the same discipline, the same high courage exhibited under most depressing circumstances.

In the meantime, at Brussels, all was confusion and alarm. The news soon spread that the Duke of Wellington was in retreat before Napoleon in person, that the Prussians had been decisively defeated, and that the French would be in the city in a few hours. The Belgians were in no condition to distinguish between retreat conducted for the purposes of better resistance and complete and hopeless rout. The dead and wounded were now arriving from the rear, and among these there was carried through the city, in the course of the day, the body of the ill-fated Duke of Brunswick,* whose chivalrous oath never to sheathe his sword until he had expiated the outraged manes of his father was to be fulfilled only by his own death. Each straggler brought news more alarming than the last, and the only hope of safety seemed to lie in prompt flight. Heartrending scenes were witnessed

* The Duke of Brunswick's father had fallen at Jéna, 1806.

## THE 17TH OF JUNE 133

in the streets, as wounded soldiers staggered to their homes in the hope—often a vain one—of dying surrounded by the care and affection of their own families. A greater contrast could scarcely be exhibited between the Brussels of the 16th, full of unreasoning hopes and boasting confidence, and the Brussels of the 17th, stricken by a panic as unreasoning as its previous elation.

### V.

As the evening closed the Anglo-Dutch army took up its position with a view to a battle on the following morning. The field of Waterloo had already recommended itself to the skilled eye of the Duke of Marlborough, during the campaigns of the War of Succession, as eminently suitable for the purposes of a general engagement; and before the campaign of 1815 opened, it had been surveyed by order of the Duke of Wellington, as being the spot where, if put to it, he would take position for the defence of Brussels. The little village of Mont St Jean, where Wellington placed his head-quarters, is situated at the junction of the high roads which lead from Nivelles and Charleroi to Brussels. In front of it was rolling ground, affording excellent cover to troops drawn up for purposes of defence, while behind it was the village of Waterloo, about two miles distant upon the Brussels road, just where it emerges from the Forest of Soignies. The village of Braine-la-Leude lay to the west, affording cover for the right of an army posted at right angles to the main road, while the hamlets of Merbe Braine on the right, of Papelotte, Frischermont, and Smohain on the left, were available to afford still further protection. In front of the right were the chateau and grounds of Hougomont, lying a little off the Nivelles road and towards the Brussels turnpike. The estate of Hougomont consisted of a house, chapel, farm buildings, a wood, a garden, laid out in the Dutch fashion with parallel walks and high thick hedges, and was surrounded by an orchard.

A mile to the southward of Mont St Jean, lying upon the west side of the main Brussels road, was the farm of La Haie Sainte, situated in the hollow just where the road begins to ascend towards La Belle Alliance. On the other side of the road, against La Haie Sainte, was a quarry, and the turnpike just about this point had been cut through the ground, leaving high banks upon either side. For purposes of defence the whole position could be turned to account most effectively, and as he retreated the Duke threw troops both into Hougomont and La Haie Sainte in order with the one to guard his right, with the other his centre. The villages to his left were also occupied.

## VI.

Such dispositions on the night of the 17th clearly indicated Wellington's intention of standing to meet the enemy, and it must now be considered what justification he had for thus accepting a battle

## THE 17TH OF JUNE 135

against a superior force when possibly the whole destiny of the campaign depended upon his determination.

It has been seen that the Duke did not receive information from Blücher as to the results of the battle of Ligny and his subsequent movements until about nine o'clock on the morning of the 17th. He had already been made aware by a patrol party which he had sent out that the Prussians were in retreat, but he could have no accurate knowledge of their intentions until he heard from Blücher. Upon receipt of news, his decision was prompt to fall back for the express purpose of maintaining communications with his allies, at the same time despatching a letter to Blücher, informing him of his resolution to stand at Waterloo if he could be assured of Prussian support to the extent " of one or more corps, as might be necessary,"* but that otherwise he would fall back upon Brussels. We may assume that this letter was despatched at the earliest possible moment, but, none the less, a reply to it could not by any possibility have been received before 3 P.M. As a fact, Blücher at that hour was in no position to give positive assurances. He was deficient in ammunition, though the train was, as it happened, upon the road, nor was he yet aware of the precise positions of his 3rd and 4th corps; marching, as they were, upon the extreme right by way of Gembloux and Sart-à-Walhain. The ammunition reached Wavre at

* Despatch to Lord Bathurst, June 22, 1815.

5 P.M. News of Thielemann and Bülow arrived just before midnight. It thus becomes a question as to the hour when Blücher sent an answer to Wellington assuring him of the support which had been requested. It may have reached the Duke on the evening of the 17th. It may have reached him only on the morning of the 18th. In any event, it is clear that the Duke's retreat was based upon his confidence in Blücher, not upon any exact assurances, and that upon the strength of that confidence he took up position at Waterloo. Chesney tells us that "Wellington, before deciding to fight on his chosen ground next day, had had the full assurance of hearty support from Blücher," and in confirmation of this statement, he quotes an extract from Blücher's letter, that "he would march with his whole army to join him, but on condition that if the French delayed to attack, the allies would give them battle on the 19th," but Chesney makes no reference to the hour when this letter was received, and, as a consequence, his contribution towards a proper estimate of the Duke's conduct is of small value. The point is this—Was there sufficient likelihood of Prussian support being forthcoming to justify the Duke in risking a battle without positive assurance of such support? A reference to the battle of Ligny may be of use in considering this question. There, entirely unsupported by his ally, Blücher had suffered a reverse. He had taken position in the hope of assistance from

## THE 17TH OF JUNE 137

Wellington, but without the certainty of it. That assistance it was impossible to afford, and in default of it Blücher had been defeated. Just as the Duke was unaware of the nature of the resistance he was himself to meet with at Quatre Bras, so he, and Blücher too, were unaware of the strength of the force which had been despatched to occupy the Prussians and separate them from the English. Grouchy's troops were estimated by Blücher at 10,000 or 11,000 men; as a fact they were three times that number; exactly the same circumstances, therefore, might intervene to keep the allies apart at Waterloo as had actually kept them apart during the engagements of the 16th. It must be remembered, too, that though the Prussians did arrive, it was not until between four and five in the afternoon of Waterloo, when the battle was four hours old. Had Napoleon begun the battle of the 18th at 6 or 7 A.M., it would have been in progress at least nine hours before the Prussians arrived, and it is, to say the least, improbable that Wellington's miscellaneous force could have held their own, unsupported, for anything like that time. The conclusion must be that the Duke's decision was marked by a boldness which closely resembles rashness; and supposing, as some critics maintain, that he received no assurances from Blücher whatever until the morning of the 18th, it will be difficult to deny that his conduct can only be justified by its success.

There is the strongest evidence to prove that the

Duke himself was fully sensible of the risks he was incurring, for, after his troops had taken position, the pickets posted, and all arrangements made, Wellington rode over to Wavre in order to interview Blücher, "that I might learn from his own lips at what hour it was probable he would be able to join forces with us the next day." The story of this night ride has been most circumstantially told by so trustworthy a witness as the Duke of Wellington himself, who related it to Mr Pierrepont in 1833, and to Mr Justice Coltman in 1838. It also appears in Lockhart's "Life of Napoleon."*

Those who assert that the Duke had no personal interview with Blücher from the time he met him at Bry, on the morning of the 16th, until they greeted each other at Genappe, at the close of the battle of Waterloo, have to contend with this story of the Duke himself, attested by independent witnesses at different times. Such a ride was certainly not unnatural in the very critical circumstances in which Wellington found himself. We may, therefore, believe the Duke when he says— " However, I saw him (Blücher), got the information I wanted from him, and made the best of my way homewards." Very possibly it is to this interview that he refers when he says, in his despatch to Lord Bathurst, that "the Marshal had promised

* In addition to the interesting pages devoted by Mr Ropes to this matter, the reader is referred to an article by Mr Archibald Forbes in the *Pall Mall Magazine* for August 1894—" Copenhagen, and other Famous Battle-horses."

me . . . he would support me with one or more corps." Some time, therefore, in the course of the night the Duke—by letter, or by personal interview, or by both—received from Blücher a definite assurance with regard to his co-operation on the morrow. Confidence was converted into certainty, and whatever may have been the Duke's misgivings throughout the 17th, as he conducted the retreat and took up his situation for the night, they must have been dispelled before morning dawned. It was then in full and clear reliance upon Blücher and Prussian assistance that the Duke stood his ground on the 18th June.

VII.

Napoleon took up his position for the night partly in front of the Anglo-Dutch army upon the high ground about La Belle Alliance and partly at Genappe. His one fear was that the enemy might escape him and continue its retreat through the forest of Soignies upon Brussels. With Blücher retreating upon Brussels from Wavre, the two armies would be concentrated in force in front of the city, and Napoleon's situation thereby rendered most critical. This was the course the Emperor afterwards insisted would have been the right one for the allied commanders to take under the circumstances, and though he had no apprehensions from the Prussians, he was much afraid that the Anglo-Dutch for their part were adopting it. In the "*Rélation fidèle et détaillée*," published in the year after the battle, it is stated that the French were astonished that the English had not only maintained their evening position, " but were prepared to defend it," while Napoleon exclaimed— "*Enfin je les tiens—ces Anglais!*" He had pushed forward his cavalry detachments in order to assure himself that the enemy was really standing, and his pickets were stationed as close to the British lines as possible in order to inform him if any attempt to withdraw should be made in the night. The Emperor himself at nightfall retired to quarters at Caillou, about three miles from Mont St Jean, and it was not until the following morning that his troops occupied the positions in which they were to fight during the day.

## VIII.

The events of the 17th of June were of the utmost importance in relation to the issue of the campaign. It was a day of manœuvres, whereas the 16th was a day of action, but the final victory of the allies was more dependent upon the manœuvres than on the actions. Want of complete and accurate intelligence is perhaps the most noticeable feature of the day, whether we regard the movements of Ney, of Napoleon, of Wellington, or of Blücher. Ney knew not or neglected the opportunity which Wellington's isolated position at Quatre Bras afforded him. Wellington was thus isolated because he knew not the results of Ligny

# THE 17TH OF JUNE

and the line of the Prussian retreat. Napoleon, owing to the remissness of Ney, knew not that by joining his centre to the left wing early in the morning he could overwhelm the Anglo-Dutch, cut off as they were from all chance of support from their allies; and equally was he unaware of the true line of march adopted by the Prussians, owing, in the first place, to an over-sanguine estimate of his victory of the day before, and in the second to his own neglect in omitting to send reconnoitring parties in any other directions than the one he wrongly assumed the Prussians to have taken. Blücher marched on Wavre, unaware of the exact situation of two of his four corps, ignorant of the situation of his ammunition trains, and trusting that Wellington would adopt a line of retreat parallel to his own, rather than knowing with any certainty that such a line was actually being taken. Wellington withdrew from Quatre Bras towards Brussels, and took position at Mont St Jean, trusting, from the nature of the case, that the Prussians would support him, if he stood his ground, not with any sure intelligence that he would be so supported. He was also misinformed as to the force the French were bringing against him, for he supposed that Napoleon had mustered his whole army, with the exception of some 10,000 or 11,000 men, whereas 33,000 men had been detached to follow the Prussians, and Girard's division of 3000 men had been left at Ligny. The movements of Grouchy were equally characterised by uncertainty, as will be seen, but this was in the nature of things, for he had been specially sent forth to obtain information, and his mission would have been useless had certainty already existed.

Uncertainty implies hesitation and delay, and hence the 17th was a day of delays. Ney delayed his attack upon Quatre Bras until Napoleon could join him. Napoleon delayed joining him until he received information from Ney. Wellington delayed his retreat until he received information from Blücher, while Grouchy's march was delayed through over-confidence that the Prussians were disposed of, and was ultimately despatched through a growing feeling of uncertainty as to whether it was really so. The responsibility for this state of things has been apportioned first to Ney, who, smarting with a sense of indignation against the Emperor for withdrawing, as he wrongly supposed, the 1st corps from his command, attributed his ill-success at Quatre Bras to Napoleon, and, as if in revenge, deliberately sacrificed his chances of converting repulse into victory. Responsibility also directly attaches to Napoleon himself, and to Soult, his chief-of-staff, for neglecting simple and feasible precautions, and wasting precious moments until it was too late to redeem them. On the Prussian side alone do we see, on the 17th, time being placed to the best account, and the time thus gained was to prove the ultimate cause of the brilliant success at Waterloo.

# THE 17TH OF JUNE

When at last the French and Anglo-Dutch troops were put in motion, we see on the one hand a retreat most skilfully conducted and a pursuit as vigorously pressed as the nature of the ground, the weather, and Wellington's dispositions would permit. At the close of the day we find one army in position, ready to fight at Mont St Jean—another at Wavre ready to support it in a decisive engagement—Grouchy, far from the main French Army, far from the Prussians, and further still from the English; while the Emperor is congratulating himself that he has but one enemy to deal with, and that it is now before him, certain to be destroyed on the morrow by his superior force, his more skilful manœuvres, and loftier military capacity.

# CHAPTER VIII.

GROUCHY'S MARCH ON THE 17TH AND 18TH OF JUNE, UP TO THE OPENING OF THE BATTLE OF WATERLOO.

I. Grouchy despatched in pursuit of the Prussians—II. Arrangements and instructions which governed his march—III. Grouchy at Gembloux; the two versions of the 10 P.M. despatch—IV. Grouchy's determination to advance on Wavre—V. The sound of the Cannonade at Waterloo —VI. General criticisms and observations on Grouchy's movements.

## I.

AT the beginning of the campaign Grouchy had been invested with the command of the cavalry upon the right wing, but upon the morning of the 16th, a letter from the Emperor, dated Charleroi, reached the Marshal, informing him of his appointment as commander of the right wing in its entirety. "My intention is that, as commander of the right wing, you should take the command of the 3rd corps commanded by General Vandamme, of the 4th corps commanded by General Gérard, and of the cavalry corps of Pajol, Milhaud, and Excelmans, which ought not to be far short of 50,000 men. My intention is that all the Generals should take directly their orders from

## GROUCHY'S MARCH 145

you. They will take mine only when I shall be present in person."

The confidence which Napoleon thus exhibited in Grouchy was not misplaced upon the 16th. His operations at Ligny were marked by vigour and resolution, and he continued to personally superintend the charges of his cavalry against the Prussians until a late hour at night. The Emperor himself withdrew from the field a little after eight o'clock in the evening, and gave orders that Grouchy should join him at Fleurus. It was not until after 11 P.M. that the Marshal's duties permitted him to obey these orders. On reaching the Emperor's headquarters Grouchy was informed that the Emperor was in bed ill, and had given strict instructions that he was not to be disturbed. Soult would not take upon himself the responsibility of issuing any orders during Napoleon's retirement, and as a consequence the Marshal withdrew in a state of cruel uncertainty as to the action he ought to pursue. He, in common with Vandamme and all Napoleon's lieutenants, expected that the retreating Prussians would be instantly pursued. It was ever Napoleon's habit to follow up success to its furthest limits— but without instructions it was impossible to take the necessary measures. Still Grouchy, on his own initiative, despatched cavalry reconnaissances under Excelmans and Pajol in the direction of Gembloux and Namur, while to Pajol was added Teste's division of infantry.

K

At daybreak Grouchy again betook himself to Fleurus, but was unable to see the Emperor or to get any instructions at so early an hour. At last he was informed that the Emperor would visit the battlefield of yesterday as soon as he was up, and that he would see Grouchy and give him his orders there.

It was not until twelve o'clock at the earliest, and more probably towards 1 P.M., that Napoleon's plan in regard to the Prussians formulated itself. He then called Grouchy to him and put him in command of the two corps of Vandamme and Gérard, of Teste's division of infantry detached from its own corps, the 6th, and of a part of Pajol's and Excelman's cavalry. The whole amounted, as nearly as possible, to 33,000 men with 96 guns. With them Grouchy received verbal orders, which were, he assures us,* to this effect—
"Put yourself in pursuit of the Prussians, complete their defeat by attacking them as soon as you shall have joined them, and never lose sight of them. I am going to reunite the troops which I lead to the corps of Marshal Ney, march against the English and fight them if they stand on this side of the Forest of Soignies. You will correspond with me by the paved road which leads to Quatre Bras."

The tone of these instructions was scarcely applicable to the situation as it existed. Had Grouchy received them the night before, upon the

* "Fragments Historiques," par le Général Grouchy. Paris, 1829. "Le Maréchal de Grouchy," par le Général de division Sénateur Marquis de Grouchy. Paris, 1864.

conclusion of the battle of Ligny, no doubt could have entered his mind as to what he was intended to do. He would have had the enemy just in front of him, and there would have been no possibility of the Prussians deceiving him as to their line of retreat. But now they had fourteen hours' start. They had been lost sight of, and the time when he would come up with them was a matter of mere conjecture. No one knew exactly which way they had gone. No wonder, therefore, that Grouchy received his command with misgivings and remonstrances. He pointed out that the troops entrusted to him were not expecting to march that day— they were the corps on whom the brunt of the battle of Ligny had fallen,—that some time must elapse before they were ready to start, that the Prussians had already gained many hours upon any pursuit that might be made, and that consequently he would not be in a position to harass their retreat or hinder the dispositions which they had already determined upon. He even ventured to point out the strategical disadvantages which might follow from detaching so large a contingent from the operations of the main army. "In a word, I conjured him to authorise me to follow him." Napoleon's reply was to reiterate his commands, and Grouchy proceeded to make the necessary arrangements for his march.

To understand Napoleon's conduct at this juncture we must forget the facts and remember only his suppositions. He supposed the Prussians to

have adopted their natural line of retreat towards
Namur. Thus they would be separating themselves
from Wellington, and were no longer to be feared
so far as the next day's battle was concerned. It
was possible that they still contemplated further
intervention in the campaign, and to effect this purpose they had two courses open to them,—to direct
their march parallel to the main Brussels-Charleroi
road, and so maintain communications with Wellington, or else they might attempt to return upon
the French as they moved towards Brussels and
take them in flank or rear. The first contingency
had obviously, from all the evidence which we have,
not even crossed Napoleon's mind at mid-day on
the 17th, and his measures were in no way directed
to meet it. The second contingency was probably
to some slight degree present to his thoughts
when he despatched Grouchy in pursuit, but he
was dominated by the idea that the Prussians
were retreating on Namur. In this event their
fourteen hours' start was a matter of slight importance. It was only of importance if they had
adopted the first course—viz., to effect a concentration with the allied army further north, and of
this Napoleon had no suspicion. He therefore
despatched Grouchy in full confidence that he
would come up with the enemy somewhere on the
Namur road, that he would complete their overthrow, and effectually check any attempts they
might be inclined to make to return upon the
march of the main French army.

## GROUCHY'S MARCH 149

The Emperor's delusion was still further strengthened by the arrival at Fleurus of a battery of eight pieces which Pajol had captured from the enemy upon the Namur road. This piece of evidence seemed convincing as to the line the Prussians were taking, and contributed more perhaps than anything else to throw dust in Napoleon's eyes.

### II.

Grouchy accordingly left the Emperor's presence to make arrangements for his march. Though still far from reassured as to the prospect before him, he none the less proceeded to his task with promptness and energy. Vandamme was ordered to get ready to advance without delay, and to proceed with his corps to Point-du-Jour, a spot where the road from Gembloux joins the main *chaussée* from Namur to Quatre Bras. Gérard's corps was ordered to follow up Vandamme. It was not, however, till about 3 P.M.—according to documents published by Gérard himself—that the 4th corps began to move, and this despite Grouchy's personal exertions to expedite its march. At about 3.30 P.M. he received reports from Pajol and Excelmans—the one informing him that the Prussian retreat was by St Denis and Leuse, so as to gain the high road from Namur to Liége—the other that the enemy was massed at Gembloux. These despatches were almost immediately followed by a letter from Napoleon himself. It was dated "*Ligny, le 17 Juin 1815, vers trois heures,*" and ran as follows :—

"Betake yourself to Gembloux with the cavalry corps of Pajol, the light cavalry of the 4th corps, the cavalry corps of Excelmans, the division of General Teste, of which you will have special care, as it is detached from its army corps, and the 4th corps of infantry.

"You will explore in the directions of Namur and Maestricht, and you will pursue the enemy; explore his march and instruct me as to its movement, so that I may penetrate what it is intending to do.

"I am carrying my headquarters to Quatre Bras, where the English still were this morning. Our communication then will be direct by the paved road of Namur. (Here follow instructions as to the occupation of Namur, should Grouchy find it evacuated by the enemy.)

"It is important to penetrate what Blücher and Wellington intend to do, and if they propose to reunite their armies to cover Brussels and Liége† in trying the fate of another battle. In any case keep your two corps of infantry constantly united in a league of ground; occupy every evening a good military position, having several avenues of retreat. Place intermediate detachments of cavalry to communicate with headquarters.

"*Dictated by the Emperor, in the absence of the Major-General, to the Grand-Marshal Bertrand.*" *

* The text of this Document has been translated literally from Pascallet, in whose biography of Grouchy it first appeared in 1842.

† There is no warrant for Mr Rope's reading "*or Liége.*"

## GROUCHY'S MARCH 151

Several reasons make it necessary to produce this order practically in full, chiefly perhaps because it was the only despatch received by Grouchy from the Emperor until the afternoon of the next day.

Here are the instructions which governed his whole march. He had no others of any kind whatever until he reached Wavre on the afternoon of the 18th.

The document assumes additional importance from the fact that for many years it was suppressed by Marshal Grouchy. Until it appeared in 1842 he always asserted that he acted under Napoleon's verbal orders only, and that no written instructions whatever were sent to him except those despatched from the field of Waterloo.

It also gives us the first indication of doubt in Napoleon's mind as to the real direction of the Prussian retreat. His suppositions on the subject have already been stated, and he did not for a moment contemplate any movement on Blücher's part towards a concentration with Wellington. In Bertrand's order, sent off about three o'clock, we see the first glimmerings of such a suspicion in Napoleon's mind. The fact was that after Grouchy's departure the Emperor had received information that a strong body of Prussians had been seen at Gembloux. This might mean anything. It did not necessarily destroy the theory that they were retreating on Namur, though to Namur from Ligny *viâ* Gembloux was certainly a circuitous route. They might, as Pajol reported, be seeking the high road from Namur to Louvain by way of Gembloux. They might be halting there in order to concentrate, and, if unmolested, effect a movement on the flank and rear of Napoleon's army; or they might be at Gembloux with a view to marching northward on Wavre, in order to keep open their communication with Wellington. It was then of the first importance that Napoleon "should be able to penetrate what the enemy was intending to do," and this was Grouchy's mission. In any event Gembloux was a good place to make for, and hence he is specifically instructed to betake himself there.

In accordance with these instructions, Grouchy made all haste to reach his destination. But his progress was necessarily slow. Heavy rain began to fall about 2 P.M., and soon the rough and narrow country roads were converted into quagmires by the march of his troops through the dripping weather. Vandamme, it is true, reached Gembloux towards 7 P.M., and pushed forward some considerable distance beyond the town, but Gérard's corps did not enter into its bivouacs till 10 P.M., and to advance further at that hour, after such fatigues and in such weather, was out of the question. In and around Gembloux, therefore, the Marshal encamped for the night. He could not advance Vandamme while leaving Gérard at Gembloux, for his orders to keep all his troops well together within a league of ground were precise. Certainly he had not got far, for from Ligny to

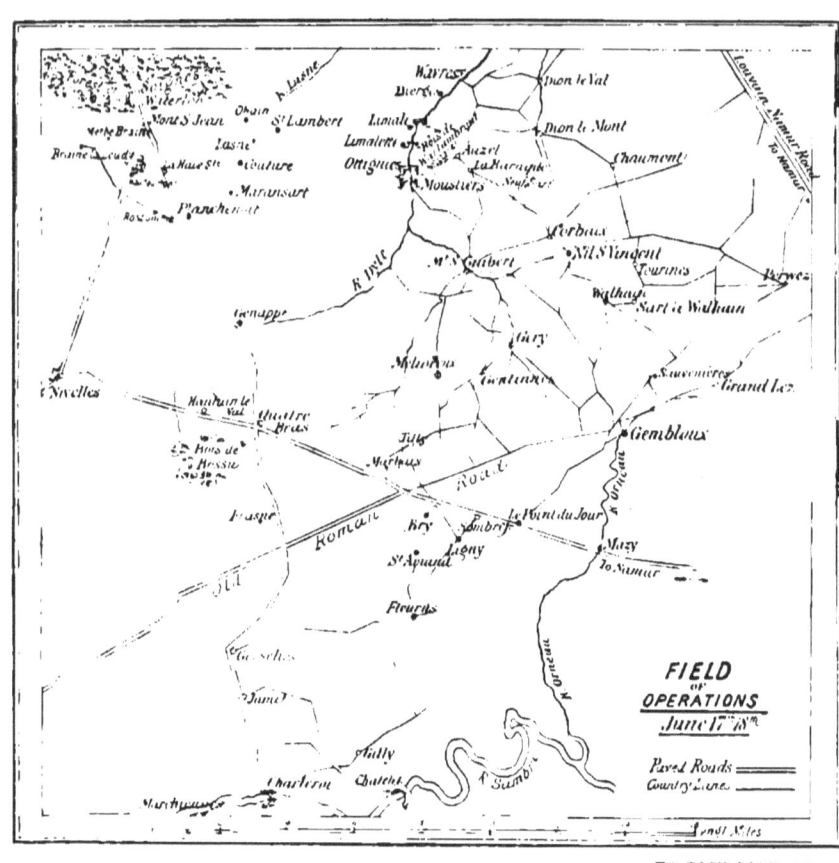

TO FACE PAGE 152

# GROUCHY'S MARCH 153

Gembloux is scarcely eight miles as the crow flies, but it is difficult to see how, in the circumstances, he could have got farther.

## III.

From Gembloux that evening Grouchy despatched a number of letters which betray an activity which can only be described as feverish. There are two to Gérard, one to Vandamme, one to Excelmans, one to Pajol,—an important despatch to the Emperor dated 10 P.M., and an equally important one (which cannot be found) at 2 A.M. on the 18th. These letters indicate a due sense of the importance of his mission, and in them he repeatedly urges upon his corps commanders the necessity of expedition. Vandamme is to put himself in motion before 5 A.M. Gérard's cavalry is to set out "*à la petite pointe du jour,*" and his infantry is to follow up Vandamme at 8 A.M. Pajol is to start "*à la pointe du jour.*" But it is with his letter to Napoleon that we are chiefly concerned, for it is clearly an answer to the Bertrand despatch, and shows us how Grouchy interpreted the obligations which that document laid upon him. Unfortunately there are more versions than one of this letter, the generally received text differing in many important particulars from that given in the Grouchy memoirs, and in the apology for Grouchy written by his son in 1864.

The versions, however, agree in this, that Grouchy

first informed the Emperor of his own position, then of what he had learned about the Prussians. " It appears, from all the reports," he says, "that the Prussians, having arrived at Sauvenières "— a village three miles north-east of Gembloux— " divided into two columns. One must have taken the road to Wavre, passing by Sart-à-Walhain ; the other column appears to be directed on Perwez. One may perhaps infer that one portion is going to join Wellington, and that the centre, which is the army of Blücher, is retiring on Liége." He is sending forward Excelmans with six squadrons on Sart-à-Walhain and three on Perwez, and will act according to the reports which he may receive, " but if the mass of the Prussians are retiring on Wavre, I shall follow them in that direction, so that they may not be able to gain Brussels, and so as to separate them from Wellington." *

The salient difference in the two versions is to be found in this last clause. In the received text Grouchy announces that if he marches on Wavre, it will be for the purpose of preventing the Prussians from gaining Brussels, and of separating them from Wellington. Now he did march on Wavre, but did not accomplish either of these purposes, nor did

* This clause in the Grouchy version runs :—" Si j'apprends que de fortes masses Prussiennes se portent sur Wavre, je les suivrai dans cette direction et les attaquerai dès que je les aurai jointes." In the ' received ' version the clause runs in the original :—" Si la masse des Prussiens se retire sur Wavre, je la suivrai dans cette direction, afin qu'ils ne puissent pas gagner Bruxelles, et de les séparer de Wellington."

# GROUCHY'S MARCH

he take the best means to secure their accomplishment. In the Grouchy version, he says his march on Wavre, if made at all, will be for the purpose of attacking the Prussians there as soon as he shall have joined them. This is precisely what he did do on the following day.

If Napoleon received the Grouchy version, he certainly sanctioned, as we shall see later on, the precise action which Grouchy took upon the 18th. If he received the other version, his sanction was given to Grouchy's intentions *as expressed in that version*—he sanctioned his design of following the Prussians, with a view to separating them from Brussels and from Wellington.

Which version, then, are we to accept? On this question must depend, to some extent, the judgment which we shall form as to Grouchy's conduct as a whole, and the matter is therefore deserving of close attention. But as in this chapter we are concerned chiefly with the narrative of Grouchy's march, it will be better not to interrupt that narrative more than is absolutely necessary in order to discuss debatable points. The main arguments on both sides are therefore appended in the form of a note,* and it must be for the reader to decide which version he will receive as the true one.

---

\* The weight of critical authority is all on the side of what we have called "the received version." Gérard, after citing it in his "Dernières Observations," published in 1830, adds the following words:—"Certifié conforme à l'original, qui nous a été remis par l'Empereur Napoléon et qui est entre nos mains."—Signé:

From Grouchy's despatch to the Emperor at 10 P.M., from Gembloux, we gather that at that hour he was still uncertain as to the line which the Prussians had taken, and as to the intentions with which they were marching. But during the next few hours he received further information, which he immediately communicated to the Emperor in a letter, dated Le Général Gourgaud." Gourgaud, therefore, is the ultimate surety for the veracity of the received version. Almost all critics accept it as the true one.

On the other hand, the security of Gourgaud is not good. He wrote in the interests of Napoleon, and notoriously falsified facts. He tells a story about two despatches, sent by Napoleon to Grouchy the night before Waterloo, containing precise instructions for his operations next day. Almost all critics agree that this story is purely mythical. Critics, therefore, are inconsistent. They cannot be allowed to treat one unsupported statement of Gourgaud as absolute truth and to discard another as absolute falsehood.

Napoleon notoriously falsified letters and bulletins to suit his interests. His interest was as great in maintaining the received version as Grouchy's in maintaining his version. Neither Grouchy nor Napoleon is entitled to absolute confidence, but the balance of confidence rests rather with Grouchy.

The author of the Grouchy "Memoirs" says he copies the letter from the original, which is under his eyes. [But Grouchy suppressed the Bertrand orders for twenty-seven years, and may have been capable of altering a document.] Gourgaud says the same thing of the received version: which of the two are we to believe?

Grouchy's son quotes the version of the "Memoirs," and says all the documents which he quotes are either in his own hands or in the archives. Some which he quotes as being in the archives are certainly not there.

Gourgaud's set purpose was to whitewash Napoleon, and to throw all the responsibility of his defeat on his Marshals, especially on Grouchy.

On the whole, I am inclined to think that Grouchy's version is quite as likely to be the true one as Gourgaud's version, and, if anything, to give the preference to Grouchy's.

# GROUCHY'S MARCH 157

Gembloux, 2 A.M., June 18th. This letter is not in existence, but Soult's reply to it, dated from the field of Waterloo at 10 A.M., sufficiently discloses its contents. Grouchy had discovered that two Prussian columns had marched by Sauvenières and Sart-à-Walhain, and he was now convinced that the Prussian retreat generally was upon Brussels. "The movement of Blücher's army," he writes to Pajol at day-break, "appears to me pronounced upon Brussels;" and it was with this idea firmly fixed in his mind that he issued his final orders for the operations of the day. These orders were to march on Wavre.

## IV.

A natural process of reasoning brought the Marshal to adopt Wavre as his first point of destination. The road from Sart-à-Walhain to Brussels is almost direct, and passes through Wavre. The Prussians, therefore, must, in their movement on Brussels, go to Wavre. There, or beyond that town, Grouchy's force would come up with them. If Blücher stopped at Wavre, the French would engage him there; if he pursued his march on Brussels, the French would either follow him up or would march by their left from Wavre to St Lambert, so as to join operations with the main army of Napoleon. The idea that Blücher, arrived at Wavre, would leave there a portion of his force to detain Grouchy, while detaching the major part of it to join operations with

Wellington in the coming battle, never seems to have occurred to the Marshal. He was wedded to a fixed idea — that the junction between Wellington and Blücher would take place in front of Brussels, on the other side of the forest of Soignies, and to prevent this, or at least to hinder it materially, an immediate march on Wavre was the best course to pursue.

Grouchy's operations, therefore, on the 18th June, were from the first conducted under a serious but rooted misapprehension, and it was this fact which caused him to be useless throughout the day—useless to Napoleon, and useless against the Prussians.

Notwithstanding his letters of the evening before, addressed to his corps commanders, urging the necessity of speed, and prescribing very early hours for their start, his force was not in movement from Gembloux until many hours after sunrise. Much recrimination has passed between the generals upon this point, and the mists of controversy have obscured the question as to who was responsible for the delay. Excelmans, with his dragoons, started at 7.30, Vandamme at 8, and Gérard at the same hour. The columns moved on Wavre by way of Sart-à-Walhain. Grouchy preceded his troops, and was at Walhain * before his advance-guard arrived. There he gathered all the information he could, and at eleven o'clock

---

* A distinction must be made between Sart-à-Walhain and Walhain. A reference to the map makes this clear.

wrote a letter to the Emperor, detailing his impressions as to the intentions of the Prussians. The 1st, 2nd, and 3rd corps of Blücher, he says, are marching in the direction of Brussels. Two of these corps have passed Sart-à-Walhain on the right, and amounted to 30,000 men at least. A corps coming from Liége (Bülow's) had effected its junction with those who fought at Ligny. The Prussians were designing to make a stand against the troops which were pursuing them, or else to unite themselves with Wellington, "a project announced by their officers, who, with their usual assurance, pretend only to have quitted the field on the 16th, so as to operate their junction with the English army on Brussels.

"This evening I shall be massed at Wavre, and shall thus find myself between Wellington —whom I presume to be in retreat before your Majesty—and the Prussian army."

The letter closes with repeated demands for further instructions.

V.

This despatch had scarcely been sent off at 11 o'clock on the morning of the eventful 18th when Colonel Lorière, Gérard's chief of the staff, announced to Grouchy and to Gérard, who had reached Walhain in advance of his corps, that he heard in the west the roar of artillery fire. The generals, surrounded by their staffs, proceeded at once to ascertain the character of the engagement which was apparently in progress on the left. At first, through the drizzling rain and heavy atmosphere, they were inclined to interpret what they heard as a skirmish of advanced guards, but very soon they were unmistakably convinced that a general action was in progress. There was little difficulty in fixing the situation of the battle-field. The plateau of Mont St Jean was marked out as being the scene of the combat. What, then, under these fresh conditions, was the right wing of the French army to do?

Gérard impetuously urged the imperative duty of marching to the sound of the cannon. The Prussian march had now definitely narrowed itself down to one of two alternatives,—either they were marching on Brussels or else were moving to join forces with Wellington at Mont St Jean. In either event, prudence and policy alike suggested the advisability of joining the Emperor as quickly as possible, for if the Prussians were moving on Brussels, they might be regarded as a negligable quantity in the battle at Waterloo. If, on the other hand, they were advancing to join Wellington, Grouchy, by marching on the cannon sound, would be most advantageously disposed to stop them, to hinder them, or to diminish the effects of their junction in the event of its having been accomplished.

Grouchy, however, thought otherwise. Undoubtedly the tone of authority adopted by Gérard predisposed the Marshal to disregard his counsels, but he had solid objections to urge to the

## GROUCHY'S MARCH

course proposed. He had, first of all, his instructions. Napoleon's verbal instructions were precise and definite in their terms. He was to pursue the Prussians, never lose sight of them, and attack them as soon as he had come up with them. He was now close upon their heels, and proposed to attack them at once. The sounds of battle at Mont St Jean created no new situation. It was exactly what Napoleon himself had anticipated at the time when he despatched Grouchy in pursuit of the enemy. "I am going," he said on the field of Ligny, "to attack the English if they stand on this side of the Forest of Soignies." They were standing there and the Emperor was attacking them. If the Emperor had intended to modify his instructions in any way he would have done so; he had not done so, therefore his original instructions still held good. It was not for a subordinate to carry out operations of inspiration, but to carry out the operations prescribed by his superior.

Moreover, there were serious practical difficulties in the way of Gérard's plan. Balthus, who commanded Gérard's artillery, considered it almost impossible to carry the guns over the muddy lanes and marshy ground, by which alone the Emperor was to be approached, in time to render any service in a battle to be fought at Mont St Jean that day. It was indeed doubtful if the troops themselves could accomplish so long and difficult a march before the day would be practically over. They certainly could not arrive before six o'clock, assuming that their progress, at the rate of three miles an hour, would be quite unimpeded by the enemy.* But was it at all likely that it would be unimpeded? The Prussians were 90,000 strong. The French right wing only numbered 33,000. If it were to commit itself to a flank march while 90,000 of the enemy were massed within a few miles of it, was it to be supposed that the Prussians would fail to avail themselves of their opportunity? Half Blücher's force would be sufficient to detain them indefinitely, while with the other half he might march unimpeded on Mont St Jean.

Such, and much more, were the arguments that passed in this momentous colloquy. Gérard endeavoured to break the resolution of his chief by proposing that he should march with his corps to the sound of the cannonade, while Grouchy with the rest proceeded on Wavre. Such a suggestion the Marshal was bound by his orders to reject. His instructions were formal to keep his corps together within a league of ground. His determination, whether for good or evil, must apply to the whole force under his command, and his determination was to march, according to his original purpose, on Wavre, and to engage the Prussians there. An hour before the discussion arose, Napoleon was replying to Grouchy's 2 A.M. despatch. His letter is dated from the field of

* For distances and calculations based thereon, see pages 171, 172.

Waterloo at 10 o'clock A.M. In it there occur the following phrases:—"The Emperor charges me to acquaint you that his Majesty is about to attack the English army, which has taken position at Waterloo, near the Forest of Soignies. Accordingly (*ainsi*) his Majesty desires that you should direct your movements on Wavre, so as to approach us, to put yourself in touch with our operations, and to bind our communications, pushing before you those corps of the Prussian army which have taken this direction, and which may have stopped at Wavre, where you ought to arrive as soon as possible."

No wonder that Grouchy congratulated himself when he received this letter at four in the afternoon, that he had decided to follow his own counsels, and had refused to be guided by the advice of Gérard.

Yet from the moment of that decision Grouchy ceased to be a factor in the campaign of Waterloo.

## VI.

The intention, so far, has been to put before the reader the more important facts connected with the first twenty-four hours of Grouchy's march. It has, however, been impossible, without encroaching unduly upon the narrative, to state the whole of the facts, or to examine them with the minuteness and care which they deserve. The present section, therefore, will be devoted to a critical examination of Grouchy's conduct during the period referred to.

It must be admitted that Grouchy was tardily despatched, and for this Napoleon alone is to blame. Mr Ropes contends that, as commander of the right wing at Ligny, it was the duty of Grouchy to send out reconnaissances during the night which followed the battle in order to ascertain the direction of the Prussian retreat, whether he received instructions to do so or not. He did send out such reconnaissances upon his own responsibility. Pajol explored the Namur road; Excelmans proceeded as far as Gembloux. No detachment, it is true, was sent along the road leading due north by Gentinnes, Géry, and Mont St Guibert to Wavre, and had this been done great results might have followed, for this was the line that Blücher and Gneisenau had actually taken. But strategical reasons seemed to render investigation in this direction unnecessary, and if Grouchy was in error here, the Emperor, when he could be prevailed on to exert himself, made no sort of effort to rectify that error.

The question that first presents itself is, Ought Napoleon to have detached Grouchy at all? If he was to be detached, would not 10,000 men have been as effective, as a corps of observation, as a force of over 30,000? How could Grouchy seriously attack and hold in check a force which was nearly three times as great as his own? If the enemy was in a state of demoralisation after defeat, to observe them and to prevent them from

## GROUCHY'S MARCH 165

rallying was all that was required. Some 10,000 men would have been adequate for this purpose. If, on the other hand, the enemy was retreating in good order, and was falling back upon a fresh corps which had taken no part in the battle—and Napoleon knew that Bülow's corps was close at hand—how could some 30,000 men be an adequate protection to the French main army from all further interference on the part of the Prussians? All that Napoleon really required was that the Prussians should not intervene in the coming battle against Wellington. If, therefore, he had concentrated his force instead of dividing it, and marched along the main road to Brussels against the allied army, he might easily have detached Grouchy at Genappe, or even at a point still further north, to manœuvre towards the right with better hopes of accomplishing his object, than by despatching him on a vague mission, under every circumstance of disadvantage, which must of necessity break off effective communications between himself and a third part of his total strength.

The next point which meets us is Napoleon's total failure to make Grouchy acquainted with his own intentions, and of the information which he had gained as to the movements of the enemy.

Except a vague intimation that he intends to fight the English should they venture to stand and meet him, it is not until an hour or so before the battle of Waterloo begins that Napoleon tells his lieutenant that a battle is imminent. There can be no clearer proof than this that he began the battle without a thought of being assisted in it by Grouchy's contingent. Certainly he had no thought that the Prussians would assist Wellington, and yet he had information on this point which, had it been communicated to Grouchy, would have been most useful in guiding that Marshal's movements and dispositions. In his first letter of the 18th Napoleon says —" You only speak of two Prussian corps. . . . Yet reports say that a third column, which was pretty strong, has passed by Géry and Gentinnes, directing its march on Wavre." Here is a piece of information of priceless value in indicating the ultimate intentions of Blücher, and yet it is withheld from Grouchy until the eleventh hour, until the opportunity of profiting by it has long since passed away, and the natural inferences to be drawn from it are entirely ignored by Napoleon himself. Grouchy's only mission, in fact, is to find out what the enemy is intending to do ; Napoleon has knowledge on the point which, by itself, could enable him to form conclusions more correct than any which, without that knowledge, Grouchy could form, yet not only does he refuse to act upon the intelligence which he possesses, but by withholding it from Grouchy prevents that Marshal from acting upon it either.

Again, with the exception of the Bertrand order, which can be characterised as nothing else than a roving commission, no instructions whatever were

## GROUCHY'S MARCH 167

sent to the right wing throughout the remainder of the 17th, or until 10 o'clock on the morning of the 18th. No attempt was made to keep communications with Grouchy open, no reconnaissances were sent in his direction on taking position for the battle which was imminent. Vague expectations, indefinite hopes held Napoleon's mind to the exclusion of vigorous measures and active precautions, and instead of two wings of a single army acting in concert and mutually supporting one another, we have two separate armies acting independently of each other's operations, and one of which drifts aimlessly for want of the knowledge, instructions, and assistance which the other could in large part supply.

The Grouchy mission, indeed, exhibits in Napoleon a strange and unwonted mixture of confidence and apprehension. Either the Prussians were still formidable or they were not. If they were, no measure of precaution, even the slightest, ought to have been omitted to render them harmless. Every route should have been promptly explored, if by any possibility the Prussians might have taken it. Every indication of their intentions should have been duly weighed and transmitted without delay from one wing to the other. And when circumstances pointed, in however small a degree, to the possibility of their junction with Wellington for the purposes of the coming battle, Grouchy should not have been left to follow his vague ideas of what was required of him, but should have been instructed decisively and without possibility of mistake as to what he was to do.

If the Prussians were not formidable, there was no need to detach the right wing from the main army at all.

Grouchy moved on Gembloux in obedience to his orders, and as a consequence of the general belief that the enemy was retreating by way of the Meuse. The Prussian columns therefore, which were marching on Wavre by way of Mont St Guibert, were left unmolested, for their very existence upon that route was entirely unsuspected. But thus a considerable detachment of the enemy was allowed to interpose itself between the two French wings. Clausewitz thinks that Grouchy might have been expected to explore this line of march with a portion of his troops, while yet proceeding with his main force by Gembloux; but this criticism ignores Napoleon's orders, that the whole of Grouchy's force was to be kept well together within a league of ground. By the terms of his instructions, the Marshal may defy criticism until the time when he learned at Gembloux that Blücher's march was on Wavre and towards the Dyle river. He had made up his mind on this point by 3 A.M. on the 18th, and his orders for the day were therefore the result of the certainty he had acquired. Was his determination to march on Wavre by Sart-à-Walhain in correspondence with Blücher's movement towards the Dyle?

The answer to this question must depend upon

# GROUCHY'S MARCH 169

the meaning to be attached to Blücher's movement. A mistake very commonly made is to suppose that the Prussian general could have no other object in view, when he concentrated his army at Wavre, than that of co-operating with Wellington at Waterloo; but his action admits of another interpretation, for he might merely be marching by way of Wavre on Brussels. Grouchy had no information that Wellington had taken position at Waterloo—he supposed him to be in retreat before Napoleon. Having no knowledge that a battle was about to take place, he could have no knowledge that the Prussians were marching to take part in it. "He thought the Prussians," says General Hamley, in his treatise on the operations of war, "if they were really moving on Wavre, intended to join Wellington at Brussels. And were they so moving, he, by marching to Wavre, would threaten decisively their communications with their base by Louvain, and so either prevent the execution of their project or render it disastrous." In fact, the fatal error of Napoleon again confronts us. A line to Grouchy that the English were in position intending to fight would have poured a flood of light upon the nature of Blücher's dispositions, but Grouchy was deliberately left to make a choice between conjectures, and for want of the information at Napoleon's disposal, he conjectured wrongly.

Grouchy's movement on Wavre, therefore, was in response to what he supposed Blücher's intentions to be, but it was entirely useless in view of the plan which Blücher was actually adopting.

The alternative to reaching Wavre by Sart-à-Walhain was to reach it by the Dyle; and, as matters turned out, Grouchy ought in any event to have taken this direction. If by chance the English were standing to fight, then Blücher's movements were certainly suggestive of an intention to join them. By marching towards his left, Grouchy would at any rate be putting himself in a position to thwart these designs; by marching towards his right he was tending, if anything, to facilitate them. Either road would bring him to Wavre, but the one would bring him nearer to the Emperor, the other would take him further away. This seems so obvious to us now that we are apt to overlook the strong reasons which influenced Grouchy's decision. He was still in bondage to the original error. He imagined that the real danger from the Prussians lay upon his right, not on his left; he was full of his own mission, not of Napoleon's necessities, and regarded himself as altogether outside the scope of the main operations of the army; he thought himself at liberty to execute his mission in the way that seemed best to him, without reference of any kind to the movements of the Emperor.

But the matter assumes quite another aspect when once Grouchy became convinced that a general action was in progress on his left. If up to this point Blücher's retreat seemed pronounced upon

# GROUCHY'S MARCH 171

Brussels, now the idea that it was not so ought to have forcibly borne itself in upon him, and in face of the bare possibility of some Prussian help being rendered to Wellington it was Grouchy's obvious duty to concentrate all his energies on the single purpose of preventing such assistance from being given. How this could best be done was now the only question.

Should he march straight upon the sound of the cannonade?

The only object in doing so was to join the Emperor, and to come up to him as a reinforcement while the battle was in progress. The question therefore hinges almost entirely on distances.

The variety of estimates given as to the simple matter of the distance from Sart-à-Walhain to the field of Waterloo, and of the time which it would take Grouchy to cover that distance, is one of the most surprising things in the history of the campaign. Authorities range between two hours, which is the least estimate, and nine hours, which is the largest. The matter of distance, however, can be authoritatively decided. To march from Sart-à-Walhain to Planchenoit necessitates crossing the river Dyle. It could only be crossed at Moustier and by bridges further north of that point. Now the distance from Sart-à-Walhain to Planchenoit *viâ* Moustier was, by the only available roads, as nearly as possible eighteen miles.

To decide the matter of time M. Quinet induced two friends of his to traverse the whole journey on foot. It took them five and a half hours. Thus they walked at a rate of a little more than three miles an hour. An army corps could not advance at anything like that rate, more particularly when the state of the roads is taken into account. Two miles an hour is a fair rough estimate for the march of an army corps under such circumstances as then prevailed. Grouchy's leading columns would therefore have debouched on Planchenoit at 9 P.M., assuming that he started from Sart-à-Walhain at twelve.*

This calculation is based entirely upon the assumption that his march would have been unimpeded by the Prussians. Such might have been the case, but at the same time it is most improbable that it would have been so. If the Prussians disputed the passage of the river, it is clear that Grouchy could not arrive on the field of Waterloo that night. If they did not do so, he could not arrive until the battle was over.

But it is urged with great force and much weight of authority that if he could not arrive himself, he might have prevented the Prussians from arriving. To accomplish this would have been to accomplish

---

\* Mr Ropes has been at great pains to show that Grouchy was not at Sart-à-Walhain but at Walhain or Walhain St Paul when the sound of the cannonade at Waterloo was heard. He has certainly established this point conclusively. This brings Grouchy a mile nearer to Planchenoit. But the point is not where Grouchy was, but where his troops were, and his troops at 11.30 A.M. had not yet reached Sart-à-Walhain, much less Walhain St Paul.

all that was necessary, for without the intervention of the Prussians, Napoleon was assured of victory over the English. Here we enter the realm of pure conjecture. It is, of course, possible that if Grouchy had displayed himself in force, the march of Bülow would have been stopped, and, as a consequence, that of Pirch, who was following up Bülow. The mere appearance of an unexpected corps (D'Erlon's) had done much to influence the battle of Ligny on the 16th. The mere appearance of Bülow at St Lambert did much, as will be seen, to influence the issue at Waterloo. But is it probable that the whole Prussian force marching on Napoleon's flank would allow itself to be stopped by so comparatively slight an obstacle as Grouchy's contingent?* It is at least equally probable that a detachment of Prussians would have been employed to detain Grouchy, while the main body continued its movement towards the battle. In this case, Grouchy's march on Planchenoit would have been altogether ineffectual, except perhaps to involve himself in the common ruin.

But in addition to the practical issues depending upon Grouchy's decision, there is an abstract strategical question involved — whether it is not, on general principles, the duty of a corps, detached from the main body, to march in the direction where heavy firing indicates a critical engagement? The authority of Clausewitz must

* Blücher was under the impression that Grouchy had only 10,000 or 11,000 men with him.

carry great weight as to this point. After referring to this contention as a dictum "hastily fabricated," he says—"This principle can only hold good in those cases when the commander of a separate column has been placed by circumstances in a position of doubt, when the originally clear and definite character of his task has been clouded by uncertainties and contradictions, which are so frequent in actual war. I admit that a commander so placed, instead of standing still doing nothing or wandering vaguely about, would do better to hasten to his neighbour's assistance if heavy firing suggests that he needs it. But to expect of Grouchy that he should trouble himself no further about Blücher, but march off to where another portion of the army was engaged with another enemy, would be contrary to all theory and practice. That General Gérard really gave such advice at noon on the 18th at Sart-à-Walhain only proves that, where there is no responsibility, consideration is apt to be hasty." *

The matter might be allowed to rest here were it not that Grouchy's alternative policy was productive of nothing. To continue his march on Wavre, and to engage the 16,000 men or so whom Blücher had left there, was the equivalent to that " standing still doing nothing or wandering vaguely about " which Clausewitz condemns. The arguments which applied against the march on Plan-

* *Feldzug von* 1815, Kap. 50.

## GROUCHY'S MARCH 175

chenoit applied in an equal degree against the march on Wavre. It was most improbable that the whole Prussian force would allow itself to be detained from its fixed purpose in order to oppose Grouchy at Wavre. And all the force which was not detained there would be available to march on Waterloo. Was it not better to run some risk in order to be of some possible use, than to run practically the same risk without the chance of being of any use at all? It cannot be shown with any degree of conclusiveness that Grouchy, by marching to the sound of the cannonade, could have exercised any appreciable influence on the battle of Waterloo. It is clear that he exercised no influence upon events by the course which he actually adopted. We are thus brought back to the point from which we started — that Grouchy's mission was from the first a mistake—that Napoleon despatched him on a vague and ill-calculated errand—and that, although perhaps a general of great intuitive genius might possibly have so dealt with the difficulties and chances of the position as to make them his instruments in achieving success for his chief, yet from no general could such results be looked for with any degree of confidence, from few could any results be looked for at all.

## CHAPTER IX.

### THE MORNING OF THE BATTLE.

I. Napoleon's Formation in Order of Battle on the 18th—II. Wellington's Formation—III. Analysis of the Duke's Force and Position—IV. Delay in beginning the Battle—V. Napoleon's Despatch to Grouchy before the Battle—VI. Prussian Movements on the Morning of the 18th.

### I.

IT has been seen that Napoleon's one fear was that Wellington might escape him, and that the stand at Mont St Jean was not really intended as an offer of battle. The astonishment of the French when they found that the English had not only taken position, but were prepared to defend it, has been noted. Should not this very fact, that the English were standing, have suggested considerations to Napoleon's mind as to the causes which had induced Wellington's determination? Instead of that overweening confidence which is expressed in the exclamation, "*Enfin je les tiens, ces Anglais!*" should he not rather have gathered from what he saw before him that the English had taken position in reliance upon some support not yet apparent? Wellington's caution was well known to Soult from experience, and to Napoleon from report, and it was inconsistent with this caution that the Duke should deliberately, and with alternatives to choose from, risk his all upon an unequal contest. The very fact that battle was accepted should of itself have sufficed to forcibly suggest the truth about the Prussian movements, even if this were the first indication that his previous surmises were incorrect. But, as we have seen, when the Emperor dictated to Bertrand his orders for Grouchy, doubts had already risen in his mind as to the intentions of the Prussians. Unable to discard the strong and convincing impression that they were *hors de combat*, yet the Bertrand order clearly shows that a suspicion of the truth was struggling with his preconceived impression. This being so, he might well be convinced by Wellington's attitude that the Prussians were near, especially when we consider Grouchy's despatches addressed from Gembloux, which explicitly warned him that one Prussian column, at any rate, was on its way to Wavre, only ten miles distant from Mont St Jean.

But nothing is more clear than that the idea of the intervention of the Prussians in the coming battle did not enter Napoleon's mind. Notwithstanding Wellington's attitude of defiance, notwithstanding the doubts which he himself evidently entertained on the day before, in spite of Grouchy's information on the morning of the 18th, Napoleon made ready for the contest with a light heart, seeing before him the prospect of a victory as decided and undisturbed as any which he had ever won. As early as one o'clock on the morning of the 18th Napoleon was in the saddle, closely examining the enemy's position, and satisfying himself that Wellington was standing for battle. There was a moment when he suspected that the Anglo-Dutch army was making ready to withdraw, but a closer examination showed him that the suspicious movement was one of preparation, not of retreat, and being satisfied upon the point, he said to D'Erlon, "Order the men to make their soup, to get their pieces in order, and we will determine what is to be done towards noon." He then proceeded to take up his own position, his whole available force being upon the ground at 8 A.M.

The Emperor established his headquarters at La Belle Alliance, a little inn upon the side of the main Brussels road, about a mile and a half from Wellington's quarters at Mont St Jean, and about half a mile from La Haie Sainte. The rising ground to the right hand and to the left gave him a commanding position, and would enable his cavalry and infantry charges to be made down-hill. On each side of the road he drew up his army in two lines, the reserve forming a third, making La Belle Alliance the centre. On the right the first line consisted of D'Erlon's 1st corps, 20,000 strong, and burning to redeem, by gallant deeds, its previous inactivity. Donzelot's division formed its left,

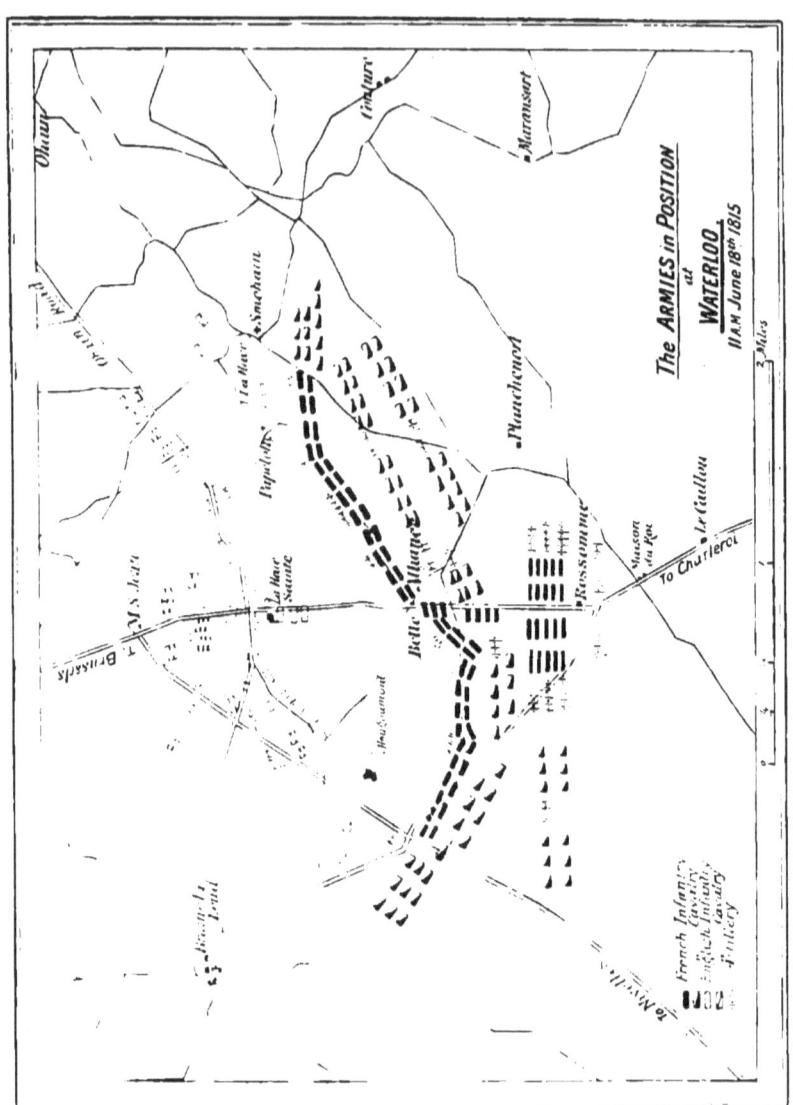

## MORNING OF THE BATTLE 179

resting on the Charleroi road, the division of Quiot rested upon Donzelot, Marcognet on Quiot, and Durutte's formed the extreme right opposite to the hamlets of Smohain, Papelotte, and La Haye. The cavalry of the 1st corps observed these hamlets, being posted to the right of Durutte's infantry. The 3rd corps of Milhaud's heavy cavalry and Jacquinot's light cavalry acted as a support to the whole line. Eighty pieces of artillery were posted partly in front of the line, and partly between and on the flank of the supporting cavalry.

The left wing consisted of the 2nd corps, with the exception of Girard's division, which had been left behind at Ligny. The three remaining divisions numbered about 13,000 men, and were posted upon the left of the Brussels road, Bachelu's division forming the right, Foy resting upon it, and Jérome Bonaparte resting upon Foy. It extended from La Belle Alliance to beyond Hougomont. Piré's cavalry continued the line upon its extreme left, and it was supported, as a whole, by Kellermann's 4th corps of heavy dragoons.

The reserve consisted of Lobau's 6th corps (with the exception of Teste's division, which was with Grouchy), together with the cavalry corps of Domont and Subervie, detached the one from Vandamme's division, and the other from Pajol. Lobau, therefore, with allowance for additions and subtractions, had about 10,000 men under his command. He formed behind the centre, the infantry resting on and across the Brussels road, the cavalry to the right.

In rear of Lobau came the Imperial Guard, 19,000 strong, their infantry posted near the farm of Rossomme, with their artillery upon their flanks. The main road divided them into two equal parts. They were drawn up in six lines, four battalions in each line, and thus they presented a formation in column, two columns on each side of the road, each column containing six battalions, the reserve artillery of the Guard, consisting of 12-pounders, being in the rear. The horse Grenadiers and dragoons of the Guard, with their artillery in the centre, were drawn up in rear of Kellermann's cavalry supporting the left wing, while in rear of Milhaud's cavalry supporting the right wing were drawn up the light horsemen of the Imperial Guard, consisting of Colbert's Lancers and Lefébvre-Desnouette's Light Dragoons. The total force amounted to close upon 72,000 men, the infantry numbering nearly 49,000, the cavalry about 15,700, and the artillery about 7300, with from 240 to 246 guns.

## II.

The position taken up by the Duke was looser than, but in many respects similar to Napoleon's. About a thousand yards from Mont St Jean the road from Ohain crosses at a right angle the main Brussels road. The Ohain road defined the

THE CORPS, DIVISIONS, BRIGADES and REGIMENTS, etc. approximately in position at WATERLOO (not to scale)

## MORNING OF THE BATTLE 181

English position. Its point of junction with the main *chaussée* marked the English centre, with La Haie Sainte immediately in front of it, not 300 yards away. The course of the Ohain road for rather more than a mile on each side of the Brussels road is along the top of a gentle ridge. Along this ridge the army was posted. Its slopes afforded protection, while from its crest an uninterrupted view was obtained of all the enemy's movements. The front was also well covered, as has been already seen, by the hamlets of Smohain, Papelotte, and others on the east, and on the west by Hougomont. The English left consisted of the 5th British division, under command of Sir Thomas Picton, the 6th British division commanded, in the absence of Sir Lowry Cole, by Sir J. Lambert, and the 2nd division of Dutch-Belgians under Perponcher. The 6th division formed the right of the left wing, and rested upon the main Brussels road. It was composed of the 4th Regiment of Foot, or the King's Own—veteran soldiers who had just returned from the war in America, and who had scarcely reached the field in time— and of the 27th, 40th, and 81st regiments. They had fought under the Duke in Spain, and constituted that "Spanish Infantry" of which he used to talk sometimes as having been present at Waterloo. Resting upon the 6th division came Kempt's 8th British Brigade and Pack's 9th or Scotch Brigade. With Pack were the 1st Royal Scots, a part of the 42nd Highlanders, the 44th and the

92nd Highlanders; with Kempt were the 79th Highlanders, the 95th Royal Rifles, and the 28th and 32nd Regiment. Best's 4th Hanoverian and Vincke's 5th Hanoverian brigades supported Pack, and continued the line, the centre of which was covered by Bylandt's Dutch-Belgians, who were drawn up in a very exposed position in front of the Ohain road, and in front of, not behind, the slope. "They were," says Sir J. Shaw Kennedy, "directly exposed to the fire of the greatest battery that was on the field, and singly exposed to the first onset of the French attacking columns." Such a formation affords a reasonable amount of excuse for the conduct of some of the Dutch-Belgian troops at the outset of the battle. Perponcher's troops continued the line to the left, while Prince Bernard of Saxe-Weimar's brigade occupied the hamlets of Smohain, Papelotte, and La Haye. Vivian's cavalry were posted on the extreme left, with the cavalry of Vandeleur upon their right.

In rear of the first line stood the Union Brigade or 2nd cavalry brigade of Sir W. Ponsonby. It consisted of the 1st Royal Dragoons, the Scots Greys, and the 6th Inniskillen Dragoons. Its formation particularly attracted the attention of Napoleon, as he observed his enemy's movements in the morning. "*Regardez ces chevaux gris*," he said, as he watched the Scots Greys, "*Qui sont ces beaux cavaliers? Ce sont de braves troupes mais dans un demi-heure je les couperai en pièces.*"

The right wing was formed on the ground

## MORNING OF THE BATTLE 183

between the two high roads from Charleroi and Nivelles, running for about 500 yards at right angles to the Charleroi road, and then inclining as it follows the bend of the Ohain road, to the south-west. Opposite the south-western extremity, where the Ohain road meets the road from Planchenoit, lies the Chateau of Hougomont. Wellington's right front, therefore, lay in a semi-circular situation from Hougomont to the main road. It consisted of Alten's 3rd British division and Cooke's 1st division, with Byng's brigade occupying Hougomont. Alten's left rested upon the main Brussels road, and his division consisted of Sir Colin Halkett's brigade, the 2nd brigade of the King's German Legion under Omptéda, and Kielmansegge's 1st Hanoverian brigade, partly in the first, partly in the second line. Maitland's 1st brigade of Cooke's division, which had been severely handled two days before at Quatre Bras, was formed next to Halkett. It consisted of the 1st and 2nd battalion of the 1st Guards, or Grenadier Guards, as they were subsequently called. Notwithstanding the hot work it had been called upon to perform at Quatre Bras, Maitland's brigade was to be put to even further proof in the coming battle, for upon it the charge of the French Imperial Guard was in a great measure to fall. Mitchell's brigade, detached from Colville's division, which was at Hal, rested its left on the Nivelles road, with Chassé's Dutch-Belgians beyond it, extending as far as Braine-la-Leude. The line was supported in the rear by Lord Edward Somerset's heavy cavalry resting close upon the main Brussels road, while the Dutch-Belgian cavalry were still further to the right.

The reserves were placed *en potence*, to the rear of the extreme right of the English army. They occupied a plateau formed by a second ridge behind that on which the first line of the army was drawn up, and owing to the undulating character of the ground at that point, it was possible to completely conceal from view the troops there stationed. These consisted of the 2nd division under Sir Henry Clinton—comprising the Light Brigade, Colbourne's 52nd, the 71st, and the Rifle Brigade (59th Rifles). With them was the 1st King's German Legion and the 3rd Hanoverian brigade. Their situation *en potence* enabled them to be used either as reserves or for a flank movement, hence their value in such a position, having regard to the defensive character of the Duke's operations, can scarcely be over-estimated. They also tended to consolidate the English right into a compact but very manageable mass. With Clinton behind, and with Hougomont in front, the right wing was certainly prepared to resist, with every chance of success, the hottest attacks which could be made upon it.

The troops of the Duke of Brunswick, now commanded by Colonel Olfermann, were posted close to the little hamlet of Merbe-Braine, but two battalions in the course of the day were moved up

## MORNING OF THE BATTLE 185

to strengthen the right above Hougomont, where they distinguished themselves by their desperate bravery. The Duke of Wellington originally posted in Hougomont the 2nd brigade of Cooke's division, commanded by Sir J. Byng, comprising three, afterwards increased to seven, companies of the Coldstream regiment, four companies of the Guards, and a battalion of the Nassau regiment. These were reinforced as occasion required, for the importance of the possession of Hougomont was very clearly recognised on both sides. Immediately the troops had taken their posts, the work of crenellating the walls of the chateau, chapel, and garden was begun, and before morning they bristled with muskets to be fired by unseen defenders upon the advancing French. The Nassauers acted as sharp-shooters in the outlying wood, the light troops of the Guards held the orchard, while the Coldstream companies and the 3rd Guards held the house, out-buildings, garden, and chapel.

The farm of La Haie Sainte was by no means so extensive as the estate of Hougomont, but relatively its occupation and retention was of equal importance. It was held by a portion of Ompteda's King's Germans—the 2nd light battalion under Major Baring—but these troops needed to be constantly reinforced throughout the day, for the position fronted the very centre of the English line, and was subjected to the first and fiercest attack of the enemy. Sir J. Lambert's 10th British brigade was specially employed as the day wore on for the defence, and afterwards for the reoccupation of La Haie Sainte, when it had been taken by the French, and the regiments composing this brigade—the 4th, 27th, and 40th—won eternal glory at the cost of 830 men out of a total effective force of 2000.

The total force under arms engaged at the battle of Waterloo under the command of the Duke of Wellington was 67,661, of whom 49,608 were infantry, 12,408 were cavalry, 5645 were artillery, with 156 guns. This force was made up as follows:—

III.

|  | Infantry. | Cavalry. | Artillery. | Total. | Guns. |
|---|---|---|---|---|---|
| British | 15,181 | 5,843 | 2967 | 23,991 | 78 |
| King's Germans | 3,301 | 1,997 | 526 | 5,824 | 18 |
| Hanoverians | 10,258 | 497 | 465 | 11,220 | 12 |
| Brunswickers | 4,586 | 866 | 510 | 5,962 | 16 |
| Nassauers | 2,880 | ... | ... | 2,880 | ... |
| Dutch-Belgians | 13,402 | 3,205 | 1177 | 17,784 | 32 |
| Total | 49,608 | 12,408 | 5645 | 67,661 | 156 |

Examining this table, it may be remarked that the number of British soldiers engaged was little more than one-third of the whole; and that even including the King's Germans, who were as reliable as the British, the strength on which the Duke of Wellington could implicitly depend did

## MORNING OF THE BATTLE 187

not amount to a half of the whole army. The Dutch-Belgians, who, next to the British and King's Germans, numbered the largest division of the whole, were suspected of being lukewarm in the cause on which they were engaged, and though by no means, as a whole, open to those charges of cowardice and inefficiency which have been so freely brought against them, it must yet be admitted that, as soldiers, they did not rank very high, and that their doubtful loyalty made them, to some extent, an unknown factor in the situation at the time when the battle began. The same remarks apply in general to the Hanoverians, Brunswickers, and Nassauers, for the conspicuous valour which they actually displayed, and which, perhaps, has scarcely been sufficiently realised by chroniclers of the battle, was not to be confidently looked for from troops whose political temper was uncertain, and whose military calibre was of doubtful quality.

The Duke's slight superiority in infantry — a superiority of about 650 men—was more than compensated for by his inferiority in cavalry—an inferiority of no less than 3300 men. Considering the important part which this arm was to play in the battle, the deficiency in cavalry was likely to have very serious results, especially when coupled with a similar deficiency in artillery and guns, Napoleon bringing to the field 1600 more artillery and about 90 more guns. Numerically, however, the forces were fairly evenly matched, and the Duke made up in position for any disadvantage he was under as to numbers. The strength of his position lay in its suitability for purposes of defence. The right wing was by far the stronger of the two, for not only did Hougomont protect its centre, but a larger proportion of troops was concentrated in line and in reserve upon that side. In this disposition the Duke was actuated by two motives—first, that under no circumstances should Napoleon be able to turn his right wing by any open or veiled movement upon the flank; and, secondly, because he was expecting the Prussians to come up upon his left, and could thus afford to leave it comparatively weak until that support should arrive. The function of the right wing was to hold its own without expectation of assistance, beyond that to be afforded by its own reserve, throughout the entire day; that of the left wing to hold its own, temporarily, till assistance arrived, and this it would probably be able to do, owing to the strength afforded it by the little hamlets which lay immediately in its front. In a similar manner the centre was protected by La Haie Sainte, and thus, before Napoleon could reach the line of battle at all, it was necessary for him to make himself master of strongly occupied positions on the left, the centre, and the right.

There were, however, 18,000 men belonging to Lord Hill's 2nd corps, whom the Duke might have employed at Waterloo, but of whose aid he deliberately deprived himself. Colville's division, consisting of the 4th and 6th British Brigades

# MORNING OF THE BATTLE 189

and the 6th Hanoverian brigade, Anthing's division and the first Dutch-Belgians, under Prince Frederick of Orange, had, in the general orders issued by the Duke before the retreat from Quatre Bras, been directed on Hal. " The brigades of the 4th division at Braine-le-Comte are to retire at daylight to-morrow morning upon Hal. . . . Prince Frederick of Orange is to occupy with his corps the position between Hal and Enghien, and is to defend it as long as possible." On the 18th these troops remained in their positions between Hal and Tubize—at a distance of about ten miles from the battlefield—nor were they called upon at any time during the day to take part in the battle, though they could have been brought up in less than four hours.

On such a critical occasion, outnumbered by his antagonist, and,* as he erroneously calculated, outnumbered by three to two, the Duke has laid himself open to severe criticism at the hands of both English and foreign military experts for these dispositions. The matter, as it lies outside the narrative of the battle, will be dealt with in a subsequent chapter. It is enough to say here that the Duke would not have thus denuded himself of so material a portion of his force unless he had

* Under the impression that Grouchy had only about 10,000 men with him, and ignorant that Girard (3000) had been left at Ligny, the Duke should have calculated Napoleon's army as nearly 99,000 strong. He himself had rather more than 66,000, or a proportion of two to three.

seen strong—even though we may consider them insufficient—reasons for so doing.

The armies were in position early in the morning, but several hours were yet to elapse before the battle actually began. We have now to consider the manner in which the Emperor employed these hours, and the motives which led him to delay, for as the attacking party he had the option of beginning the fight at any time that seemed good to him.

## IV.

It has been seen that when Napoleon was examining the English position about eight o'clock in the morning, in company with Count D'Erlon, he gave instructions to that General to order the men to make their soup, and to get their pieces in order, and "we will determine what is to be done about noon." It is evident, therefore, that he was in no hurry, and that he had no idea that the issue of Waterloo depended very largely upon moments. He saw before him the opportunity for which throughout the campaign he had been working. His opening moves had all been directed to secure the chance of meeting Wellington, unsupported by his Prussian ally, and the chance, as he supposed, was now before him. It offered him the practical certainty of success, for his force was superior in numbers to that of his opponent; the quality of his soldiers was superior to that of the Anglo-

# MORNING OF THE BATTLE 191

Dutch soldiers; retreat was for them, he presumed, if not impossible, at any rate difficult and hazardous, because of the forest through which they must withdraw. The Prussians were occupied by his army under Grouchy, and, therefore, were not to be reckoned with. Everything pointed to the certainty of a great victory, which seven or eight hours would amply suffice to secure. There were therefore no reasons for hurry, and several reasons for delay. The rain had fallen heavily all night, but the weather cleared in the morning. A few hours' bright, hot sunshine would do something towards drying the sodden ground and making it fit for the operations of artillery. Considering the superiority of the French in this arm, and the great use to which Napoleon always put it in his battles, this in itself was a sufficient ground for delay, supposing there were no very urgent necessity for haste. Accordingly he determined to modify his original intention of attacking the enemy at nine o'clock, and to use the interval in reviewing his army, and in exhibiting a great spectacle of military pageantry before the eyes of his opponents. The sight would be likely to produce a disspiriting effect upon such of the Anglo-Dutch divisions as had at some time themselves served under the Emperor's banner—who were still in awe of his military genius and his reputation for invincibility, and who, perhaps now hesitating between their fears and their loyalty, might under the influence of a splendid military display be led to desert their ranks and join his own. The review was over about half-past ten, and when it was ended Napoleon dictated a despatch to Grouchy, and then proceeded to formulate his plan of attack for the battle, which was to begin as soon as it had been communicated to the divisional commanders.

## V.

The despatch to Grouchy is written in a tone of easy confidence as to the general situation of affairs. It is dated—

> "*In front of the Farm du Caillu,*
> "*the* 18*th of June, at* 10 *a.m.*"

After acknowledging Grouchy's last report from Gembloux, and calling attention to a third Prussian column advancing on Wavre by Géry and Gentinnes, it proceeds—

"The Emperor charges me to inform you that at this moment his Majesty is about to attack the English army which has taken position at Waterloo, near the forest of Soignies; thus (*ainsi*) his Majesty desires that you should direct your movements on Wavre, so as to approach us, put yourself in touch with our operations, and connect communications, pushing before you the corps of the Prussian army which have taken this direction and which may have stopped at Wavre, where you are to arrive as soon as possible.

## MORNING OF THE BATTLE 193

"You will cause the enemy's columns which are upon your right to be followed by some light corps, so as to observe their movements and pick up their stragglers. Instruct me immediately as to your dispositions and your march, as well as of the news which you have of the enemy, and do not neglect to connect your communications with us. The Emperor desires to have news of you very often.
"THE DUKE OF DALMATIA."

This despatch was the first that Grouchy received from Napoleon since the Bertrand order of the day before. In Gourgaud's narrative of the campaign, written at St Heléna, and in Napoleon's "*Mémoires pour Servir*," &c. there is, it is true, a story of an order sent in duplicate to Grouchy in the course of the night, informing him that an engagement was imminent, and instructing him as to the part he was to play in it.

But the story may be summarily dismissed as a fabrication. "The two officers sent by Napoleon," says Quinet, "were never seen by Grouchy. No one has ever been able to give their names. The orders they are asserted to have carried are not to be found registered on the staff-records. What is still more to the purpose, in the despatches which followed, Napoleon made no mention whatever of these orders of the night. He does not even refer to them, contrary to his invariable custom." This criticism admits of no answer.

The 10 A.M. despatch, in fact, is, upon the face of

it, an answer to Grouchy's 2 A.M. letter from Gembloux, and although we may read in it some uncertainty as to the Prussian movements and a strong desire for information, it is quite impossible to read into it any real apprehension as to the issues of the coming battle being affected by Prussian intervention. Though the facts which it contains were known to Napoleon ten if not twelve hours before, he only thought it worth while to inform Grouchy of them as the engagement was about to begin. The despatch was written at leisure, was sent off at leisure, and was conveyed leisurely to Grouchy, for he did not receive it till after four in the afternoon, when he was definitely committed to his action at Wavre.

Taking this letter in conjunction with the other circumstances which have been related, it is clear that the Emperor contemplated the coming battle, and formulated his plan for the conduct of it, with a mind at ease both as to Grouchy and as to the Prussians.

## VI

While Napoleon was consuming the morning in delay and suffering a golden opportunity to slip from him, Blücher was profiting by the inactivity of his rival.

The four corps which constituted his army were concentrated at and around Wavre before midnight on the 17th, and were in readiness to move to the

## MORNING OF THE BATTLE 195

support of Wellington at any early hour on the 18th. Bülow was to head the advance, for he had not yet been employed in action, and consequently might be expected to display more energy and promptitude than troops which, in addition to the fatigues of severe marches, had undergone the strain of a general engagement. Bülow was to be followed up by Pirch with the 2nd corps, and the duty of these commanders was to take Napoleon on the flank, their ultimate destination being Planchenoit, by way of St Lambert.

The 1st and 3rd corps, under Ziethen and Thielemann respectively, were to march first on St Lambert, and striking off from there in a northerly direction, to come up upon the rear of the English left by the Ohain road. If, however, Grouchy's force should display any activity before Wavre, Thielemann's corps was to remain behind in order to detain the French and to secure for the rest of the Prussian army an unmolested march.

In conformity with these arrangements, Bülow was in motion at break of day from Dion-le-Mont, where his corps had bivouacked the night before. Dion-le-Mont is some two miles east of the town of Wavre, and it was certainly a faulty arrangement that the column which was to lead the advance in the morning should have been stationed for the night on the extreme left instead of on the extreme right of the army. It took many hours for the 4th corps to reach the town of Wavre and to get clear of it, and accordingly Bülow's leading division did not reach St Lambert until noon.

There a halt was made for three hours in order to allow the rear divisions to come up, and it also happened that Ziethen's columns had to cross the road on which the 2nd and 4th corps were advancing. It was not, therefore, until 4.30 P.M. that Bülow debouched upon the field of Waterloo.

Pirch and Ziethen did not leave Wavre till noon, reaching their positions upon the field a little after 7 P.M. Thielemann's 16,000 were left behind to engage throughout the afternoon the very superior force of Marshal Grouchy.

# CHAPTER X.

## THE BATTLE OF WATERLOO.

I. Napoleon's general plan and the attack on Hougomont — II. D'Erlon's infantry attack — III. First appearance of the Prussians at St Lambert—IV. Observations on Napoleon's conduct of the battle and on the difficulties of ascertaining the facts—V. The attack on La Haie Sainte—VI. Cavalry charges on the British right and centre—VII. The battle with the Prussians around Planchenoit—VIII. The charge of the Imperial Guard—IX. Wellington's advance and rout of the French — X. Lobau at Planchenoit protects the line of retreat for the main army—XI. Pursuit of the French by the Prussians.

## I.

Such were the dangers which were gathering on Napoleon while he, all unconscious of them, was reckoning only with the army in front of him.

To cope with Wellington he formulated a plan at once simple and comprehensive, a plan which, if efficiently executed, must be productive of decisive results.

His design was to break the enemy's centre and gain possession of Mont St Jean. If successful, the Anglo-Dutch army would be broken in halves, and the road to Brussels open to the French.

To prevent Wellington from concentrating all his attention upon the point which was specially menaced, the attack was to be general all along the line, and was to be so evenly sustained that the Duke would have difficulty in deciding where his danger particularly lay.

With these views Napoleon drew up his Order of Battle, which contained his general plan, as well as the measures which were to be taken to execute it.

"When once the whole army shall be drawn up in order of battle, at one o'clock P.M. as nearly as possible, at the moment when the Emperor shall give the signal to Marshal Ney, the attack will begin for the purpose of gaining possession of Mont St Jean."

The road to Mont St Jean was, however, blocked for the French by the two positions of Hougomont and La Haie Sainte. It was necessary to occupy them both, and as the former lay quite close to the French lines it was to be attacked first.

The prompt occupation of Hougomont would, moreover, assist the Emperor's projects in several ways. From it, when once in possession, his troops could operate directly on Mont St Jean, and also a demonstration in force upon the position would be likely to divert the attention of the English commander from his centre, and so facilitate the French operations upon that point.

Accordingly, about 11.30 A.M., as a preliminary to the main battle, Jerome's division of Reille's corps was sent forward against Hougomont to the sound of a general cannonade by the artillery, which was posted in advantageous positions all along the line. As the columns moved down into the hollow ground below them two brigades of artillery attached to Cooke's division opened fire, and so accurate was the range of the English nine-pounders that many of Jerome's men were killed and wounded before they reached the outskirts of the position against which their attack was directed.

But soon a battery was brought to bear upon Cooke's guns, and under its cover the French succeeded in gaining possession of the wood. But every step of the way was most desperately contested. The defence of the wood had been entrusted to some Hanoverian troops of the line and a battalion of Nassauers, and it was not until Jerome put in Soye to assist the brigade already engaged that the Hanoverians and Nassauers gave way.

The buildings of Hougomont, the walls surrounding the garden, the chateau itself and the chapel, were held by Lord Saltoun with four light companies of the Coldstream Guards and two companies of the 3rd Guards. To these Wellington quickly added three more companies of the Guards and a Brunswick battalion. By the nature of the place it was capable of being stubbornly defended, for the thick hedges and high walls gave cover to the defenders, from which, themselves unseen, they could pour destruction on their assailants. Against the main position, therefore, the attack of the French was unavailing. They displayed heroic courage and resolution, but even more necessary than these was artillery to beat down the defences of the place. It is strange that Jerome should have attempted, at such cost of life and time, to take by assault a position which could easily have been demolished by either artillery or siege appliances.

Yet there was a moment when the impetuous valour of the French seemed as if it would carry everything before it. A few companies of the 1st light infantry succeeded in reaching the northern entrance of the castle, and a sub-lieutenant, Legros, penetrated within the courtyard. As, with his handful of men, he advanced against the open door of the building, Sir James Macdonald, with a sergeant and corporal of the Guards, hurled himself against it. The door was shut in the face of the French; Legros and his companions were all of them killed.

In view of the desperate resistance offered by the English, Reille ordered Foy's division to support Jerome. But the character of the engagement was not materially altered, the advantage continuing to rest now with one side now with the other. Throughout the buildings remained in the hands of the Guards.

# THE BATTLE OF WATERLOO

At last eight howitzers were brought to bear upon the chateau and its out-buildings, which were soon in flames; but still the high walls of the garden served as a protection, and when the flames drove them to seek shelter in the garden the Guards maintained themselves there.

And thus Hougomont was attacked and defended throughout the entire day. Originally designed to be a preliminary attack, subsidiary to the main operations, it became in itself a main operation to which other movements were subsidiary. The stanza of Thackeray's "Ballad of the Drum" applies with telling force to the defence of Hougomont—

> "At noon we began the dread onset,
> We charged up the enemy's hill;
> And madly we charged it at sunset—
> His banners were floating there still."

## II.

Though foiled in his attack upon Hougomont, and disappointed of his expectations there, Napoleon determined that the grand attack which he had fixed for one o'clock should none the less proceed.

It was to be made under the general orders of Marshal Ney, who was instructed to make the first movement upon the enemy's left and centre with the 1st corps under Count D'Erlon.

D'Erlon's men were smarting under the reproach

of having been so far useless in the campaign, and were burning to redeem their reputation. In their hands, the attack was likely to be conducted with extraordinary vigour and impetuosity. At one o'clock, or a little later, the order reached D'Erlon to advance.

Already, since 11.30, a battery of eighty pieces of artillery, posted in front of the French line, had been playing upon the English left front, dealing havoc among the Dutch-Belgians, who, as has been seen, were stationed in a very exposed position in front of the road behind which the English line extended. So heavy a fire would, it was expected, have the effect of demoralising the British left and centre, and of weakening its power of resistance when the French infantry attack should be made in force.

Each of the four divisions of D'Erlon's corps, with the exception of one brigade, specially detached against La Haie Sainte, were formed in columns. Each column consisted of the various battalions composing the division. Each battalion was drawn up in three ranks. There were thus three times as many ranks as there were battalions in the division. The battalions were separated from one another by a distance of five paces.

The arrangement will probably be best understood by means of a diagram.

It will be observed that this formation was very unwieldy for purposes of attack. The overthrow of the leading battalions would involve in confusion

## THE BATTLE OF WATERLOO 203

those behind. No room was afforded for deploying in line, and similarly there was no room for formation in squares in the event of the enemy's cavalry charges rendering such an operation advisable. There were no advantages, except perhaps that of weight, to counterbalance these disadvantages, and moreover, the formation was one not usually employed. The charge, however, of such a body of men, 20,000 in number, was likely to prove, from mere weight and impetuosity, exceedingly formidable. To resist it there were drawn up, as has been seen, Bylandt's Dutch-Belgians in front, with the 5th British Division behind under Picton. The attack would chiefly fall upon the brigades of Kempt and Pack, that is to say, upon the 1st Royal Scots, the 42nd, 44th, and 92nd Highlanders, the 79th Highlanders, with the 95th Royal Rifles and the 28th and 32nd English Regiments. Behind them were the cavalry of the "Union Brigade," the Royals, the Scots Greys, and the Inniskilling Dragoons, and thus it was largely upon the infantry and cavalry of Scotland that there fell the burden and the glory of repelling the first great and general attack made by Napoleon upon the day of Waterloo.

D'Erlon was supported in his advance by a considerable body of Cuirassiers, though his was essentially an infantry attack. A more generous measure of cavalry support, in which arm Napoleon's superiority over Wellington particularly lay, would undoubtedly have rendered the movement more effective. Scarcely had D'Erlon's charge traversed the intervening ground between his position and the enemy than the Dutch-Belgians broke and fled. Exposed as they had been to the fire of the French battery, this was scarcely surprising, and the charge of cowardice urged so frequently against them will scarcely bear examination when their exposed situation and their political temper are fairly taken into consideration. The duty of repelling the French charge now fell upon Pack's Highland Regiments. These troops had suffered severely at Quatre Bras, but their courage and spirit were unimpaired, and taking up their line in rear of a cross-road, the bank of which served to some degree as a protection to them, they prepared to meet the enemy's advance. Formed up in squares, they met the shock with invincible determination not to yield an inch, and when at last the enemy began to give way before the deadly volleys poured in upon their front, with fixed bayonets the Scotch brigade rushed upon the right flank of the column, and the fight was waged hand-to-hand with desperate bravery on both sides —the muskets almost muzzle to muzzle, and the colours of the 32nd Regiment being for a moment in danger. It was now that Kempt's Brigade was ordered to charge, an order conveyed by the voice of Sir Thomas Picton, who was shot down and killed at the moment of uttering it. D'Erlon's men resisted with the greatest steadiness and determination, but, unable to deploy, and huddled to-

## THE BATTLE OF WATERLOO

gether in unwieldy masses, they were forced to give ground, while the Highlanders and English Regiments rushed over the bank of the road in pursuit. There was, however, great danger of the British being taken in the flanks by the immense masses who composed D'Erlon's right and left columns, and to avert this disaster Lord Uxbridge ordered up the Union Brigade of heavy Dragoons, commanded by Sir William Ponsonby. The Highland infantry opened out its ranks to let the Dragoons pass, some of the 92nd in their enthusiasm seizing the stirrup-leathers of the horses that they might be carried along to share in the glories of the cavalry charge. The shriek of the bagpipes contended with shouts of "Scotland for ever," and above all, the roar of artillery, and the cries of the wounded, combined to make a music in harmony with the wild rush of battle which now began. The Greys were directed against the centre columns, and nothing could stand against their impetuosity. The Eagle of the 45th Regiment was captured, and the enemy fled in confusion up the incline, down which they had just charged, to regain their original positions. In the meantime the Royals were equally active upon the French left columns, and not to be outdone by the Scots Greys, the Eagle of the 105th Regiment was captured by Sergeant Styles. On this side the enemy offered a less determined resistance. Numbers threw down their arms, and the Inniskilling Dragoons, sweeping them upon the flank, those who were not killed were taken prisoners, to the number in all of between 2000 and 3000 men. The rout of D'Erlon's columns was, however, to some extent checked by the French Cuirassiers, who formed to receive the charge of the heavy brigade, and the effect of the British success was also materially diminished by the fact that enthusiasm carried it beyond the limits of discretion. The British cavalry followed their beaten enemy almost up to their lines, sabring the gunners and disabling many guns; thus they fell victims in great numbers to the cavalry of Milhaud, which took them in a position of isolation. Sir William Ponsonby, getting separated from the Royals, was killed by a detachment of Polish Lancers, and when eventually, after three-quarters of an hour of dreadful carnage, the remains of the regiments engaged were collected under cover of a small wood to the left, it was found that the Royals were almost completely destroyed, and of the Inniskillings and Scots Greys scarcely one-half remained. To cover the pursuit of the broken British cavalry, the Light Dragoons of Vandeleur were advanced from the left, and they handled severely some of the French infantry still in the hollow between the contending lines. They then advanced against the pursuing Lancers and Chasseurs. Durutte's column, however, which had not shared in the general rout of D'Erlon's corps, directed a heavy fire from a protected position behind a ridge upon the advancing light troops,

## THE BATTLE OF WATERLOO 207

with such effect that they were compelled to withdraw and reform slightly to the right of their original position.

Three out of the four French columns had, however, been thrown into confusion, and the main attack, which, if successful, would have broken the English line and surrendered Wellington's central position into the hands of the enemy, had failed. It failed partly because of its unwieldy formation, partly because it was not efficiently supported by cavalry, but chiefly because of the steadiness and splendid pluck of the troops opposed to it. The least wavering at the moment when the French were upon the crest of the British position, and the battle would have been compromised, if not lost. At any rate, a great measure of success would have been won by the French, which, coming at the very beginning of the engagement, would have animated them for further efforts in proportion as it would have dispirited the British for further resistance. In fact, D'Erlon's charge was critical in the extreme. The Duke of Wellington regarded it as the most serious attack made during the day, and though its repulse must not be taken as absolutely decisive of the general issue, yet its influence upon the final victory can scarcely be over-estimated.

In the meantime, while the Highlanders were repelling the attack of the centre columns, Quiot was assailing La Haie Sainte, which was held by Baring with the light troops of the King's German Legion.

The ground in the neighbourhood of the farm was intersected by sand-pits, from which the riflemen could keep up an unseen and deadly fire upon the French should they occupy the walls. The King's Germans resisted desperately, but none the less the French occupied the orchard, and were pressing up to the buildings, driving the riflemen to seek refuge from their rifle-pits among their own ranks. At this moment a reinforcement was despatched by the Duke to the support of Baring, who, thus strengthened, sought to regain the orchard and garden which had been lost. The French Cuirassiers now dashed in, and were carrying all before them, when Lord Uxbridge ordered the advance of the Household troops under Lord Edward Somerset, consisting of the 1st and 2nd Life Guards, the Royal Horse Guards Blue, and the 1st Dragoons. The impact of the opposing bodies of cavalry was terrific, the troops engaging hand-to-hand, the steel clashing and flashing upon helmets, casques, and cuirasses. The French were compelled to give way, the Household troops in hot pursuit, until the high road, off which La Haie Sainte stands, was choked with a seething mass of horses and of men, penned in between the high banks on each side. In such a situation it was difficult to recognise friend or foe. Many of the Life Guards fell victims to the fire of the French infantry gathered on the banks above, while the British artillery was sending in a heavy fire upon the serried masses of the enemy gathered in the high road. La Haie Sainte, however, was for the time relieved, and the repulse of D'Erlon's left by this operation was made even more complete.

### III.

This great general movement, beginning between 1 and 1.30, was not over till 3 o'clock. While preparations for it were being made, and before D'Erlon had advanced from his position, Napoleon had seen upon his right some troops advancing by way of St Lambert. He believed them, or affected to believe them, to be the troops of Grouchy advancing to his support, and seems at first to have had no apprehension that they were the advance guard of the Prussian army. He was at the moment writing a despatch to Grouchy, which is dated, "The Field of Waterloo, June 18, 1 P.M.," and he therein acknowledged the receipt of Grouchy's letter of 2 A.M. "You have written this morning at two o'clock that you would march on Sart-à-Walhain. Your design, then, is to move on Corbaix or Wavre. This movement is conformable to his Majesty's arrangements, which have been made known to you. However, the Emperor orders me to tell you that you should constantly manœuvre in our direction, . . . and be always prepared to fall upon any of the enemy's troops which may endeavour to annoy our right and crush them.

"At this instant battle is engaged* on the

\* Grouchy read "gagnée" instead of "engagée."

line before Waterloo. The enemy's centre is at Mont St Jean. Manœuvre, therefore, to join our right."

This letter serves to illustrate the confusion in Napoleon's mind relative to Grouchy's march. When he sees troops at 1 P.M. at St Lambert, he imagines them to be Grouchy's, though at the moment he is writing to Grouchy, supposing him to be directing his march from Gembloux by way of Sart-à-Walhain and Corbaix or Wavre. Assuming that the Marshal started from Gembloux at 4 A.M., an eight hours' march could not have brought his leading columns to St Lambert by noon. Again, the directions to manœuvre towards the right of the main body are repeated twice over, conveying the impression that there was some uneasiness on the Emperor's part lest his previous instructions should not have been sufficiently precise. When, therefore, he saw the strange troops at St Lambert, he ought to have been certain that they were not Grouchy's, or, at any rate, he should have had so much doubt upon the subject as to justify the detachment of a considerable body of men from his own right to observe their movements, and, if necessary, impede their progress. Instead of this he merely sent a part of Domon's and Subervie's light cavalry, amounting to about 2400 men, to act purely as a corps of observation. In a very short time a Prussian hussar was brought in as a prisoner, and it was found that he was the bearer of a despatch

## THE BATTLE OF WATERLOO 211

from Bülow, announcing the arrival of his corps at St Lambert, 30,000 strong, and asking Wellington's instructions as to the disposition of it. Napoleon immediately added a postscript to his letter to Grouchy, which ran thus—

"*P.S.*—A letter, which has just been intercepted, tells that General Bülow is about to attack our flank. We believe we see this corps on the heights of St Lambert, so lose not an instant in drawing near and joining us in order to crush Bülow, whom you will catch red-handed (*en flagrant délit*)."

The divisions of Lobau's 6th corps, about 7000 men, were now detached in support of Subervie's cavalry, and thus the force which was to have supported D'Erlon found itself, at the moment when it was wanted for that purpose, actively engaged on quite another part of the field.

This letter, addressed to Grouchy, could have no influence upon his movements. It is an indication that Napoleon needed his assistance sorely, but is in no way an indication that Grouchy could have come. Had that Marshal, very early in the morning, directed himself upon the Bridges of the Dyle he might have been to some extent within touch of the main army by the afternoon, but he had adopted a different course, believing that by marching direct upon Wavre he was best fulfilling the Emperor's intentions, and by the time the 1 P.M. despatch reached him, at a late hour in the evening, he was fully engaged with Thielemann's corps, and could not abandon that engagement, even with the strongest inclination to do so.

Still, even without Grouchy's assistance, the Emperor had an opportunity, which he entirely let slip, of delaying the Prussian advance materially. The ground between St Lambert and the battlefield was intersected by the Lasne stream and its various tributary rivulets, and was rendered peculiarly difficult by the heavy rains of the preceding days. The Prussian march had already been arduous, and its last stages were to be more arduous still. A comparatively small body of men detached as far as the main stream could have easily occupied 30,000 men for a very considerable time, even if insufficient to stop their progress altogether. The artillery could have been thrown into confusion before Bülow could place it in position, and the weary Prussian soldiers, knee-deep in mud, would have been ill-fitted to break their way through troops refreshed by food and sleep, and animated by a due sense of the importance of their mission upon the main operations of the day. The Anglo-Dutch left was originally weak, and Wellington was in no position to detach a portion of it to take the French marching to the Lasne in flank and rear. Instead of adopting a plan which could scarcely have been more disastrous than that actually adopted, and which offered, at any rate, very fair chances of delaying the Prussians, the Emperor allowed them, practically unchecked, to

## THE BATTLE OF WATERLOO 213

take position in the field, and limited his own movements to detaching 10,000 men to oppose them only when actually in position. The Prussians were descried at 1, were recognised by 1.30, but were not upon the field, ready to begin, till 4.30. Why were they permitted a period of three hours in which to move unmolested without any serious attempt being made to impede their advance?

### IV.

But in the interval between the repulse of D'Erlon's corps and the active intervention of the Prussians, the battle continued to rage along the whole line, and two episodes between the hours of three and six conspicuously demand attention. The first is the renewed attack by the French on La Haie Sainte, and their eventual occupation of it. The second is the great cavalry charge under the command of Ney, which offers many points of analogy with D'Erlon's grand infantry charge a few hours before. Having described these movements and their effects, it will then be time to relate the story of the Prussian attack, and the final scene of all, the advance of the Imperial Guard and its overthrow, involving the overthrow of the whole army.

But there is one fact which must be noticed in regard to all the movements of the battle,—that they were conducted outside the immediate control of the Emperor in person. One of the first effects of the Prussian advance, as soon as it was recognised, was to fully occupy Napoleon's attention. The orders to Lobau to prepare to meet this flank attack, the careful observation of his movements which led to the despatch of the Young Guard as a reinforcement, the consequent repulse of the corps of Bülow, all this closely engaged the Emperor till six in the afternoon, and the movements of the battle in front were left to the conduct of Marshal Ney. If those movements were brilliant or were faulty, it is to Ney that the credit or the blame is chiefly due; and brilliant as they undoubtedly were, it must be acknowledged that they are not altogether beyond the reach of hostile criticism. This fact of the absence of Napoleon from the main battle is duly noted in almost every account, whether contemporary or otherwise, but the natural inference from it is seldom drawn with sufficient force. From three o'clock in the afternoon we must regard the action at Waterloo as two battles and not as one, requiring two commanders and not one, demanding their presence in very different parts of the field, and rendering any superintendence by one of them over the operations of the other practically impossible.

Any further description of these two battles, which were taking place at the same time upon the same field, must be prefaced by a remark, which is doubtless of general application to all battles, but which, in a special degree, applies to the engagement at Waterloo. It is almost impossible

## THE BATTLE OF WATERLOO 215

to be sure that any view of the fight is absolutely correct. This uncertainty arises not from any lack of materials, but from the multiplicity of materials by which the subject is overlaid. The ultimate testimony must of necessity be that of those who were present on the occasion, and in the multitude of eye-witnesses there is confusion.

To the common soldier, fighting in the ranks, everything outside the little circuit of his own operations is chaos. His impression of the whole is distorted by his experience of a very small part, and at the moment of a general victory, he may be under the impression that defeat stares him in the face.* Even the regimental officers know little beyond that which immediately concerns them, and their narratives must be received with the greatest caution. And with the generals in command, and even with the general-in-chief, it is much the same. On matters of detail they speak with many and with contradictory voices, and yet it is on details that campaigns are lost and won. The relations of eye-witnesses, in short, are in a large degree untrustworthy, but it is from such relations alone that descriptions of battles are compiled. The fierce excitement of the fray annihilates time and space, and hence discrepancies, which are little short of grotesque, invalidate the evidence on which, perforce, we must form our judgments. A simple illustration of this may be

* See Conan Doyle, "A Great Shadow"; and Erckmann Chatrian's "Waterloo."

found in the various statements given by those most competent to speak with authority as to the time when the action began. Contemporary letters say, "towards eleven" or "about half-past eleven." Wellington says, "at about 10." Alava, the Spanish attaché on Wellington's staff, says "at 10.30." "Towards noon," says Pozzo di Borgo, the Russian attaché. "About 1," says Alten, and Ney corroborates his statement. "About noon" is the statement of Napoleon.

When there are such variations of opinion about a matter open to the accurate observation of all, we must expect to find even greater discrepancies as to the occurrences which took place in the heat of action, and so it is that in reference to the occupation of La Haie Sainte by the French, we have the testimony of eye-witnesses to the effect that it took place at 2 o'clock, at 3.30, about 5 o'clock, while Lord Wolseley is convinced that it was about 6 P.M.

Thus, in attempting to describe the defence and capture of this important post, we are met at the outset by difficulties and doubts exactly where certainty is the first essential, for the hour at which La Haie Sainte was captured by the French is the very governing point of subsequent criticism. If the French were in possession of the place before their grand cavalry charge, Ney is open to the imputation of neglecting to profit by all the opportunities which the position afforded for the support of that charge. If, on the other

## THE BATTLE OF WATERLOO 217

hand, the charge was made before the occupation, it is obvious that La Haie Sainte could not be used as a support to the French cavalry. The Duke of Wellington, of all men on the field, was likely to know best when the place was taken. Writing to a correspondent two months after the battle, he says, "This (position) they got, I think, at about two o'clock. . . . At about two in the afternoon, as I have before said, they got possession of the farm-house on the high-road, . . . and they then took possession of a small mound on the left of the high-road going from Brussels, immediately opposite the gate of the farm, and they were never removed from thence till I commenced the attack in the evening." *

Yet, if this be true, it implies that La Haie Sainte was seized by D'Erlon's left column, which, as a fact, was driven back by the charges of the Household troops. A non-commissioned cavalry officer, who was engaged in the action round the farm, declares that it fell into the hands of the French "soon after five o'clock." Critics are as much at variance as eye-witnesses, and this being so, it is well to walk circumspectly through the details of Waterloo, and to temper judgment with some amount of prudent doubt as to whether it all was as we suppose it to have been. "In an action such as Waterloo," says Quinet, "it seems that the

* The Duke, believing the battle began about 10, means to say that La Haie Sainte was captured when the fight had been in progress about four hours.

most decisive incidents should to-day be known with sufficient exactness to make mistake impossible, and it is the contrary which is the case. However superficially one enters into the history of that day, it is astonishing to see how many obscurities and contradictions still remain, how many uncertainties in the relation of important events. Did such a phase of the battle precede or follow another phase? Was such a village taken? or such a farm occupied? At what moment was it lost or regained? Each narrative differs on each of these points, and yet it is on the interconnexion of causes and effects that the real character of a battle depends. Throughout these hundred days there is a chronology which is implacable. Invert it for a moment and everything escapes you."

M. Quinet then proceeds to give a most vivid description of the fight. His chronology—so implacable—adapts itself to his glowing picture, and not a sign betrays the man who, a few pages before, has so clearly warned us that when we think we know, then, perhaps, we are most mistaken. "The history of a battle," wrote the Duke of Wellington, six weeks after Waterloo, "is not unlike the history of a ball. Some individual may recollect all the little events of which the great result is the battle won or lost, but no individual can recollect the order in which, or the exact moment at which, they occurred, which makes all the difference as to their value and importance."

But as to the hour when La Haie Sainte was occupied there are certain probabilities which must be taken into account, and it is certainly more incredible that Ney, in possession of the farm, should have neglected to use it in support of his cavalry charges than that he was not in possession of the place at the hour when the charges were made. The statements, too, of Sir J. Shaw Kennedy, who was throughout the battle upon the English right centre, and of Heymès, who was Ney's chief-of-staff, and therefore close to him all day, should carry more weight on such a point than even the testimony of the Duke himself, whose mind was occupied with the direction of the whole action, and who, while repelling an attack, would probably be oblivious of time. These officers state that it was after the cavalry charges that La Haie Sainte fell. Though with much diffidence and hesitation of judgment, we may conclude, with strong probability of being correct, that there was no fixed and formal interval between the one operation and the other; that the attack on La Haye was contemporaneous, at any rate to some extent, with the charges of the cavalry; that both movements were cheered on and stimulated by the enthusiasm of Ney, and that the moment the farm was seized, he made use of it to the best advantage as a *point d'appui* against the English centre. Just as the attack on Hougomont is a distinct phase of the battle, though it went on all day and at times blended with other movements, so the atack upon and capture of La Haie Sainte is a distinct phase, though other operations in the battle were being carried on side by side with it.

V.

The repulse of D'Erlon's columns was followed up by a tremendous cannonade from each side, and by the descent of clouds of skirmishers into the hollow ground between the positions. Further operations against Wellington's left were impossible until the French right wing had some time allowed it to re-establish itself, and the reserves which might have supported it in its renewed attack were now needed for the battle on the flank. Moreover, there still stood, immediately fronting the allied centre, the stronghold of La Haie Sainte, occupied by Baring's Hanoverians, now reduced to a mere handful of men.

It was then, to the roar and thunder of the cannonade, that Ney collected first of all such infantry as might be efficient for his purpose. There were but few of these, for the right had not yet recovered from its repulse, the left was too hotly engaged at Hougomont, the reserves were marching to confront Bülow. He had to rely upon D'Erlon's left division, or such part of it as was available, and upon two battalions of Donzelot's division, which had already suffered severely. With these La Haie Sainte was vigorously beset. The garden and orchard were carried at the first assault,

## THE BATTLE OF WATERLOO

but no sooner were the French in possession than Baring's Hanoverians drove them out. Again they returned to the attack, and seized the ground once more, the Hanoverians retreating step by step and contesting every inch of the way. As they advanced within the protecting walls of the building, a deadly fire was poured in upon the French from the crenellated walls, and from scaffoldings erected hastily for purposes of cover and defence, but the undaunted enemy pressed on up to the very muskets as they protruded, seeking to snatch them from the hands of the besieged. In the meantime Baring was sorely in need of reinforcements and ammunition. The last was hard to obtain, for ammunition was running short all along the line, and the road which would bring it to La Haie Sainte was full under fire of the French batteries. Each shot, therefore, was carefully husbanded and aimed with deadly effect. Help at length arrived in the shape of some Nassauers, but the besiegers, now as five to one, were hammering upon the main doors, which opened on to the high-road, with axes and crowbars, while the gates on the western side were being forced in the same manner. In addition to the work of defence, the defenders were called upon to extinguish the flames which were blazing up in the farm buildings. The great camp kettles of the Nassauers served as buckets, and under a constant stream pouring from them the flames were extinguished; but, the work of active resistance being for a brief space intermitted, the Hanoverians and their supporters were unable to check the rush of the French upon the western door. It was broken in, and La Haie Sainte was in the hands of Ney, Baring and his little band retreating under fire upon the main position. At once great masses of men poured in through the open doors and took up their positions immediately under the ridge which defined the British line. By this time it must have been between five and six o'clock, when Wellington was hard put to it to find men to resist the cavalry attack. Accordingly the 5th and 8th battalions of the King's German Legion were advanced down the ridge in order to check the fire from La Haie Sainte. A small body of Lord Edward Somerset's cavalry was sent in support of the 5th, so that regiment suffered but slightly, but the 8th battalion was terribly mauled, losing more than half its men and its colours.

But, on the side of the French, the cost of gaining and maintaining the position was enormous. Two thousand of their men were reported to have fallen in the operations at and around La Haie Sainte, though these figures probably represent the total number, French and allies, who fell there. In any case the French loss was enormous, and what was more serious, to a large extent unnecessary. For here, as at Hougomont, the impetuous ardour of the French blinded them to considerations of prudence. A hand-to-hand attack, however

## THE BATTLE OF WATERLOO 223

gallant, against an enemy defended by stone walls is never economical of time or life, and time and men were, at this juncture, what Napoleon chiefly required. If, instead of trying to carry La Haie Sainte by assault, the walls had first been demolished by artillery, the capture of the place must have been more easily effected and at much less cost. The French justly pride themselves upon their *élan* in the field, but reckless impetuosity dissociated from wise precaution, unquestionably cost them dear upon the field of Waterloo.

However, La Haie Sainte was won, and general success began to attend upon the French right. The troops of Donzelot and Marcognet, now resting on La Haie Sainte, were engaging Kempt, Pack, and Bylandt, while Durutte was successful in driving Prince Bernhard of Saxe-Weimar from Papelotte and making himself master of that position.

### VI.

While the French were gaining these advantages upon the right, Ney in the meantime was organising a grand cavalry movement upon the allied right-centre. The infantry of Reille's corps should have occupied the space intervening between Hougomont and La Haie Sainte, but it was already so fully engaged at Hougomont that no part of it could be spared for operations elsewhere. Lobau's divisions, which might have supported Reille, were already moving against the Prussians towards Planchenoit. Accordingly this space was unoccupied, and a considerable gap left in the French line of attack between these two positions.

Shortly after 3 P.M. Milhaud's Cuirassiers were ordered to take position upon this open ground. With them were the light cavalry of Lefèbvre-Desnouettes and Kellermann, and Guyot's dragoons were also advanced forward in support. The attack was heralded by thunders of artillery from the French batteries, which maintained a continuous fire, while Ney was receiving the cavalry squadrons which defiled in the hollow on the left of La Haie Sainte. To avoid the cannonade, which was dealing serious destruction in his ranks, the Duke of Wellington withdrew his troops from the summit of the ridge and formed them in squares *en échiquier* upon the sloping ground behind it. The artillery alone were left upon the crest, and an incessant fire was poured in upon the advancing cavalry until the gunners were compelled to abandon their guns and take refuge in the protecting British squares. Cuirassiers and lancers dashed up the slope, and soon held the summit of the ridge, which a moment before had been the allied position, but their task was only now begun. In front of them were the infantry of Alten's and Cooke's divisions, formed in impenetrable squares, constituting two lines—seven squares in the first line, six in the second—each resting upon the other

## THE BATTLE OF WATERLOO

as the spaces on a chess-board. The redcoats of the English guards alternated with the dark uniforms of the Hanoverian and King's German Legion. All alike, as the flashing torrent broke upon them, held firm as if rooted to the ground, "pouring in a deadly fire of musketry from the lines and of small shot from the guns posted at the corners of each square." The ground was heavy from the recent rains, and this took off something from the impetuosity of the French charge, but none the less it was tremendous in its intensity and earnestness, and the fate of Europe at this crisis hung trembling in the balance. The short stern order "Close up the ranks" mingled with the sharp rattle of the musketry and the fierce shouts of "Vive l'Empereur," and if a breach was made, at once the ranks were closed and the serried front remained, still impenetrable. And now the French horsemen, exposed to the pitiless fire, front and flank, of the allied squares, began to fall into confusion. They had gained the plateau, but there was no supporting infantry to maintain it. Herein lay the cause which rendered the cavalry charge ineffectual. Unsupported by infantry there was no alternative between breaking the line and retreat, and the line could not be broken. Ney recognised the inevitable and sounded the rally. At once the Duke of Wellington seized the favourable moment, and while the French were still in disorder they were charged by the allied cavalry under Somerset. As they descended the slope,

Wellington's artillerymen at once sprang from the protection of the squares to their guns, which still crowned the ridge, and directed a heavy fire upon the discomfited mass below. The danger, however, was only averted for a moment. Though the cuirassiers had failed, Lefèbvre Desnouettes still commanded two thousand sabres, while the heavy dragoons under Kellermann and Guyot remained untouched. Ney promptly put himself at the head of the lancers and charged the pursuing cavalry of the allies, which paid the penalty of an over-rash impetuosity by fearful losses, and by a forced retreat behind the English lines. And now, refreshed by a short breathing space, cuirassiers and lancers once more invaded the plateau, nerved for an effort more strenuous than before. The attack was characterised by all the features of the former one, and the result was the same. The want of infantry was fatal to success, unless the squares could be broken. "Infantry!" said Napoleon bitterly, in answer to Ney's urgent request, "where can I get them from? Would you have me make them?" It is at this juncture of the battle that we can first form an estimate of the influence of the Prussian advance. Had Lobau's ten thousand men been now available, to hold the plateau which the cavalry had won, there can be no doubt that Wellington's line would have been broken and that he would have experienced a disastrous defeat. But Lobau was now holding Planchenoit against Bülow, and failing his or other support,

# THE BATTLE OF WATERLOO 227

these repeated cavalry charges ought not to have been made. The issue, however, was now definitely committed to the touch of cavalry, and every available man was called upon for a supreme effort. Even the brief respite between the attacks was charged with destruction, for the artillery fire from the English position kept plunging in upon the ranks below, cutting deep pathways through them. Inaction was as fatal as action, and the English squares must be broken. Accordingly Guyot and Kellermann were ordered to support the remnant of Milhaud's and Lefèbvre's men, and for two hours cuirassiers alternated with dragoons in desperate assault against the allies. The Duke of Wellington had anticipated these renewed onsets by reforming and materially strengthening his position. Chassé's division of light infantry was drawn in from Braine L'Alleud and formed behind the Brunswick contingent: two brigades of Clinton's division were brought up from around Merbe Braine and posted upon the right flank: Maitland's guards, together with Mitchell's brigade of Colville's division, hitherto stationed in the rear as a reserve, were brought forward to the front, while Vincke's Hanoverian brigade was moved across the Charleroi road in support of Alten's division, which had especially suffered from the repeated charges of the French.

The resources of each army were now employed to the full, and each was resolute for victory. If the Duke's position were forced, the day was lost.

His left was barely holding its own, and unless Ziethen's column arrived soon, it must give way. Hougomont was in flames; the centre was menaced by the full force of Ney's cavalry, and Bülow's corps was held by Lobau. No further reserves were to be had. "Tell him," said the Duke to Halkett's request for relief, "that we must stay where we are while one man remains alive." Disaster at any one point meant disaster everywhere, while successful resistance to Ney meant victory all along the line. Delay in winning implied for the French ultimate defeat, for Ziethen's arrival must soon re-establish the allied left, while the co-operation of Pirch, who was rapidly marching to support Bülow, would render the main Prussian attack irresistible.

Ney was ignorant of the near approach of the Prussian reinforcements, but none the less he conducted the attack with more than his wonted ardour. The allied squares were beset on every side. "The cavalry surrounded us," wrote the Duke to Beresford, "as if it had been our own." The Duke himself, with the Prince of Orange and several other general officers, sought safety within the squares, and animated the men with stirring words of encouragement. "Stand firm, 95th," he cried; "think what they will say of this in England!"

A few isolated cavaliers succeeded in penetrating the position, and turned to charge it *en revers*. To a man they fell victims to their heroic temerity.

The allied cavalry were once more brought into play, but were soon reduced to a force less than that of an ordinary regiment. Cumberland's Brunswick Hussars turned and fled; not a man of them responded to Lord Uxbridge, as he called them on to the charge. Omptéda was killed, Alten seriously wounded, and scarcely a staff officer was left to carry the Duke's orders. Still the squares stood unbroken, and the force of the attack was wearing itself away. The French loss was as great as ours, if not greater; only the prompt support of infantry could render effective such success as had been attained. It was now that, having relieved Lobau at Planchenoit, Napoleon determined to advance the remaining battalions of the Imperial Guard—his last reserve—to clench the work that through so many hours his cavalry had been doing upon the plateau of Mont St Jean, and it was now, too, that upon the extreme left of the allies was heard the sharp rattle of musketry, which announced to Wellington that Ziethen had debouched upon the open ground, and was joining his forces to those of Prince Bernhard, to drive the French from Papelotte.

VII.

The Prussian dispositions on the morning of the 18th have already been shown. Between twelve and one Bülow's corps was observed by the Emperor, and two squadrons of light cavalry were despatched to watch it. An order was sent to Grouchy to manœuvre towards his left, so as to join forces with Napoleon, and catch Bülow *en flagrant délit*. Later still, Lobau's corps was moved upon Planchenoit, so as to guard against an attack from the rear, which, if successful, would cut Napoleon's communications and close his line of retreat. But while thus taking precautions against Bülow, the Emperor by no means realised the full gravity of his situation. He knew nothing of Pirch, who was already well forward from Wavre to support Bulow. He knew nothing of Ziethen, who was marching under cover of wood and undulating ground to co-operate directly with Wellington's left. He believed that he had before him an isolated corps, which would be taken between two fires—Grouchy's and his own—and which would consequently soon be annihilated, thus rendering his victory on that day even more decisive than he had anticipated. Lulled by such false hopes, he omitted to intercept the Prussians at the passages of the Lasne, and allowed them to deploy, practically unmolested, upon the open ground beyond the wood of Paris towards Planchenoit. Bülow's difficulties, however, were very great. His men had been marching since early morning, his divisions were not together, and the ground was so heavy as to be almost impassable for artillery. It was not, therefore, until 4.30 that two of Bülow's four divisions were in position, together with their cavalry, under Prince William of Prussia; these, however, promptly joined action with Lobau, and the flank attack was vigorously begun.

Lobau's command numbered rather less than 10,000 men, and consisted of two brigades of cavalry under Domon and Subervie, and two divisions of infantry under Simmer and Jeannin. Teste's division, which formed a part of the 6th corps, was with Grouchy. Bülow's force was nearly three times as great, though of very inferior calibre. At first able to hold his own, and indeed to gain some success over the Prussians, yet when Bülow's corps was consolidated, disparity of numbers compelled Lobau to retreat. This he did, in close order and with admirable steadiness, upon Planchenoit. Here he took position, determined to sacrifice the last man for the protection of the rear of the main army. Napoleon now despatched to his assistance eight battalions of the Young Guard, and these troops held the village, enabling Lobau to cover the entire flank of the main army, his right resting on Planchenoit, his left in touch with Durutte's division in and about Papelotte, a movement which had the effect of separating Bülow from Wellington, and which might have been decisive of the battle, but for the appearance of Ziethen later on in the day. And now this battle on the flank was carried on with desperate determination on both sides, but with doubtful fortunes almost to the end. Blücher's artillery, posted most advantageously upon the high ground which overlooked the field, poured a shower of shot and shell upon Planchenoit and its defenders. Under cover of this cannonade the Prussians vigorously assaulted the village, but were repulsed by the Young Guard. A second assault was more successful. Overpowered by numbers, the French were driven out, and several Prussian batteries were successfully posted in such close proximity to the main *chaussée* that Napoleon's reserve around La Belle Alliance was threatened by their shot. Three additional battalions were at once moved forward by the Emperor to the support of the Young Guard, and this timely reinforcement once more established the fight. Planchenoit was again invested by the French, the Prussians being driven from the village at the point of the sword, and rolled back as far as Maransart. The advantage thus won was followed up by Lobau upon the left, who, engaging Bülow's remaining divisions, forced them also to retire in considerable confusion. The danger from the Prussians seemed now to be over. So long as the French held Planchenoit, Napoleon's position could not be turned, and while Lobau continued to present a steady front along the entire flank of the main army, any active co-operation with Wellington on the part of Bülow was impossible. But the real danger remained unseen. It was about seven o'clock that two divisions of Pirch's corps— some 15,000 strong—came up to the support of Bülow, and about the same hour, or a little later, Ziethen's columns effected a junction with Wel-

# THE BATTLE OF WATERLOO 233

lington's left. The arrival of these reinforcements turned the day against Napoleon. So far the intervention of 30,000 Prussians had but postponed his victory. They had, it is true, occupied the entire corps of Lobau, as well as several battalions of the Imperial Guard, which had been destined to support the earlier attacks upon the allies, but in their main object, to turn the Emperor's position and take him at once in flank and rear, they had entirely failed ; it even seemed as if they would be involved in the defeat which threatened to overtake the army of Wellington. But, reinforced by Pirch and Ziethen, the Prussians by mere weight of numbers became irresistible, and a battle which for eight hours had waged with indomitable steadiness on both sides, but on the whole with advantage to the French, was in an hour converted into a deplorable rout, into total ruin at the very moment when success seemed imminent.

## VIII.

At the moment when Napoleon judged the crisis of the battle to have arrived, he determined, as at Ligny, to put in the Imperial Guard, or rather those battalions of the Guard which still remained at his disposition.

Among the many glorious deeds which shed lustre upon the allied army upon the 18th June, there still remains to be related perhaps the most glorious deed of all, when splendid gallantry and fine soldiership combined to repulse an attack made by the flower of Napoleon's armies, troops whose mere intervention in an engagement had hitherto been regarded as an assurance of victory.

The infantry of the Guard were all picked soldiers, distinguished by length of service and brilliant achievements. The Old Guard (Grenadiers) consisted exclusively of those who, in addition to distinguished exploits, could show twelve years' service in the army. Every member of the Middle Guard (Chasseurs) had served eight years, and of the Young Guard at least four years. Each of these corps of Guards contained eight battalions, with about 500 men to each battalion. At the beginning of the campaign of Waterloo the total muster of the infantry of the Guard was about 13,000 men.*

Of this number, however, only a small proportion was available for the final attack upon Wellington. Duhesme's eight battalions were already

---

\* Young Guard—Duhesme, . . . 3800
  Middle Guard—Morand, . . . 4250
  Old Guard—Friant, . . . 4420
  Artillery—320 men with 16 guns to each corps.
                                                  GOURGAUD.

But Gourgaud under-estimates Morand and Duhesme. The official statement of the chief of the staff of the Imperial Guard is—
    Duhesme, . . . . . 4283
    Morand, . . . . . 4603
    Friant, . . . . . 4140

## THE BATTLE OF WATERLOO 235

engaged at Planchenoit, and to these had been added one battalion of Grenadiers and two of Chasseurs under Morand. Thus eleven out of twenty-four battalions were fully occupied with the Prussians, and of five other battalions two were disposed between Planchenoit and the main *chaussée*, one near Caillou, and two at La Belle Alliance. Thus but eight battalions were available for the final charge, numbering, when allowance has been made for losses at Ligny, at the most 3500 men, and probably little more than 3000. These were formed by Napoleon himself in columns of battalions, with a front of two companies in three ranks. As there were four companies to a battalion, the front of the column would consist of between seventy and eighty men—"about seventies in front," says Captain Powell of the English Guards. Halting in the dip by La Haie Sainte, the Emperor addressed his invincible bodyguard in a few stirring words, and then entrusted them to the hands of Ney, who led them in person against the English position. The point of attack for the head of the column was that part of the ridge just behind which Maitland's Guards were lying down. With drums beating and colours flying the French infantry moved steadily forward, "as if on parade," and reaching the foot of the ridge, dashed impetuously up it, seeing no enemy to contest their progress. Scarcely, however, had they reached the ridge, when the British Guards sprang to their feet, and from a front of 450 men, four deep, so deadly a volley was poured into the advancing column that it suddenly stopped, as if from the impact of an irresistible mass, then wavered and fell into confusion as the front ranks dropped under the British fire, and finally, when Lord Saltoun opportunely gave the word to charge, fled down the hill, hotly pursued by our Household troops. The rear battalions of the Imperial Guard were not, however, involved in this overthrow. They, as the advance column proceeded, inclined, according to Maitland's account, towards their own left, and proceeded in a line parallel with that of the leading battalions, and thus, as the English Guards charged down the hill, they found themselves exposed upon their flank to what they imagined to be a second column of the Imperial Guard, though, in reality, it was a part of the original column, deflected from the prescribed line of advance.* Thus menaced upon their flank, the English Guards withdrew to their original position behind the crest of the ridge.

In the meantime the rear battalions of the Imperial Guard were advancing independently of their routed comrades, towards that part of the

* This seems to be the true solution of the problem which has vexed all writers upon the Battle of Waterloo from that time until now, and which will doubtless continue to vex the critics of the future—viz., Were there two separate columns of Guards or only one? The solution, as given in the text, is simple; it fairly reconciles much conflicting testimony, and it embodies Maitland's idea of what he saw himself. No other theory can pretend to harmonise all the facts to the same degree.

## THE BATTLE OF WATERLOO 237

British line which was held by Adams' Brigade, recently called up from their station in reserve at Merbe Braine. The brigade consisted of the 2nd battalion of the 95th Rifles, the 52nd Regiment, under Sir John Colborne, and the 71st, under Sir Thomas Reynell. As the enemy's column advanced, Colborne, on his own initiative, ordered his regiment to move directly forward to its front, and when its left at the foot of the slope was in line with the leading company of the French column, by a skilfully executed movement, the regiment was formed in line four-deep so as to flank the French column. The position thus assumed by Colborne was hazardous in the extreme, for the regiment was entirely unsupported —detached, in an exposed position, from the main army, liable to be rendered powerless for offensive purposes by a charge of cavalry, liable also to very rough handling from the French artillery if at that time any batteries had been mounted against them.

But the fatal error in the French dispositions for this last attack was now made apparent. The batteries which accompanied the Imperial Guard were rendered useless by the deflection of the rear battalions from their true line. There were no other batteries to do duty for them, and the left of the column was consequently entirely unsupported either by cavalry or artillery. Under these circumstances Colborne's advance was not a desperate act of rashness but an inspiration of genius, which knows how to seize the chance which the moment offers, and the claim of the 52nd—that their movement was decisive of the battle— must be allowed. For the Imperial column, thus taken on the flank, halted in its advance. " Then as many files as possible, on the left of each company of their leading column, faced outwards," and a furious musketry fire was exchanged, by which the gallant 52nd suffered severely, but which, on their own admission, simply overwhelmed the French (*une attaque très vive, qui nous écrasa*). The light troops followed up their fire by a charge, before which the French infantry broke and fled, the companies immediately exposed to the attack in a state of complete confusion—the rear battalions withdrawing in fairly good order towards their position in front of La Belle Alliance.

## IX.

It was now eight o'clock. About half an hour earlier, distinct above the din of the main battle, there rose the roar of some new firing upon the extreme left of the allies. It could indicate nothing but the arrival of a reinforcement to one side or the other. If it were Grouchy, all was well for Napoleon—and indeed the rumour circulated that it was Grouchy, arrived in the nick of time— but if it were a fresh detachment of Prussians, then Napoleon's chance was gone. It was not Grouchy, but Ziethen with his corps of 20,000 men

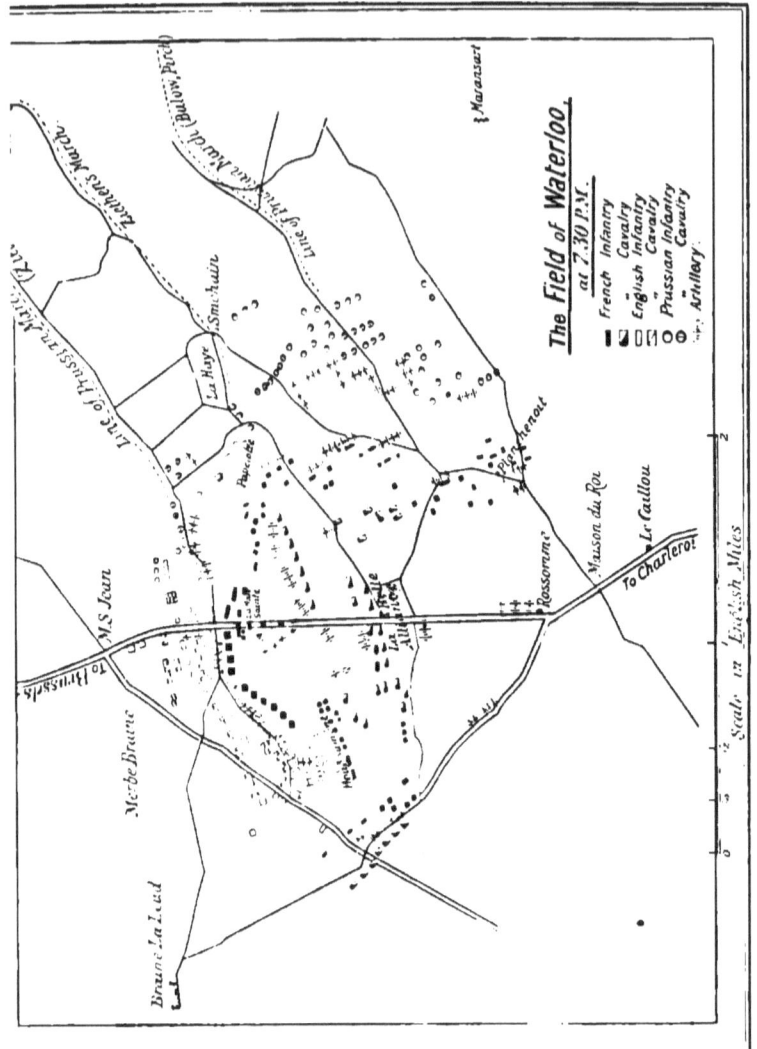

## THE BATTLE OF WATERLOO 239

and 32 guns, who, debouching from the woods around Ohain, now at length, after incredible exertions, came to take his stand by the side of Kempt's hardly-pressed division. Ziethen's leading battalions, under Steinmetz, after a brief moment of confusion, when friends were mistaken for foes, joined the troops of Prince Bernhard of Saxe-Weimar, and they together renewed the assault against Papelotte, which, since the first irruption of the Prussians, had become the pivot of the French position, for upon it Durutte's right and Lobau's left respectively rested. The place had been gallantly forced by Durutte two hours before, and as gallantly held against all efforts to retake it; but now, borne down by force of numbers, the French were compelled to retire, and thus the right of the main army and Lobau's position on its flank were simultaneously turned. Confusion rapidly spread all along the line. Marcognet, Quiot, and Donzelot, holding the crest from Papelotte to La Haie Sainte, were compelled to cease their attack in order to act on the defensive. The brigades of Lambert, Pack, and Kempt, animated with fresh courage by the arrival of the Prussians, drove the French down the slope, while Ziethen's guns, which now crowned the crest, carried destruction into their ranks. At this moment the cavalry brigades of Vivian and Vandeleur, no longer needed as reserve upon the left, were brought over to the centre, and their charge completed the distress of the French infantry. Many of the battalions broke and fled, all semblance of discipline or of resistance was lost, and their line of flight, crossing as it did the retreat of the routed Imperial Guard, paralysed all the efforts of the latter to rally, and completed the panic and confusion.

This was the moment chosen by the Duke of Wellington to order a general advance all along the line. His work was now accomplished, and the Prussians might well have been left to complete the victory, but the Duke had no desire to relinquish to his allies the full glory of dealing the last and crowning blow. The advance, therefore, was made by the whole allied force, on front and flank concurrently, and with overwhelming effect. The 52nd followed up their advantage over the Guard by an impetuous advance, which drove everything before it. "Well done, Colborne! well done! Go on, don't give them time to rally," was Wellington's greeting to his intrepid lieutenant. Exposing himself freely, the Duke was often in a position of imminent danger, but no remonstrances would induce him to retire, "until I see those fellows go." Lord Uxbridge, as he rode by Wellington's side, had his leg shot off, but the Duke himself and his good horse "Copenhagen" seemed proof against every danger, and remained unscathed throughout the day.

It is needless to dwell further on the last desultory efforts of the French main body to rally from the disasters which had overwhelmed them. Such of the battalions of the Imperial Guard as

# THE BATTLE OF WATERLOO 241

still retained any organisation did all that was possible, but nothing could now retrieve the demoralisation which prevailed. The Emperor himself was at last compelled to seek safety within one of the squares of the Guard, and thus sheltered he abandoned the field, passing through the wreck of his army along the great *chaussée*, through Genappe to Charleroi, scarcely drawing bridle. From Charleroi a letter was sent to Grouchy to announce the issue of the day. This was Napoleon's last military despatch. It is with a confession of hopeless and irreparable failure that the great warrior sinks down from the sphere of active affairs into the dull, pitiable obscurity of captivity and exile.

## X.

Great as was the overthrow of the French, it would have been even more complete but for the heroic resistance of the 6th corps and of the Guard at Planchenoit. Bülow had signally failed in his attack against these gallant troops, and had been compelled to withdraw to some distance beyond his first position. Lobau, with his left resting on Papelotte, his right on the battalions of the Guard in possession of Planchenoit, completely covered the French main battle, and from five o'clock until after 7 P.M. relieved it from all anxiety in regard to the Prussians. The appearance of Ziethen, however, changed the situation, for his successful attack on Papelotte at 7.30 had the effect of turning the

French left and flank simultaneously, and almost at the same moment Pirch, with 15,000 fresh troops, came up to the support of Bülow. The situation of Lobau was now critical in the extreme. Turned upon the flank, attacked by 40,000 men in front, his own men by comparison a mere handful, the main army behind him utterly demoralised and in retreat, none the less he contested stubbornly and with a deliberate courage little less than sublime every foot of ground which the Prussians won. For he recognised to the full the responsibility which now lay upon him. He alone interposed between the Prussians and the French line of retreat, and if he failed retreat would be cut off, the army would be turned in rear as well as in front and flank, and scarcely a man could escape from the field. The fate of the army, the Emperor, and for aught he knew, of France, rested upon Lobau at this supreme moment of the day, and splendidly he did his duty. Dusk had given away to darkness, only illuminated by the blazing ruins of the village he had held so well, before Lobau retired from Planchenoit, but by that time the rear of the flying army had cleared that point, and comparative safety was assured. Still steady and in good order he took position on the high road to close the line of flight and block pursuit, and thus the gallant remnant of the 6th corps and of the Young Guard had to bear the full fury of the combined advance of the allies.

# THE BATTLE OF WATERLOO 243

Many deeds of splendid daring were done at Waterloo, but none can excel for coolness, courage, and devotion, the heroic resistance of Lobau.

## XI.

The battle was over, the enemy in full retreat, and Wellington now felt that his share in the day's operations was done. His troops were in possession of the ground on which, in the morning Napoleon's lines had stood, and were thoroughly exhausted by the excessive labours of the day. The task of further pursuit was therefore surrendered to Blücher, and it was a peculiarly congenial one. There was in Blücher a depth of concentrated and venomous hatred against Napoleon and the French, nourished by years of defeat and humiliation, and the sentiments of the commander were fully shared by the men. Not a moment of respite was granted to the panic-stricken army, huddled together in pell-mell flight within the limits of a single road. Darkness was no protection to the vanquished, for the struggling moonlight lent its aid to the victors, rendering concealment impossible. At Genappe there was but one bridge across the Dyle, and this was thickly blocked with artillery waggons and surging masses of men too hopelessly disorganised to think of fords or other means of passage. The Prussian batteries, posted on the high ground above, poured destruction among the mass, and confusion became despair. There Lobau was made prisoner, Duhesme of the Young Guard died of his wounds, and Ney, reserved for an even more bitter fortune, barely escaped. Beyond Genappe to Quatre Bras, ghastly with its unburied corpses in the moonlight, from Quatre Bras to Frasne the work of vengeance was carried on, until even revenge yielded to exhausted nature, and the drama of Waterloo closed. So ended the greatest battle of our modern epoch—great by virtue of the military skill, courage, and tenacity which distinguished all the actors in it; greatest perhaps for the unparalleled career which thereby was brought to an end. An obscure Belgian village, till then unknown, has become the centre of the admiration of the world, and to it the eyes of all succeeding generations of Englishmen, Frenchmen, and Prussians will be turned when they desire to think on the stuff of which their forefathers was made. "All is lost but honour," said Francis at Pavia. Frenchmen, when they think of Waterloo, may still find consolation in the same reflection, for of glory they won full measure; while Englishmen and Prussians may add to their pride in a hard-fought battle splendidly won the thought that that success was due, not to the single arms of either, but to the well-planned and skilfully-conducted co-operation of both. The day of petty jealousies and acrimonious prejudice about Waterloo has gone by. We admit that without the timely intervention of the Prussians the battle would have gone against

## THE BATTLE OF WATERLOO 245

us, though to admit this detracts in no way from the gallantry which throughout the long day opposed unflinching resistance to a vastly superior army. Prussians admit that but for this unflinching resistance their intervention would have come too late, without detracting in the smallest degree from the stubborn constancy of Blücher, by which all the immense difficulties of the march from Wavre were overcome. Instead of tending to divide the great Teutonic nations of the North, the recollection of Waterloo should serve to unite them as they were united then, should serve to remind them of the common origin of both, and strengthen the ties of kinship by the ties of a common glory.

# CHAPTER XI.

### CRITICAL EXAMINATION OF THE BATTLE OF WATERLOO.

### (FRENCH SIDE.)

I. Napoleon's delay in beginning the battle—II. His methods of attack at Hougomont and La Haie Sainte — III. D'Erlon's formation in columns of attack—IV. Ney's employment of the cavalry—V. The expediency of retreat at various periods of the battle—VI. The attack by the Imperial Guard—VII. Napoleon's physical condition at Waterloo—VIII. Napoleon's generals at Waterloo.

### I.

THE losses in the battle of Waterloo were very heavy. In round numbers, 203,000 men took part in the engagement, and of these 48,000 were killed, wounded, or made prisoners—more than 23 per cent. The allies under Wellington lost over 15,000, the Prussians 7000, while of the French, Gourgaud, writing for the Emperor, admits a loss of 25,000 men. Such figures do more than prove the desperate character of the encounter. They suggest considerations as to whether the circumstances of the battle justified such a wanton destruction. Here it is obvious that the responsibility—and the blame, if any—rests not upon

# CRITICAL EXAMINATION 247

Wellington, who could do no less than defend himself to the utmost, nor upon the Prussians, whose attack was prescribed by the nature of things, but upon Napoleon; and the question to be considered is this—Could his operations during the day have been as effectively carried on without such a sacrifice of human lives?

The question is a convenient one as affording an opportunity to review in order the various movements of the fight, and we shall consider it under the following heads:—(*a*.) Napoleon's delay in beginning the battle. (*b*.) The methods employed in the attacks on Hougomont and La Haie Sainte. (*c*.) The formation of the French right for D'Erlon's attack. (*d*.) Ney's cavalry charges. (*e*.) The expediency of retreat. (*f*.) The attack of the Guard.

The reasons which actuated Napoleon in deferring the engagement until noon have already been sufficiently explained.* With his mind at ease as to the enemy in front, and strangely oblivious of the dangers to be apprehended from the enemy on his flank, delay appeared to him to offer advantages without any corresponding drawbacks.

His original intention, however, was to open his attack at nine o'clock. He might certainly have done so at that hour, if not considerably earlier, and thereby he might have gained at least three hours upon the Prussians, for it is questionable if

* *Vide* pp. 190, 191.

the Prussian movements would have been materially hastened by such a decision on Napoleon's part. Therefore we are confronted with the question whether Wellington could have maintained his resistance until the Prussians came up if three additional hours of resistance had been demanded of him. When we reflect that, in these changed conditions, Lobau's 10,000 men would have been used to second D'Erlon's attack—that the full strength of the Guard would have been available at Waterloo—as at Ligny—and that, as it was, the Duke's army at eight o'clock was in a state of extreme exhaustion, we may from these considerations conclude that, begun at 9 A.M., the battle would have been over at five in the afternoon, and Napoleon master of the field. The loss of the allies might have been greater, of the French certainly less, while of the Prussians there would have been no loss at all.

## II.

The methods adopted against the two positions of Hougomont and La Haie Sainte were both marked by lavish indifference to life. The troops of Jerome, then of Foy, and lastly those of Bachelu, were in turn employed against the former, and endeavoured to effect by reckless courage what the judicious employment of artillery might have accomplished more speedily, more effectually, and at infinitely less cost. The loss to both armies in and around Hougomont was certainly 6000 men, and of these the French lost considerably more than half. 1500 fell in the first half-hour of the attack. The position was eventually fired by Reille's howitzers, and there is no reason why it should not have been stormed from the French batteries before such fearful loss was incurred. On a day when every available man was needed to support the main attacks upon the allied front, practically the whole of the Emperor's left was occupied in fruitless attempts against an advanced position, and was thus incapacitated from playing its due part in the general operations of the day.

A like criticism applies to the attack on La Haie Sainte. Hundreds of lives were sacrificed in an assault which might have been saved had the place been stormed by the fire of heavy guns. The French, indeed, may be said to have exhausted a superabundant courage upon brick walls and heavy doors, but against these artillery would have been as useful as impetuosity was futile.

### III.

The faulty formation of D'Erlon's attack has already been noted. It is a subject which has much engaged the attention of critics. There can be little doubt that it was some misunderstanding of orders which brought about a formation so cumbrous and unwieldy, formidable indeed by virtue of the weight which thereby was concentrated against the allied left, but far from possessing those qualities of strength which come from manageability, suppleness, and mutual support. Napoleon ordered but did not organise D'Erlon's attack.* The duty of organisation was left to Ney and to D'Erlon himself, and in such lieutenants the Emperor was justified by all past experience in placing implicit confidence. Yet it is almost impossible to conceive that the formation which they adopted was in conformity with Napoleon's intentions. What his intentions were we may perhaps surmise, as Quinet has well pointed out, by examining the formation of the Guard, which Napoleon personally supervised, for the last attack as the day was drawing to a close. There we see columns of battalions, formed in echelon, as in the case of the 1st corps, but instead of being massed one upon the other, without facilities for deploying or for forming square upon the flanks, so as to resist any cavalry charges which might be made upon them there, the column of the Guard advanced with its battalions in the centre deployed in line, supported on the flanks by battalions in columns in such a way as to secure the maximum of attacking force, of mobility, and of resisting capacity.

This latter formation in columns of attack was moreover the one usually adopted in the French

* "I had not myself sufficient leisure to occupy myself with the secondary details of the organisation of my troops." Napoleon to O'Meara.

# CRITICAL EXAMINATION 251

army at that epoch. D'Erlon's formation was unusual, if not unheard of, and carried no advantages beyond that of weight to counteract its defects. It was vicious in its conception—*une folie*, says Charras — ineffective in execution, and disastrous in its results. For 5000 men were killed, wounded, or made prisoners in this movement alone.

Various conjectures have been hazarded to account for these unwonted dispositions. The materials before us, however, supply no sufficient explanation, though it seems most probable that, in the passage of orders from Napoleon to his lieutenants, a misconception as to his design in some way arose.

Another tactical point must be noticed as contributing to the failure of the attack of the 1st corps. The infantry battalions were altogether unsupported by cavalry. It may, indeed, be urged in addition that they were not supported by reinforcements of infantry, but this was owing to circumstances, not to negligence. Lobau was to have seconded D'Erlon's efforts, but the appearance of the Prussians necessitated his presence on the flank. There was, however, no sufficient reason to account for the absence of cavalry support. In this arm Napoleon was vastly the superior of Wellington. Sufficient cavalry were promptly forthcoming to retrieve disaster, but not to avert it. Had Milhaud's cuirassiers and the lancers of Jacquinot been employed directly in seconding the infantry, the French losses must at least have been appreciably diminished, while it is by no means impossible that the success of Picton's infantry and of the Union Brigade would never have been attained at all. When we consider that, notwithstanding its unwieldy formation, D'Erlon's corps did gain the crest of the allied position, it is something more than idle speculation, when estimating the chances and losses of the day, to enquire what results would have been likely to follow had the formation been sound and the cavalry advanced in support.

## IV.

Want of proper support by infantry is the criticism which applies generally to Ney's cavalry charges. It is convenient to state this here and at once in order to emphasise Napoleon's essential fault throughout the battle of Waterloo. "In general," says Brialmont, and Chesney endorses the remark, "all the attacks made during this day had the defect of being badly supported." Over and over again the French cavalry gained the crest of Wellington's position, but there was no infantry to maintain it when won. Napoleon petulantly exclaimed that he had no infantry, and could not manufacture it upon the spot. But a due economy of the infantry which he had would have rendered the process of manufacture unnecessary. As the afternoon wore on, in fact, he began to feel bitterly the unnecessary losses which

## CRITICAL EXAMINATION 253

he had already incurred. Moreover, Reille's corps was by no means employed to advantage. To maintain a whole wing of the French army at and around Hougomont was to waste the services of half of it. It may therefore be asserted that this deficiency of infantry to support the cavalry charges was not inevitable, but was due to faulty dispositions all along the line.

But these general observations by no means exhaust the adverse criticism which may be directed against the cavalry attacks upon Wellington's right centre. Napoleon consistently maintained that they were made too early in the day, that they were premature, and that Guyot's heavy cavalry were sent in without orders, thus depriving the army of its last cavalry reserve. Too much confidence, of course, is not to be given to Napoleon's statements after the event; yet there is a concurrence of testimony upon this point which cannot be ignored. Gourgaud, who was by the Emperor's side all that day, says that the officers who surrounded Napoleon, observing the success of Ney's charges, shouted victory, and made every demonstration of joy. The Emperor did not share in this exultation. He observed to Marshal Soult, "this is a premature movement, which may be attended by fatal consequences." Soult expressed himself with considerable warmth respecting Ney, and said, "He is compromising us, as he did at Jéna." That the attack was ill-timed was so generally conceded, that Ney himself disclaimed in part the responsibility for it, and declared, through Colonel Heymès, his aide-de-camp, that the heavy cavalry of the Guard went in, not by his orders, but independently of them. If we believe this we must conclude that the last reserve of cavalry engaged without orders from either of the responsible commanders—a conclusion which, when all allowances are made for the confusion incident to a battle, can leave us no very high opinion of the organisation and discipline which prevailed. The fact is that these cavalry charges were marked by the same reckless impetuosity which has already been noticed at Hougomont and La Haie Sainte. They supply another instance of splendid courage wasted for want of control. Nor can they be properly understood without a due comprehension of the character and position of Ney on the day of Waterloo.

Michel Ney had long before worthily earned the title of "*Le Brave des braves.*" In the long roll of Napoleon's generals none had displayed greater brilliancy in the field, or greater constancy in disaster. To him the cause of the Empire was the cause of France, and he had served it gloriously. But the time came, in 1814, when these two causes appeared to him distinct. The fatal issue of the Russian campaign, the disaster at Leipsic, and the hopeless struggle on the frontier, seemed to him to separate the interests of his master from those of his country, and he was consenting to Napoleon's abdication. He gave his allegiance to the Bour-

## CRITICAL EXAMINATION 255

bons and served Louis XVIII. But in the conditions of this new attachment there was much which was uncongenial to him. Regarding the course of events from the point of view of a soldier, not of a politician, he saw with disgust the humiliations which the new *régime* imposed upon the army, and keenly resented humiliations to which he was himself subject at Court. Still, upon the news of Napoleon's escape from Elba, he hurried to the King, and, governed by impulse rather than by studied reflection, declared that Bonaparte's attempt was that of a madman, and that, if taken, he deserved to be brought to Paris in an iron cage. Thereupon, at the head of 6000 men, he advanced to oppose the Emperor's progress. In proportion as he moved forward, the more the conviction grew upon him that the course of the Bourbons was lost. The co-operation of the troops under Monsieur, the King's brother, and under the Marshal Macdonald, was not forthcoming. "He was expecting reinforcements and artillery, but he received none. He hoped to be informed of Napoleon's march, and of the resolutions taken at Paris, but he obtained no information. What he did know was that the troops sent to fight against the invader were either uniting themselves to him or beating a retreat." His situation was indeed one of cruel embarrassment, and it is not surprising that at such a juncture his personal griefs against the Bourbons should have recurred to his mind, and that placed between his oath of allegiance and civil war, which he had it in his power to avert, he should see duty, self-interest, and patriotism all combining to force him on to Napoleon's side. The result of this conflict was not long in doubt. The proclamation of Lens-le-Saunier declared frankly for Napoleon on the ground that the glory of the army and the liberties of France were alike in jeopardy under the Bourbon rule.

For Ney at Waterloo, therefore, the stake was nothing less than his fortune, his honour, and his life, and throughout the campaign he realised this fact to the full. "For you and me," he cried to D'Erlon, as his fourth horse was shot under him in the battle, "if we do not die here under the English bullets, there will remain nothing more than to perish miserably under the bullets of the *émigrés*." It puts no strain upon the facts to conclude that the balance of his mind was disturbed by the tremendous consequences which depended on the game he was playing, and that the conditions at Waterloo would naturally tend to intensify a spirit of dare-devil impetuosity in a man at no time distinguished for restraint.

When, therefore, the responsibility for the movements in the front was imposed upon Ney, we are helped towards a comprehension of those movements by a knowledge of the man who conducted them.

It only remains to be added that Ney was a cavalry officer, that his most brilliant exploits had

# CRITICAL EXAMINATION 257

been performed with that arm, and that he was perhaps disposed to believe that more could be accomplished by cavalry than, in fact, they are capable of accomplishing in war.

In any case, the result of all these considerations taken together is clear. Throughout the day the cavalry was squandered. The loss in that arm was altogether out of proportion to the advantages they obtained. Incapable of securing victory, they were wanting to cover the retreat; but, effectively supported, victory perhaps might have been won, or, if not, a sufficient force of cavalry would have been available to stem the tide of disaster and to prevent an orderly retreat from becoming a disorganised rout.

## V.

For the French the disaster of Waterloo lay not so much in the victory of the allies as in the nature of their own defeat. It was overwhelming, absolute, final. The army was the last hope of the Empire, and in the evening that army had ceased to exist. Scattered and demoralised groups of men flying pell-mell for safety, relaxed from discipline, their arms abandoned, their *moral* shattered, were all that remained of those splendid corps which had defiled so proudly before Napoleon in the morning. Was this the inevitable result of defeat? Was catastrophe so great unavoidably associated with failure?

It is urged by some critics that Napoleon's action was that of a ruined gamester hazarding his last stake upon a desperate chance. He should, it is said, have recognised the true state of affairs either when the Prussians first appeared, or, at any rate, after the failure of his front to break the allied line. In the first case he might have withdrawn an effective army from the field, have operated a junction with Grouchy, and with his forces thus consolidated have carried on a war of manœuvres against the allies until some favourable opportunity should occur for striking a great blow. In the second case, what remained of his army might have retired in good order under cover of the Imperial Guard. On the lowest reckoning, 40,000 men might thus have been withdrawn. Grouchy would have joined him with at least 25,000 more; 3000 had been left behind at Ligny. Thus the Emperor would have found himself still at the head of nearly 70,000 men — as many as he had with him at Waterloo—and with these he might have carried on a war upon the frontier under better auspices than in 1814, when, with a smaller army, he performed such prodigies of skill and daring.

The weakness of this criticism—if it be weak—consists in the fact that it comes after the event. Few things are more difficult than to abstract ourselves from theories which subsequent knowledge of events suggests, in order to limit ourselves to the actual facts of the case at the time. Theory

## CRITICAL EXAMINATION

and fact have a tendency to confuse themselves together, and to become in our minds one and the same thing. Seated in the study there are doubtless hundreds of persons—not one of whom could dispose a regiment in the field—who could on paper defeat Napoleon with more ease and precision than did the Duke,—who could, theoretically, win the whole campaign ten times over for either side. The student, after the event, has all available documents before him—his *coup d'œil* ranges over the movements of all the antagonists together. He is independent of aides-de-camp, accidents, or mistakes. But in the field it is far different. There the commander, for the positions, resources, and intentions of his opponent, must depend largely upon divination. Even as to his own army his information must be limited, and the favourable moment has sometimes passed before he knows that it has arrived. He is in a measure the sport of circumstances, for his pieces are human beings and not pawns upon a chess-board. His critics, if their criticism is to apply, must recognise these limitations upon their subject. The question is not how, under ideal circumstances of information, a campaign may be conducted to the best advantage, but how, under the practical conditions of the moment, a commander should act.

Applying these principles of criticism to the question under consideration, we must first look at Napoleon's position at the time when the Prussians were sighted upon the heights of St Lambert. It is almost beyond question that he did not anticipate the intervention of any Prussians whatever in the battle between himself and Wellington. His measures had been taken to prevent such intervention, and he supposed his measures to have been effectual. When, therefore, the Prussians actually appeared, he had to consider the effective capacity of this unexpected enemy, and his impression that it was the corps of Bülow, and of Bülow only, was strengthened by all his subsequent information and observation as the day wore on. The idea that three out of the four Prussian corps were in march for the field of Waterloo never occurred to him until the fact was declared by their presence. Confident that Blücher's retreat had been towards the Meuse, confident that Grouchy intervened between Blücher's main army and himself, Napoleon was forced to the conclusion that what he saw at St Lambert was merely a column, though perhaps a pretty strong one, detached from the main body, and that it represented the total amount of assistance which Blücher would be able to send to Wellington that day. If this was so, the appearance of even 30,000 additional antagonists was scarcely a sufficient reason for immediate retreat. On the contrary, it was a reason for pursuing the contest with redoubled vigour; for now not only the allied army under Wellington, but also a considerable detachment of Blücher's army as well, might be involved in a common destruction. Such an opinion was based

## CRITICAL EXAMINATION 261

on something more than arrogant self-confidence. Events were to show that it was very nearly, if not quite, the truth. Napoleon's army of 71,000 men was so vastly the superior of that of Wellington in calibre, *moral*, and experience, that he might well reckon himself a match for Wellington and Bülow combined. It is scarcely necessary to include here, as influencing Napoleon's decision, the anticipations which he had, or pretended to have, from Grouchy. Of course if Grouchy arrived almost simultaneously with Bülow, then matters remained as they were; but leaving Grouchy entirely out of the calculation, the first appearance of the Prussians was rather a cause of congratulation for Napoleon than a circumstance to induce him to retreat.

If this be admitted, the case against retreat at a later period of the day is even stronger. All Napoleon's calculations were turning out correctly. The Anglo-Dutch army was being very severely pressed throughout the afternoon and evening. La Haie Sainte had fallen, and Wellington's centre was dangerously threatened. The Dutch-Belgians had been driven from Papelotte and La Haye. Hougomont, though still a centre of obstinate resistance, was in flames. Bülow's attack upon Planchenoit had been repulsed, and the Prussian contingent was thoroughly held by Lobau. The Imperial Guard was committed to its attack. In fact, at seven o'clock every *known* consideration influenced the Emperor to believe that victory was well within his grasp. Facts, which were *unknown* to him at this critical hour, were really decisive of the contest against him. The unperceived arrival of Ziethen's corps, the unsuspected advance of Pirch to the support of Bülow, turned a doubtful battle into a ruinous defeat, but it was then too late for an orderly retreat. The repulse of the Imperial Guard, taken by itself, was a disaster from which Napoleon might have recovered himself, but the repulse of the Guard, coming simultaneously with the irruption of Ziethen upon the right, and of Pirch upon the left, meant nothing else but irretrievable ruin. Had the Emperor known the true facts of the situation, then retreat, while yet there was time, was the only safe policy to adopt. He only knew a part of the facts, and the part which he knew justified him in resolutely maintaining the combat. He began the battle of Waterloo under grave misconceptions, and under a wholly false sense of security. That it was so was largely, if not entirely, his own fault, but with that, for the purposes of this argument, we have nothing to do. Given the position, as he understood it, on the 18th June, ought he, as events developed themselves, to have ordered a retreat? Is his action that of a desperate gamester or of a responsible commander? With the issue thus narrowed it may be asserted with much confidence that retreat was at no time called for until it was too late advantageously to effect it.*

* For an opposite view, see Clausewitz.

CRITICAL EXAMINATION 263

VI.

The attack by the Imperial Guard becomes, for purposes of criticism, two distinct questions. (1.) Ought such an attack to have been made at all? (2.) Was the attack organised in the best possible manner to secure success?

The first of these must be decided by much the same criticism as has already been applied above to the question of retreat. They must stand or fall together. If it be maintained that Napoleon's true policy was retreat early in the evening, then it follows that the Guard should not have been put in; if it is conceded that retreat was uncalled for, then some such attack as that by the Imperial Guard was simply indispensable, for if successful it must be decisive of the battle, if unsuccessful the contest would still be an open one. Napoleon at least must so judge the situation, ignorant as he was of the Prussian reinforcements which were so close at hand.

When, however, we turn our attention to the dispositions of the attack, we see that it was by no means so effective as it might have been. It could not be an attack in force, for owing to circumstances now beyond Napoleon's control, only a third of the battalions of the Guard were available, but such as it was it might have been rendered far more effective by due support upon its left. It was solely in consequence of this want of support that Colborne's flank movement was possible. A timely charge of cavalry would, even when the movement had been made, have compelled the 52nd regiment to form square, at once relieving the Imperial Guard from the pressure of its attack, but neither infantry was at hand to check Colbourne's movement in its inception, nor cavalry to thwart it when made. So too with the artillery. Two batteries, consisting in all of twelve pieces, accompanied the charge, but they were masked, and so rendered useless when the rear columns deviated from the true line of attack. In fact, in no particular, in infantry, cavalry, or artillery, was the Guard adequately backed up, and to this fact its repulse was due more than to any intrinsic deficiencies of its own. It is idle to assert that Napoleon did all that was possible, but that he had no cavalry or infantry available. If this be true, then the whole scheme of the attack stands condemned *ipso facto*. To hazard his last reserve in so desperate a venture would have been the work of a madman. But the assertion, at least as far as infantry is concerned, is untrue. Reille's corps was wasting itself away around Hougomont, and no compensating advantage was being gained. A part of it might have been employed with great effect to support the Guard, and it was undoubtedly Napoleon's intention that this should be done. But it was not done, "it does not seem to have been even attempted," and disaster was the inevitable consequence. A commander of course is

CRITICAL EXAMINATION 265

not quit of all further responsibility because his intentions are good. It is his business as far as possible to enforce them. To shift the blame from himself on to the shoulders of his subordinates multiplies the blame but does not remove it. However, in this matter it may be said that the design was good but the execution of it faulty. The attack itself was imperative; its details were adequately conceived, but it was very imperfectly executed.

It is perhaps impossible to explain satisfactorily the non-fulfilment of the Emperor's intentions in regard to this last charge of the Guard. The fault lay somewhere between Napoleon and his lieutenants, but it is difficult for lack of evidence to say exactly where.

## VII.

It must not be forgotten that throughout the campaign Napoleon, though often so precise in his instructions, had yet for the fulfilment of them left a large latitude to his generals. Already at Quatre Bras Ney had exercised a semi-independent command. A command of like character had been given to Grouchy after Ligny. The organisation of D'Erlon's first attack had been left to Ney and D'Erlon himself, and throughout the afternoon of the 18th Ney had acted in a position of almost supreme command against the Duke of Wellington. The cavalry attacks had been prematurely engaged, contrary to Napoleon's intentions, and had been pushed too far, against his will. A certain want of harmony and of efficient co-operation between the commander-in-chief and the commanders-in-part marks the whole history of these days, and is an explanation in part of the blunders and disaster of the campaign. Allowance must be made for the fact that Napoleon himself was occupied very closely with the Prussian attack upon his flank, and was thus bound to delegate a large part of his authority in the front to others. It was, too, undoubtedly a misfortune for him that Mortier, the Commander of the Guard, had fallen ill and was unable to be present during the campaign, but when all this is said, the fact remains that it was before the eyes of the Emperor in person that the Guard moved forward to the charge, and that, if the organisation of their movement was faulty, upon Napoleon primarily must rest the blame. All generals must make mistakes, and Napoleon was at no time an exception to this rule; there are some kinds of error from which not even the greatest commanders can in the nature of things be exempt, but when we see in Napoleon's tactics precisely those faults which had always been most foreign to his practice in war, the very faults by which in his adversaries he had so often profited, and which he had taught them to discard, we are led to seek an explanation in the conditions personal to himself and to his lieutenants, and are forced to conclude that the Napoleon of Waterloo

## CRITICAL EXAMINATION 267

was not the same Napoleon as in the old days of Austerlitz and Jéna, and that his generals were not characterised by the same ardour as in the days when their *bâtons* and their fortunes had yet to be won.

Both these considerations demand attention from a student of the campaign, for both contributed largely to the loss of it. Exactly how largely it is perhaps impossible to determine, for critics arrive at very different conclusions when they attempt to solve the personal equation of Waterloo. Some, looking at the whole strategy of the campaign, consider that it exhibits Napoleon's military genius at its highest point, and maintain that such conceptions and combinations could not have emanated from the brain of a man who was physically unfit. Others, bringing forward many particular examples to prove their contention, urge that throughout the campaign Napoleon was incapacitated by disease and in a semi-comatose condition at the moment when energy was of all things the most needful. The truth seems to be that Napoleon was suffering under the influence of a strange and mysterious malady, the nature of which has not yet been accurately defined. A life such as his, spent in privations, fatigues, and exposure, so full of mental and physical labours, with brief flashes of dissipation, would not unnaturally generate diseases from which the ordinary man is free—diseases, therefore, which but rarely present themselves to the observation of medical men. There still remains to be written a work, which would prove as interesting as it should be valuable, upon the maladies of great men, and scientific investigation might be worse employed than in examining the physical and mental condition of such men as Pope, Swift, and Napoleon Bonaparte.* What is certain in Napoleon's case is that his malady had been growing upon him with increasing force since 1806, that its attacks were notified by a sudden lethargy amounting to complete prostration, and that "its effects were that at some critical moment of a battle his wonderful power of quick and correct decision seemed to desert him; so much so, that for the time being he almost abandoned the reins to chance." † At Wagram and at Bautzen he slept

* Since writing this I learn that a work entitled " Les Maladies de Napolèon " is to be produced this year (1895) by Dr Cabanès, author of "Marat Incounu."

† Napoleon at St Helena, referring to this tendency of his to sleep upon the battlefield, explained it in an ingenious and characteristic way. "'Quand je donnais des batailles qui duraient trois jours, la nature devait aussi, avoir ses droits : je profitais du plus petit instant ; je dormais où et quand je pouvais.' Il disait sur cela qu'indépendamment de l'obligation d'obéir à la nature, ces sommeils offraient au chef d'une très-grande armée le précieux advantage d'attendre avec calme les rapports et la concordance de toutes ses divisions, au lieu de se laisser emporter peut-être par le seul objet dont il serait le temoin." Las Cases. This means of course that Napoleon endeavoured to disguise from himself and others the real nature of his attacks of lethargy.

It is not a mere supposition that Napoleon was attacked by his malady during the Waterloo campaign. There is ample evidence, apart from his lethargy during a critical period of the 18th, to prove it.

while the noise of battle was rolling around him ; at Waterloo, seated on a wooden chair, his head drooping upon his arms stretched on the cottager's table, which was brought out to accommodate his maps and papers, he slumbered heavily, oblivious for the moment, even at this crisis of his fortunes, of the events which were deciding his destiny.

But, on the other hand, these attacks, though tending in his later years to become more frequent and more severe, were passing in their character, and affected Napoleon only during the period of their duration. When not immediately under their influence, his intellect was as unclouded as ever, his genius as entirely unimpared. He was thus as capable in 1815 of devising great military schemes as at any time in his life, but he was not so capable of effectively superintending their execution. His physical condition, in fact, gives us a clue to some of the anomalies of Waterloo. It explains that extraordinary combination of energy and prostration, of force and weakness, which is so conspicuous throughout the campaign. The delay in pursuing the Prussians after Ligny, the tardy despatch of Grouchy in search of them, the inade-

Thus, although the battle of Ligny continued till past eleven o'clock P.M., Napoleon left the field at eight and went to bed. When Grouchy came for orders at twelve o'clock he was told that the Emperor "était couché, souffrant, et avait défendu qu'on entrât chez lui." He remained in this state of strict seclusion, issuing no orders, till after 8 A.M. on the 17th, and was not really alive to the situation till twelve mid-day.—Lord Wolseley, "The Decline and Fall of Napoleon," *Pall Mall Magazine*, January 1894.

quate prosecution of his own conceptions for the conduct of the battle, become intelligible to us, if we regard them as the natural consequences of an untimely seizure.

## VIII.

When we turn to Napoleon's lieutenants, we no longer find in them the same *élan*, the same enthusiasm, as in their early days. They had won honours and wealth, and they wished to enjoy them. "Gorged with all the favours that human vanity can dream of, the marshals and generals of first rank had become grumblers. One exclusive desire animated them all, to live peaceably on the benefits which the bounty of Napoleon had conferred on them." \* "These men," says Mellernich, "wished to enjoy their fortune, and had no idea of risking their possessions and their lives every day in the midst of the vicissitudes of war." "The men whom I have overwhelmed with favours wish to enjoy them," said Napoleon to the Duke of Vicenza. "They no longer wish to fight. They do not understand, poor reasoners that they are, that to fight is still necessary, if the repose for which they thirst is to be conquered. And have not I, too, a palace, a wife, a child?" In addition to this, they lacked also something of that confidence in the fortune of their chief which had animated them in the old days. The campaigns

\* Arthur Lévy. *Napoleon Intime.*

## CRITICAL EXAMINATION 271

of Russia and the Peninsula, the days of Leipsic, and the frontier struggle of 1814, had shaken their faith in the Emperor's star, and had engendered some distrust, perhaps, of his genius. "My generals were discouraged," Napoleon said at St Helena, "and imagined that they saw everywhere armies of a hundred thousand men, and I had not myself sufficient leisure to occupy myself with the secondary details of the organisation of my troops." "Many of the generals," says Gourgaud, "were no longer the same men. They had lost that energy and that enterprising genius which formerly distinguished them; they had become timid and circumspect in all their operations. Their personal bravery remained, but for them the grand object was to compromise themselves as little as possible." Thus, while some among the marshals were bent upon conducting the campaign so as to compromise themselves as little as possible, however the issue might turn out, others, as in the case of Ney and D'Erlon, were committed beyond possibility of redemption, should Napoleon be defeated. A mixture of calculated temporising with headstrong impetuosity is thus a notable characteristic of the campaign—a characteristic which it would be difficult adequately to understand and appreciate, were it not for our knowledge of the circumstances and inner feelings of the chief actors in the scene.

No estimate of Waterloo can therefore be satisfactory if the personal element is ignored. The state of Napoleon's health was as vital to the issue as the state of his army, for the dispositions of his army were largely dependent upon the state of his health. The motives and emotions which animated his lieutenants must no more be left out of account than the technical questions of strategy and tactics on which campaigns are too readily supposed exclusively to depend. It is this which gives its enduring fascination to the study of Waterloo, and removes the campaign from the exclusive domain of the military specialist. It is a drama of real life, teeming with human interest, with dramatic contrast, and the ingredients of tragedy. The serene confidence with which the battle was begun, the proud display of military force and pageantry which heralded the combat, stand out in glaring opposition to the utter ruin and despair in which it closed. The hopes and fears which alternated so rapidly; the Nemesis which was so surely, because unseen and unsuspected, overtaking the greatest genius of his own or perhaps of any age, but who had degraded that genius to the uses of a transcendent egotism; the fate of Europe, which hung trembling in the balance; the constancy and matchless fortitude which decided the issue,—these are the magnetic forces which have focussed upon Waterloo the attention of all succeeding years, and which render it as much the theme of moralist and poet as of the military expert, critic, and historian.

# CHAPTER XII.

## CRITICAL EXAMINATION OF THE BATTLE OF WATERLOO.

### (WELLINGTON AND BLÜCHER.)

I. Wellington's Defence—II. Colville's Division at Hal—III. Blücher's Co-operation; could it have been earlier or more effective?

### I.

IN the last chapter criticism has been confined to the French movements in the battle. In the present chapter criticism will be directed to the allied armies under Wellington and Blücher.

No very extended remarks are necessary to this part of the subject, for the function of Wellington was merely to defend himself, while that of Blücher was first to arrive and then to make his co-operation as effective as possible. We have simply to ask (*a*) Could the resistance of Wellington have been made more vigorous and less expensive than it was? (*b*) Could the assistance of Blücher have been rendered more speedily, or when rendered, could it have been made more effective?

(*a*) At whatever point on the battlefield or at whatever period in the battle we look, there is seen the same spectacle of dogged, obstinate resistance opposed to impetuous attacks. At Hougomont practically the whole French left was employed to secure that position, but it remained in the hands of its defenders when the day closed. At La Haie Sainte Wellington was not so fortunate. A failure in the supply of ammunition, and the impossibility of remedying this failure in time, compelled Major Baring to evacuate the position, but the dauntless tenacity with which it was held as long as it was possible to hold it has never been called in question. So, too, with the attacks, both by cavalry and infantry, upon the front. No defence could have been finer, more resolute, and more effective than was that of the allies all along the line. Some of the foreign regiments, it is true, broke and fled, carrying consternation and panic in their flight, but the causes of this need not be considered here. It is proposed to treat separately the question of the conduct of the foreign troops at Waterloo. For the moment it is sufficient to notice that the resistance of Wellington's army as a whole was only the more obstinate in proportion as panic seized upon some isolated parts of it. The very circumstances in fact that would half excuse vacillation and despondency were actually productive of exactly contrary effects.

## II.

The only serious fault which can be urged against Wellington's defence is that he failed to employ all the forces which were available for use.

# CRITICAL EXAMINATION 275

In reviewing in a previous chapter the dispositions of the Duke of Wellington on the eve of the battle of Waterloo, it was pointed out that some 18,000 men, constituting Colville's division, had been stationed at Hal—a point within four hours' march of the field—a distance from Mont St Jean of about ten miles. The present section will discuss the reasons which induced Wellington to deprive himself of the assistance of Colville's division in the action of the 18th June.

Hitherto critics have for the most part referred to this matter merely in order to express their condemnation of the Duke's determination. Few have thought it worth while to treat in any detail a point which is certainly of the first importance. For the absence or presence of Colville might at a crisis have turned the scale one way or the other.

And yet it is impossible to conceive that it was through wantonness, lack of care, or insufficient reflection that the Duke acted as he did. He must have been actuated by strong motives when, in the face of all the risks of his situation, he voluntarily increased those risks by detaching 18,000 men from his side. He must have supposed that advantages would accrue from this course which would more than counterbalance the additional dangers which their absence implied.

Wellington's general orders to his troops at the close of the 17th give the first clue to the problem. His instructions to Colville's division were as follows:—"The brigades of the 4th division at Braine-le-Comte are to retire at daylight to-morrow morning upon Hal. . . . Prince Frederick of Orange is to occupy with his corps the position between Hal and Enghien, *and is to defend it as long as possible.*" Now the sentence which has been placed in italics demonstrates beyond the possibility of doubt that the Duke expected an attack to be made upon the position which he had ordered the Prince to occupy. The Duke clearly was anticipating the possibility of an attempt on the part of Napoleon to outflank him upon his right, and the presence of Colville between Hal and Enghien would effectually prevent this. No such attempt was made by Napoleon, and so Colville was wasted for the purposes of Waterloo; but none the less it was the duty of Wellington to guard against all chances, especially seeing that if such a movement had been successfully made it would have brought confusion and disaster upon the allied right wing, on which, for purposes of resistance, Wellington chiefly depended.

There is an interesting passage bearing upon this point in Napoleon's "*Mémoires pour Servir*," &c., compiled at St Helena, in which the Emperor asserts that on the evening of the 17th he detached a column of 5000 cavalry to make a detour in order to gain the high roads, or one of them, leading from Enghien and Braine-le-Comte to Brussels. The force thus detached was, when it had gained its object, to make a march upon the

## CRITICAL EXAMINATION 277

English rear, taking them unawares at the very crisis of the next day's engagement. Nothing was ever heard of this detachment of cavalry; no account is to be found of how it was composed, who commanded it, or what its operations were, and the whole story is generally regarded as a figment of Napoleon's brain—an afterthought conceived in his retirement, and suggestive rather of what he might advantageously have done than what he actually did. The Duke of Wellington, however, in his Memorandum relating to the battle, published in 1842, accepts this story and defends the employment of 18,000 troops at Hal on this ground, that they were there to repel Napoleon's project of falling upon the English rear. If we accept these statements of the "*Mémoires*" and of the Memorandum, it speaks volumes for the foresight of the Duke that he should have so accurately divined the precise action which Napoleon asserts that he adopted, but the testimony of both documents is generally rejected as untrustworthy. It is pointed out that the Memorandum of 1842 is full of inaccuracies as to details and matters of fact, and that it was composed from the Duke's recollections of the engagement, twenty-seven years after the event, when his memory was clouded by the great mass of misstatement and invention about the battle which so long a period had naturally produced, and when the true circumstances of the case had to some extent faded from his mind. As to this particular statement of the Memorandum it is asserted "that in his old age he unhesitatingly accepted the story told in the '*Mémoires*,'"\* and that it was from that source that he first heard of it.

It is, however, to be noted that this precise story is related as a fact in the "Additional Particulars to the Battle of Waterloo," published by Booth in 1817. Napoleon's "*Mémoires*" were not published till 1820, three years later. The story was, therefore, current two years after the battle, and three years before the "*Mémoires*" appeared. It was regarded at the time as an explanation of the Duke's dispositions, and, at any rate, it throws doubt upon the assertion that it was from the Emperor's book that the Duke first learned of the projected manœuvre. There is no evidence whatever to show that Napoleon did detach, or ever thought of detaching, a corps to act upon the enemy's rear, and the story is, without doubt, a creation of his fancy; but it is by no means improbable that the Duke contemplated the possibility of some such movement being made, and thought it well to be prepared against any event. It is, in fact, more probable that a due consideration of the Duke's dispositions suggested to Napoleon at St Helena the advantage which such a movement might have gained for him (and that consequently he wished it to be thought that he had executed it), than that the Duke should have

\* Chesney.

## CRITICAL EXAMINATION 279

first heard in 1820 a story which was current in 1817, and should have utilised it in 1842 to explain certain of his dispositions in 1815.

It is, therefore, very possible that the troops were posted at Hal to prevent any veiled movement on the part of Napoleon upon the right flank and rear of the Anglo-Dutch army. But there were other reasons to account for the Duke's dispositions, and of these the one most currently received is this—that the Duke placed so considerable a force out of his reach upon the right in order to ensure support for his retreat in the event of defeat. In this connexion we have to consider what the Duke's line of retreat would have been. It is generally assumed that it would have been direct on Brussels by the roads leading through the Forest of Soignies, but retreat through a forest is always hazardous. The nature of the situation must afford great opportunities to the enemy of harassing an army in retiring through thick woods, and Napoleon always maintained that to post an army in front of a forest, through which alone retreat was possible, was contrary to the principles of military science. Indeed, he goes so far as to assert that it was only the circumstance that retreat was practically impossible that prevented Wellington twice upon the day of Waterloo from giving the order to his army to fall back. To these criticisms of Napoleon the Duke subsequently retorted that had he been compelled to retire he would not have withdrawn through the forest, but upon his right by Hal, and in support of this statement he instanced the troops which he had posted there. Just as after Ligny the Prussian corps of Thielemann retired upon its reinforcements in the shape of Bülow's corps, stationed near Gembloux, so after Waterloo the Duke would, he asserted, have retired upon his reinforcements stationed, to the number of 18,000 men, in the neighbourhood of Hal, or, at any rate, his right would have so retreated in the event of the centre being pierced during the battle.

There is still one further point to be noticed in regard to this matter. It has been seen that Wellington, from the very first, was doubtful as to the true line of Napoleon's advance. He delayed the concentration of his army upon the main Brussels-Charleroi road until the last moment, because he thought Napoleon's advance by Charleroi might only be a feint, and that the real object was to cut his communications with the sea, or to advance on Brussels by way of Mons. Even as late as midnight on June 15th, Nivelles rather than Quatre Bras was the point on which the army was directed, Nivelles lying six miles further to the west than the latter place. Moreover, the Duke always maintained that to attack him first (and not Blücher), and by his right would have been the best policy for Napoleon to adopt. It is therefore clear that the Duke's judgment throughout the opening days of the campaign was biassed by a preconceived opinion,

# CRITICAL EXAMINATION 281

and feeling strongly that an advance by way of Mons was a contingency always to be guarded against, he posted an effective number of reserve troops to meet such an event, should it occur, content to run the risk of the loss of their services in return for the sense of security which their presence at Hal afforded him.

Such, then, is an explanation of the Duke's dispositions. The troops were at Hal and not at Waterloo—

(*a.*) To prevent any flank and rear movement by Napoleon, such as might very likely be made.

(*b.*) To support the army in case of retreat, for it was by Hal rather than Soignies that the Duke would have withdrawn.

(*c.*) To guard against the possibility of any movement by Napoleon upon Brussels by way of Mons.

These reasons, taken together, seem to form a strong justification for Wellington's action. They are not, however, admitted by critics to be an excuse. Chesney speaks of the Duke's "strategical error," and considers that "this blot is the single one of several once charged against Wellington for this day's conduct, which time has not long since cleared away." Sir J. Shaw Kennedy says, "The Duke ought certainly to have had Colville . . . on the field." Sir E. Hamley is equally emphatic, while foreign critics are practically unanimous in the same sense.

Notwithstanding this weight of authority, there

was much force, it is contended, in the Duke's apprehensions, and much caution and good sense displayed in the measures which he took to allay them.

But, while admitting this, there still remains another question,—whether every purpose would not have been equally served by posting Colville nearer to the main army than Hal, or, at any rate, by gradually drawing him nearer as the fight wore on. Had he been stationed, say at Braine-le-Chateau, six miles nearer to the field, he might have served a double purpose. He would have been equally useful to guard the right wing from the chance of a surprise attack upon its flank, and would also have been available to take his part in the battle, should it become evident that no danger upon the flank was threatened.

A student of the campaign has forcibly stated this aspect of the question in a letter to the author of this study. "I never doubted the wisdom of this precaution of Wellington, nor questioned his excuse for it. My only trouble is in his apparent oversight in placing the 18,000 Dutch and Hanoverians *at a fixed point*, some twelve miles away on his right rear, instead of gradually, *as the fight wore on*, drawing them nearer and nearer, so that, at a critical moment, while having them in hand to cover his retreat, he might have turned them into an attacking force on Napoleon's left, if opportunity occurred—as it did. When Bülow was active upon Napoleon's right

# CRITICAL EXAMINATION 283

the latter had no chance of operating on Wellington's right. If at that time the Hal force could have been brought up, Napoleon, at the time of Blücher's arrival, would have been caught between *three* fires, and the French would have been annihilated. As it was, the Hal force was stuck fast all day, and never fired a shot nor sought a chance of firing one. In short, the Hal force might have had alternative offices instead of one."

This, however, is judgment after the event. Wellington had to judge while events were in progress, and with only a very limited knowledge of all the elements in the situation. With the full information which we possess of the whole history of the campaign, we can see that his precautions were unnecessary. But he could not know this at the time, and, moreover, it was always his habit to carry caution to its extreme limits.

Again, if the disposition of the force at Hal was intended to prevent a French advance upon Brussels by way of Mons, it is clear that he must have troops stationed close to the line of communication between those cities. For this purpose they would not have been effective, or so effective if posted at Braine-le-Chateau as at Hal and Tubize.

Their presence nearer to the field also would have offered strong if not irresistible temptation to use them. Could the Duke have known for certain that to use them would ensure him the victory, he would have disregarded all ulterior consequences in order to gain his ultimate end, but with no such certainty before him, and with a possibility of being compelled to retire, there was prudence in removing beyond the reach of any temptation to employ them the troops on whom he relied to support his retreat. While the troops were at Hal he was certain, should he have to withdraw, that he would be able to withdraw in good order. With the troops nearer the field there was the chance of their being involved in the general ruin.

If, after examining the question as a whole, we are desirous of forming some definite conclusions, it must be borne in mind that controversial topics seldom admit of any dogmatic conclusions. The object of this section is to point out the strong grounds which exist for reserving judgment upon Wellington's arrangements, not to insist that he was right and wiser than his critics. The justification, in fact, for devoting a separate section to a matter which, after all, is only of secondary importance, is that most treatises on Waterloo dismiss this subject in a few sentences of unqualified censure, whereas the case warrants a careful examination. Attention has also been called here, possibly for the first time, to the fact that, whereas Wellington's own explanations in 1842 are generally regarded as an afterthought, suggested by the commentaries of his antagonist, those explanations in truth exactly coincide with the view of the matter put before the public shortly after the

CRITICAL EXAMINATION 285

battle was fought, and some years before Napoleon's book was written.

III.

It has been clearly seen that the Prussians were the determining factor in the situation at Waterloo. They were so at the beginning as much as at the end of the day, for it was in the full assurance of their intervention that Wellington determined to stand and meet Napoleon in battle. Without such assurance it is certain that no battle would have been fought at all—at any rate, at Waterloo. What precise arrangements were arrived at between the two commanders—what transpired at that mysterious midnight interview which Wellington assures us took place between himself and Blücher, it is impossible to say, but it is certain that while the Duke was prepared to risk an engagement upon the security of the co-operation of two Prussian corps, Blücher's impetuous eagerness would only be satisfied if he brought up his whole army to share in the overthrow of the traditional enemy of his country.

The corps of Bülow was naturally marked out to lead the van of the Prussian advance. This corps had taken no part in the battle of Ligny, and was therefore quite unaffected by the exhaustion of a great contest or by the depression caused by defeat. Bülow had effected his junction with the rest of the Prussian army in the course of the 17th, and could have bivouacked for the night at or beyond Wavre, ready at break of day on the 18th to begin an uninterrupted march. As a fact, however, Bülow bivouacked at Dion-le-Mont, three miles to the east of Wavre, while the other three corps were stationed in and about the town. The troops which were to lead in the morning were stationed in the extreme rear the evening before, and thus, instead of starting in the morning clear of the town, they had first to march to it and then through it. Wavre was already encumbered by the troops and military equipage of the other corps composing the Prussian army, and Bülow's march was consequently much impeded. It was still further impeded by a fire which broke out in the streets of Wavre, and as a consequence of these delays the two leading divisions of the corps only reached St Lambert at noon—three hours before its two remaining divisions. Bülow, in fact, ought not to have been stationed at Dion-le-Mont, but considerably further westward, or, at least, he should have skirted Wavre in his march instead of passing through it.

The 2nd Prussian corps, under Pirch, was under orders to follow the march of Bülow. It did not actually start from Wavre till mid-day. This was perhaps in conformity with the arrangements, for the rear divisions of Bülow could scarcely have been clear of the town much before noon, but in the case of Ziethen's corps—the 1st—there was a delay which is highly significant. Its march was

# CRITICAL EXAMINATION 287

not to be in any way dependent upon that of the 2nd or 4th corps ; it was not to traverse the same road, being directed on Ohain by Bierge, and it might well have started at daybreak. It did not start till close upon noon.

These facts clearly show that it was not until mid-day on the 18th that Blücher began seriously and vigorously to prosecute his march. It was not until nearly mid-day that the sound of the cannonade at Mont St Jean was heard at Wavre. It is difficult to avoid the conclusion that there is some connexion between these two circumstances. It would seem as if Blücher scarcely cared to commit his army finally to the hazard of a march to Waterloo until he was thoroughly assured that Wellington meant to stand and await his arrival. That he should have some doubts about Wellington's good faith was not unnatural, and it is well known that Gneisenau, his chief of the staff—on whom the direction of affairs very largely rested—entertained grave, though quite unfounded, suspicions as to the Duke's trustworthiness and intentions. The wholly inaccurate account of the position of his troops which Wellington had given to Blücher on the morning of Ligny, his failure to support the Prussians at Ligny, even to the extent of a single division, his known prudence and caution, coupled with the very hazardous position in which he stood at Mont St Jean, were all facts calculated to arouse some amount of suspicion and distrust. What, again, would be the situation of the Prussian army if Wellington were not standing to fight a battle, but retreating on Brussels? Engaged in a dangerous oblique march with the main French army in front and Grouchy behind, it would be advancing to inevitable disaster, perhaps to utter and irretrievable ruin. Every dictate of prudence counselled delay, until all doubt and hesitation gave way to certainty. At noon the sound of the cannonade gave the necessary assurance, and at noon the march began in earnest.

This view of the case will also go far to account for the somewhat tardy and ill-arranged march of Bülow with the 4th corps, and for the long halt of his two leading divisions at St Lambert until the other divisions came up. Though he left his position at Dion-le-Mont so early, yet, as has been seen, he gained no advantage from this early start, nor was he actually on the field of battle till 4.30 P.M., little less than twelve hours after he had broken camp in the morning. It is only reasonable to conclude, with Mr Ropes, "that Bülow had been ordered to be very cautious and to proceed with all deliberation."

But if misgiving and hesitation mark the attitude of the Prussian commanders, Blücher and Gneisenau, up to noon on Waterloo day, nothing but vigour, energy, and resolution is to be found from that hour. Through miry roads and over marshy ground, three of the four Prussian corps—the third, under Thielemann, was left behind to engage Grouchy at Wavre—laboured and struggled

# CRITICAL EXAMINATION 289

upon their way. No effort of human endurance was left untaxed if only the old Field-Marshal might be true to his plighted word. The strenuous vigour which he exhibited now stands out in inverse proportion to the suspicion which filled him before. The spirit which animated the Prussians was that of enthusiasts, confident in their powers, marching fresh to gain their laurels in a first campaign, rather than that of wearied soldiers who, for the past four days, had been continuously in movement, had experienced nothing but defeat and discouragement, who were saturated with rain and caked with mud, and who with every step were abandoning their natural base of supplies in order to commit themselves to the perilous chances of a possible success, to which complete ruin was the only alternative.

The spirit of desperate resolve which characterised their march equally characterised their action upon the field of battle. There every corps surpassed itself. In the headlong impetuosity of their pursuit of the routed French the sentimentalist may see vengeance let loose rather than discipline acting under restraint, but the peace of the world and the cause of humanity is served in proportion as success is absolute and defeat irretrievable. The armies of Wellington and Blücher must be indissolubly and without reservations associated together in the glories of Waterloo. The parts of each were separate and distinct, but it is to the fact that each played its part so well that the ultimate triumph must be ascribed.

T

# CHAPTER XIII.

## THE FOREIGN TROOPS WITH WELLINGTON AT WATERLOO.

I. The King's German Legion—II. The Hanoverians—III. Brunswick Contingent—IV. The Dutch-Belgians.

## I.

IT is not only with Prussia that England is called upon to share the laurels of Waterloo. More than half of Wellington's army was made up of foreign troops, and for good or evil, these foreign regiments played a considerable part in the battle of Waterloo. Here at home the opinion seems still to prevail that it was rather in spite of his allies than by their assistance that Wellington secured the victory. It may be useful to examine this view a little in detail, and to endeavour to estimate exactly the extent of the burden of defence which lay upon the various foreign contingents.

The total Anglo-Dutch force present at Waterloo numbered rather less than 68,000 men. Of these only 24,000 were British. Forty-four thousand men, therefore, belonged to other nationalities.

## THE FOREIGN TROOPS 291

First in military qualities comes the small contingent of the King's German Legion. It consisted at Waterloo of two brigades of infantry under Duplat and Ompteda, two regiments of cavalry under Dörnberg and Arentsschildt, and numbered, with its artillery equipment, rather more than 5800 men.

Duplat, with four brigades of infantry, was attached to Clinton's division. He was stationed above Hougomont upon the right, where he was opposed to Bachelu. It would be impossible to distinguish between the capacity and bravery displayed by these troops and by their British comrades.

Ompteda was attached to Alten's division, and was stationed in the front to the right of the Charleroi road. The cavalry of Dörnberg and Arentsschildt were posted immediately in rear. These troops, therefore, formed part of Wellington's centre. They were exposed to the full shock of the cavalry charges as well as to the fire of the French artillery which preluded the cavalry attacks. "The enemy's artillery," says Alten, in his report to the Duke of Cambridge, "played upon our squares at the distance of 150 paces. Not one of them gave way; the dead were pushed aside and the ranks filled up again. Several went to meet the enemy's cavalry, and by their heavy fire, compelled it to retreat. At length some of them, which were almost entirely cut in pieces, fell back. They retreated, however, in good order, and immediately advanced again when they were ordered. . . . The greatest part of our most distinguished officers have fallen. Among these I reckon particularly Colonels Von Ompteda and Duplat. . . . We have, to be sure, this consolation, that these men have covered their graves with glory."

In addition to these services rendered by the King's German Legion must be reckoned the defence of La Haie Sainte. The position, it is true, was taken by the French, but not until late in the afternoon — towards six o'clock, probably — and throughout the day its chief defenders were the men of Baring's battalion (2nd light infantry of the King's German Legion), reinforced by the Lüneburg battalion of the same force. The post was held until ammunition failed; as it was impossible to introduce fresh supplies, nothing was to be done but withdraw. The struggle for La Haie Sainte cost Baring's battalion half its effective force.

II.

The Hanoverian troops at Waterloo, exclusive of the King's German Legion, numbered rather more than 11,000 men. Of these one brigade, under Count Kielmansegge, was attached to Alten's division, and fought side by side with Ompteda's brigades. Alten reports that "Major - General Count Von Kielmansegge gave the most brilliant example of courage and intrepidity to his brigade, and constantly supported me with all his might."

The Osnabrück brigade, under Colonel Halkett, was attached to Clinton's division, and exhibited

## THE FOREIGN TROOPS 293

great gallantry upon the right. The brigade, indeed, was to Duplat what Kielmansegge was to Ompteda. As the action drew near its close Halkett moved down the slope, together with the 71st regiment, in rear of the movement of the 52nd. His men shared in the pursuit of the French Imperial Guard when its rear column had been broken by Colborne's flank fire, and thus they were associated with one of the most critical and glorious exploits of the day. Their performances, however, are somewhat magnified in the Hanoverian official report, for there it is said that "the Osnabrück Landwehr fought against Napoleon's Guards, *and overthrew them.*"

The two brigades of Hanoverians, under Vincke and Best, formed a part of Wellington's left, and were attached respectively to the 5th and 6th divisions, which seem to have been under the general command of Sir Thomas Picton.* Upon this part of the line the attack of Marcognet and Durutte with their divisions of D'Erlon's corps was very severe. The Hanoverians were roughly handled, and Vincke's brigade was subsequently withdrawn from the line into reserve in front of Mont St Jean; but the whole of Picton's division displayed conspicuous courage and sound soldierly qualities throughout the day, and no distinctions need be made between the Hanoverians and the other brigades of which it was composed.

* It is impossible to define exactly how far Picton's command extended.

A detachment of Hanoverian Jagers served in Hougomont throughout the engagement, and a Hanoverian regiment despatched by Kielmansegge as a reinforcement to Baring in La Haie Sainte was almost cut to pieces by a charge of the French Cuirassiers.

Such, then, were the services rendered by the Hanoverian contingent at Waterloo. It is astonishing that they should have done so much rather than they did not do more, for they consisted for the most part of raw untrained troops, of whom but very little was expected by Wellington. It is to be noticed that he intermingled them as much as possible with his British regiments or with the men of the King's German Legion. Thus disposed, they would have before their eyes an example of steadiness and determination, and it was, moreover, a measure of precaution, for the Duke had as little confidence in their loyalty as in their fighting powers. His suspicions, however, though not unnatural, were entirely misplaced, and we may certainly consider that the Hanoverian infantry performed their duty in a thoroughly efficient manner on all parts of the field.

The Hanoverian cavalry under Estorff was with Colville's division at Hal, with the exception of one regiment known as the Cumberland Hussars. These were placed, together with the rest of the cavalry, under the general command of Lord Uxbridge, but he did not find it necessary to use them until the close of the afternoon, when the

## THE FOREIGN TROOPS 295

heavy cavalry of Guyot and Kellermann had been driven back. At this point the Cumberland Hussars were ordered to assist in the pursuit of the beaten enemy. But scarcely had they responded to the call when they turned rein and fled from the field, deaf to all remonstrances, and carrying panic and confusion with them in their abject flight to Brussels.

### III.

There were nearly 6000 Brunswick troops at Waterloo. They were stationed in reserve when the action began, between the village of Merbe Braine and the Nivelles-Brussels *chaussée*. They were moved forward in order to restore the Duke's right when it had been weakened by the repeated charges of the French cavalry. There, in company with the British and Hanoverians, the Brunswickers formed squares and were exposed to the full fury of the renewed cavalry attacks. Leeke, who was ensign in the 52nd, tells us that, as his regiment advanced, it " passed over the spot on which one of the Brunswick squares had stood, and found lying there many of their killed and badly wounded men. They had suffered most severely from round shot and shells. It was one of the most shocking sights we saw, even on that most bloodstained battlefield. Close to this was a Brunswick square, prepared to receive cavalry, the front rank kneeling, as steady as a rock." Other eye-witnesses speak of the Brunswickers as seeming to revel in the fire "like Salamanders." Later in the day, as the infantry of the Imperial Guard were beginning their advance, the Brunswick contingent was exposed to the charge of Donzelot's and Quiot's divisions, and was very severely handled, being indeed broken and forced back by the fury of the onset; but according to General Alava's report to the Spanish Government, "the Duke, who felt that the moment was most critical, spoke to the Brunswick troops with that ascendancy which every great man possesses, made them return to the charge, and putting himself at their head, again restored the combat, exposing himself to every kind of personal danger." "The gallant and noble conduct of the Brunswickers was the admiration of everyone," wrote an English officer of the Guards, three days after the battle.

Not alone at Waterloo, but at Quatre Bras, the Brunswick contingent earned just titles to fame. It was there that "Brunswick's fated chieftain" fell. In the roll of brave men who fought through this campaign, the Brunswickers stand high, nor should the noble service which they rendered ever be forgotten.

IV.

Last in this review come the Dutch Belgians, Nassauers, and troops of Orange Nassau. This force was by far the largest of all the foreign

## THE FOREIGN TROOPS 297

contingents at Waterloo, numbering over 20,600 men, but it was also by far the most unreliable. In military qualities and in loyalty to the cause for which they were fighting they left much to be desired, and the possibility that they would desert to the enemy was constantly present to the mind of the Allied Commanders. Every care was taken by the Duke to prevent such a mischance, by breaking them up into comparatively small detachments and intermingling them with the stable elements which composed his force. One brigade— Prince Bernhard of Saxe-Weimar's—was posted on the extremity of the allied left, and occupied the villages of La Haye, Papelotte, and Smohain. Chassé's division, including the brigades of Ditmers and D'Aubremé, were posted on the extreme right at Braine-la-Leud, and extending as far as the farm of Vieux Forêt. Thus the line on each side was flanked by Dutch-Belgians—that is to say, the greatest possible distance was put between Chassé's and Saxe-Weimar's men.

Two other brigades were stationed towards the centre. Bylandt's was attached to Picton's division, and was associated with such splendid British regiments as the 28th, 79th, 95th, and 42nd, while Kruse's Nassauers, nearly 3000 strong, leaned their left upon the Charleroi-Brussels *chaussée*, and their right upon Kielmansegge's Hanoverians and Ompteda's King's Germans.

A detachment of Nassauers was employed as sharpshooters in Hougomont, while Dollaert's cavalry (Trip, de Ghigny, and Van Merlin) were held at Mont St Jean in reserve.

Special ignominy has always in England attached to the Dutch-Belgians, for almost every Englishman believes that they turned and fled at the first charge. It is well to understand the truth of the matter, and for this purpose it is necessary to study the part played by the various Dutch-Belgian brigades in detail.

The first to be attacked was Bylandt's brigade. These troops were posted in a very anomalous manner. The ground rises sharply from the Wavre-Ohain road, which may be taken as indicating roughly the direction of the British line. Behind the road and beyond the slope the allied troops were posted, and their position was therefore covered by the rising ground, with the exception of Bylandt's brigade, which was stationed in front of the road, entirely without cover, and exposed to the full fire of the greatest French battery. This disposition, says Sir James Shaw Kennedy, was most unaccountable, and was followed by its natural results. Having endured the fire of the battery for an hour and a half, Bylandt's men were also to endure, unsupported and " singly exposed," the first shock of D'Erlon's charge. " Utterly unable," says Mr Ropes, " to resist alone the impact of such an enormous force, they broke in confusion and fled to the rear amid the undeserved curses of their English allies," and they were of little further use throughout the day. We may fairly

## THE FOREIGN TROOPS 299

conclude that if Bylandt's brigade had received fair treatment—if only such a measure of constancy and endurance had been demanded of them as was demanded from the other troops of the line upon the left—they would have rendered as good an account of themselves as their comrades on other parts of the field.

Prince Bernhard's brigade held the villages entrusted to it with great courage and tenacity, and were only expelled from their positions by Durutte's final onset between 6 and 7 P.M. Scarcely were the villages lost than they were regained, for shortly after 7 Ziethen's leading division (Steinmetz) came upon the field.

At first the Nassauers were mistaken by the Prussians for enemies, for, as Prince Bernhard tells us, the uniforms of his men were still "very French." The mistake was serious, for the Prussians "made dreadful fire" upon them, drove them from their post, nor could they be rallied until they had fled "a quarter of a league from the field." They did rally, however, and performed good service till the day was over.

On the other extremity of the line, Chassé's division was ordered up from Braine-la-Leud in order to restore Wellington's right, shattered by the French cavalry. They were thus not called upon till late in the afternoon. Massed in deep columns to the left of Maitland's brigade, they awaited with steadiness the onset of the French dragoons. They were still in position when the

Imperial Guard advanced, directing its charge, it will be remembered, full on Maitland's brigade. Thrown into confusion by the charge of the Imperial troops, they were rallied by Vandeleur's cavalry closing up behind them, and a Belgian battery, that of Van der Smissen, was most opportunely brought forward by Chassé to the support of Napier's battery of nine-pounders, and helped to render even more decisive the rout of the French Grenadiers.

The services rendered by the Dutch cavalry were so unequal as to be of scarcely any value. An occasional charge seems to have been made with vigour and resolution, but the troopers were liable to be seized with panic at the moment when their co-operation would have been most useful.

On the whole, the Dutch-Belgians on the right can scarcely be said to have covered themselves with glory, but some solid work was done by them : the intervention of Van der Smissen's battery was most timely, and their conduct generally entirely belied the suspicions formed of them before the battle began.

When we turn from the Dutch-Belgians, whose operations have already been reviewed, to Kruse's brigade, we can feel nothing but unreserved admiration for the devoted gallantry which it displayed. Stationed just to the left of that part of the line which was most fiercely beset by the French cavalry, it was upon the Nassauers in part that the duty fell to re-establish the broken front

## THE FOREIGN TROOPS 301

of the allied army. Just as the crisis of the French attack arrived, the Prince of Orange put himself at the head of Kruse's battalions. For the moment their courage failed them when they saw their hereditary Prince severely wounded and obliged to quit the field, and before the point-blank fire of the French musketry they turned and fled. The Brunswick battalions also failed before so furious an attack, but it was only for a moment. Encouraged by the advance of Kielmansegge's Hanoverians and some battalions of the King's Germans, supported by the 10th British Hussars, both Nassauers and Brunswickers resumed their formation, and threw themselves into the thick of the fight. In the contest they amply redeemed their momentary failure, and showed the grit and stuff of veteran soldiers in a *melée* engaged with some of the finest troops in Europe.

Of the Nassauers in Hougomont it is unnecessary to speak, except to say that the splendid defence of that position in no way depended upon their exertions or assistance.

It may then be conceded that the Dutch-Belgian and Nassau troops exceeded expectations in the battle of Waterloo, and occasionally gave glimpses of conspicuous gallantry. No one pretends—outside official reports and laudatory accounts of the battle emanating from Belgium—that they contributed in any special way to Wellington's victory. Any troops might have done as well, and many, doubtless, would have done better. But by troops from whom little was expected, effective work was done, and not only did they not desert, but contributed a fair share towards the success of the day. If they ran upon occasions, it was, it must be conceded, when skilled and tried troops could scarcely be expected to stand, and when they ran they could generally be rallied to render good service to the allied cause.

In the case of the King's German Legion, the Hanoverians, and the Brunswick corps, it has been seen what they were called upon to do, and how they did it. It is with no wish to detract from the splendid services of the British troops, but simply in a spirit of justice to those to whom the British owe so much that this chapter has been written.

# CHAPTER XIV.

## GROUCHY AT WAVRE.

Grouchy follows the Prussians to Wavre—Receipt of Napoleon's 10 A.M. despatch—Grouchy confirmed in his design of attacking the Prussians—Prussian dispositions at Wavre—The battle at Wavre on the 18th—Receipt of Napoleon's 1 P.M. despatch—Its effect on Grouchy's dispositions—Early morning of the 19th—Thielemann's determination to attack—Success of the French on the 19th—Grouchy receives the news of Waterloo—Determination to retreat on Namur—Grouchy's conduct of the retreat—Conclusion.

THE operations of Grouchy at Wavre upon the 18th are, in a technical sense, a part of the campaign of 1815, though for all practical purposes that campaign ended with the rout of Napoleon's army at Waterloo.

Nothing which Grouchy could do against the Prussians left behind at Wavre could have any effect upon the main issue which was decided between the French and the allies at Mont St Jean.

With a view to completeness, however, it may be well to devote a few pages to the fortunes of Grouchy from the moment when he came to his fateful decision to neglect the main battle upon his left in order to follow up the Prussians to Wavre. Grouchy was at Walhain, but his troops were in the neighbourhood of Sart-à-Walhain at the time when the cannonade of Waterloo was first heard, about 11.30 A.M. From Sart-à-Walhain to Wavre the distance is at least nine miles. It was not, therefore, till between 4 and 5 P.M. that Vandamme with the 3rd corps appeared upon the high ground which overlooks the town of Wavre upon the left bank of the river Dyle.

It was while the 3rd corps was taking position that Grouchy received the Emperor's despatch, dated from the field of Waterloo at 10 A.M. He was there informed of Napoleon's immediate intention to attack Wellington. "Accordingly (*ainsi*) his Majesty desires you to direct your movements on Wavre, so as to approach us, put yourself in touch with our operations, and connect communications; pushing before you the corps of the Prussian army which have taken this direction, and who may have stopped at Wavre, where you ought to arrive as soon as possible."

Whatever Napoleon's real meaning may have been—and critics have laboured with much ingenuity to prove that this despatch does not instruct Grouchy to proceed to Wavre, but to march on Waterloo—Grouchy read in it an unmistakable sanction for the course which he had pursued. He at once gave orders for a vigorous attack on Wavre, exclaiming to his lieutenants, " Vous voyez bien que j'avais raison." *

* La Tour d'Auvergne.

The task of holding the town had been entrusted by Blücher to Thielemann, commanding the 3rd corps of the Prussian army. The three remaining corps—of Bülow, Pirch, and Ziethen—were already well on their way to Waterloo, Bülow, in fact, taking position on the Emperor's flank almost at the very moment when Vandamme was preparing to attack Thielemann.

The position of the latter was hazardous in the extreme. His troops numbered scarcely a half of those which Grouchy could oppose to him, nor was any reinforcement to be looked for from Blücher. Originally estimating Grouchy's force at less than 12,000 men, the Prussian commander-in-chief confidently reckoned that one of his corps would be sufficient to occupy it. Nor when undeceived as to its strength, did he see cause to modify his existing arrangements. Blücher, in fact, determined to abandon to the chances of total destruction a whole *corps d'armée* if only thereby he might be enabled to punctually fulfil his engagements to Wellington. The immediate advantage of supporting Thielemann against Grouchy was sacrificed to the greater advantage of inflicting a crushing defeat upon Napoleon. Few commanders would have been capable of such a decision, involving, as it did, the abandonment of his fellow-countrymen in order to march with his army to the assistance of a stranger-ally.

Thielemann's business, then, was to stand at Wavre throughout the remainder of the day, and

so fully to engage the attention of Grouchy that it would be impossible for him to send assistance to Napoleon or to impede in any way the movements of the main Prussian army. This object was successfully accomplished. Vandamme opened a sharp fire from his batteries upon the town, and under cover of it his infantry columns descended on to the low ground bordering the river, and made a desperate effort to seize the bridges and to occupy the town. The Prussians offered a furious resistance, the contest raging for two hours hand to hand without any conspicuous success being gained by the French. Indeed, upon the left, the attack of Lefol's division of Vandamme's corps upon Bierges was a signal failure; so much so that Grouchy ordered up Gérard's 4th corps to relieve Lefol, and himself headed the charge. While the fight was thus in progress along the whole line from Wavre to Bierges, the marshal received Napoleon's second letter, dated from the field of Waterloo at one o'clock. From it he learned that Bülow's corps had been sighted at St Lambert, and that the Emperor expected his lieutenant not to lose an instant in approaching the main battle in order to catch Bülow redhanded (*en flagrant délit*). It was now six o'clock, and Bülow had been actively engaged for an hour and a half against the French before Grouchy even received the despatch which summoned him
¹ from Wavre to Waterloo *pour écraser Bülow*. It was now too late for anything to be done which

GROUCHY AT WAVRE 307

could serve Napoleon. None the less, Grouchy promptly set himself to obey instructions. Leaving to the unassisted efforts of Vandamme's corps the task of taking Wavre and Bierges—a task which had proved too severe for Vandamme and Gérard together—the marshal moved the 4th corps to Limal, a hamlet some distance to the west of Wavre, where a bridge crossed the river. A Prussian detachment stationed there was quickly driven in, the bridge was seized, and Gérard's corps, supported by Pajol's cavalry and Teste's infantry division, crossed the river and formed up in order of battle upon the ground beyond it. There the attempts of the Prussians to regain the lost position were successfully resisted, the French became masters of the ground from Limal to the wood of Rixensart, two miles and a half due west of Wavre, and Thielemann's position in the town was in danger of being turned. Such was the situation upon the left when darkness put an end to further hostilities. In the meantime Vandamme was maintaining a vigorous attack along the right bank of the Dyle from Wavre to Bierges, but all his efforts to make himself master of those positions were unavailing. At nightfall the Prussians still held Wavre, Bierges, and the bridges across the Dyle, which gave access to the town.

At an early hour upon the 19th the Prussians renewed the combat. No authentic information from the field of Waterloo had yet reached Thielemann, and Grouchy was altogether without news. It is, however, probable that some rumours of Napoleon's defeat were current in Wavre, for otherwise Thielemann, outmatched as he was, would scarcely have ventured upon an offensive movement. But if Napoleon was in retreat Grouchy must retreat too; and it would be exceedingly difficult for him to withdraw in good order in face of an attack in force by which he found himself committed to a general engagement. Moreover, the longer Grouchy was detained fighting at Wavre the more likelihood there was that one of the Prussian corps from Waterloo would come up to aid Thielemann. Or perhaps Blücher would despatch a force from Genappe or Quatre Bras to circumvent Grouchy and intercept him as he retreated on Namur. In any event, therefore, the French force before Wavre was likely to be annihilated if only its retrograde movement could be delayed for a few hours. At 8 o'clock A.M. vague rumour gave place to certainty, for it was at that hour that official information arrived at the Prussian headquarters of the result of Waterloo. Grouchy, however, remained ignorant of the issue of the battle for three hours longer, and cherishing the hope that the allies had been defeated, and that he would soon be supported by a detachment from the main army, he had no hesitation in accepting Thielemann's offer of battle.

In the engagement of the 19th Grouchy was everywhere successful. His left remained masters

## GROUCHY AT WAVRE

of the wood of Rixensart, notwithstanding determined efforts to dislodge them. Bierges was taken by Teste's infantry at the point of the bayonet. Thielemann, finding himself menaced upon the right flank, evacuated Wavre, which was promptly occupied by Vandamme. The pursuit of the Prussians was vigorously pressed, and thus it was when in the full tide of success that Grouchy, at 11 A.M., received the news of the Emperor's total overthrow. His situation was now desperate in the extreme, and his successes against Thielemann only made it the more so. He was beyond Wavre, in complete isolation from the main army, the shattered remnants of which were by this time across the Sambre, surrounded by enemies elated by a splendid victory, and outnumbering him by at least four to one, utterly unable, with his 30,000 men, to do anything to retrieve Napoleon's disaster, and with very little prospect of being able to effect his own retreat. It was, however, precisely when things were at their worst that Grouchy was at his best. Compelled to rely upon himself alone, and with a full sense of his position, he exhibited at this crisis powers of initiative, resource, activity, coolness, and skill such as have compelled the warm admiration of his bitterest detractors.

Masking his designs from Thielemann by maintaining an appearance of force at Wavre and at Limal throughout the day, with his main force he retired in good order, but with great rapidity, upon Namur. He succeeded in eluding the vigilance of

Pirch, who, with the 2nd corps, had been despatched from Waterloo to cut off his retreat. On the 20th he was at Namur, the Prussians now in hot pursuit. A little to the north of the town an engagement took place between the Prussians of Pirch and Thielemann and Vandamme's corps assisted by Teste's division. The Prussians were severely handled, and under cover of this action Grouchy, with the 4th corps, passed safely through Namur. Vandamme followed, leaving Teste to hold the town. Teste delayed the Prussians till nightfall, when he in turn retired, having succeeded with a mere handful of men in covering the retreat of Grouchy's whole force. At 4 A.M. on the 21st the 30,000 men under Grouchy's command were united at Dinant, soon to be distributed in cantonments at Soissons, Rocroi, and other neighbouring towns. Grouchy received from the provisional government the office of commander-in-chief, for in the days which immediately followed the campaign of Waterloo, he was not its scapegoat, but its hero. Was it not he who, in the midst of appalling defeat, had redeemed the honour of France by victory, who, in the hour of headlong flight and utter consternation, had, by a coolness and intrepidity which recalled the best traditions of the Grand Army, secured the safety of his whole command in the face of tremendous odds, and so provided France with the nucleus of another army with which the disasters of Waterloo might even yet be repaired?

# APPENDIX.

## NOTE TO CHAPTER V.

IN a recent article in the *Preussische Jahrbuch*, Herr Delbrück has emphatically condemned Wellington's conduct as a breach of faith to Blücher. He asserts that English writers on the campaign, and notably Lord Wolseley, are accustomed deliberately to ignore the evidence which goes to prove that the Prussian commander was deluded into taking position at Ligny on the strength of false assurances. He declares that such assurances were given, not only on the morning of the 16th, but also to Müffling on the evening before, and roundly asserts that it was the Duke's intention to induce Blücher to fight in order that the concentration of the Anglo-Dutch army might be effected quietly while the Prussians were occupying the French. Blücher, in fact, was to be the scapegoat of the Duke's blunders. These are serious charges, and certainly should not be ignored; nor, under the circumstances, can we affect much surprise that such charges should be made. The situation of the Prussians at Ligny on the 16th was not at all unlike that of the Anglo-Dutch army on the 18th, and when we remember the splendid and strenuous determination which brought the Prussians to our aid at Waterloo, we can scarcely wonder that their vigour should be favourably contrasted with Wellington's apathy as regards the contest at Ligny.

To admit that such charges are natural is not, however, to admit that they are true. The only really serious thing about them is the assertion that the Duke gave definite assurances of his support, that Blücher took position on the strength of them, and that there is documentary evidence to prove this. Where are the documents? If Herr Delbrück can produce anything over and above Wellington's letter to Blücher, which has been already quoted, English writers will unquestionably be prepared to examine it with attention, but if, as we shrewdly suspect, the Duke's letter is the only and ultimate *pièce de conviction*, few will be inclined, on the strength of that letter alone, to endorse the sweeping charges of the *Preussische Jahrbuch*.

Misleading as that letter is, at least it was written in good faith, or, if this be disputed, it still remains certain that Blücher had already taken his position at Ligny before the Duke's letter was received. For a letter despatched at 10.30 from Quatre Bras cannot have influenced the orders of Blücher, which were issued at an earlier hour. Now Ziethen and Pirch were both in position before 10 A.M., and Thielemann completed the line before noon. It was not, therefore, Wellington's letter which caused the Prussians to be formed up in order of battle at Ligny, though the receipt of it must have done much to establish Blücher in the conviction that he had acted wisely.

www.ingramcontent.com/pod-product-compliance
Lightning Source LLC
Chambersburg PA
CBHW030002240426
43672CB00007B/790